You're Retired Now What?

Wiley Personal Finance Solutions

Suddenly Single: Money Skills for Divorcées and Widows
by Kerry Hannon

New Families, New Finances: Money Skills for Today's
Nontraditional Families
by Emily W. Card and Christie Watts Kelly

How Can I Ever Afford Children? Money Skills for
New and Experienced Parents
by Barbara Hetzer

The Cost of Caring: Money Skills for Caregivers
by Anne Johnson and Ruth Rejnis

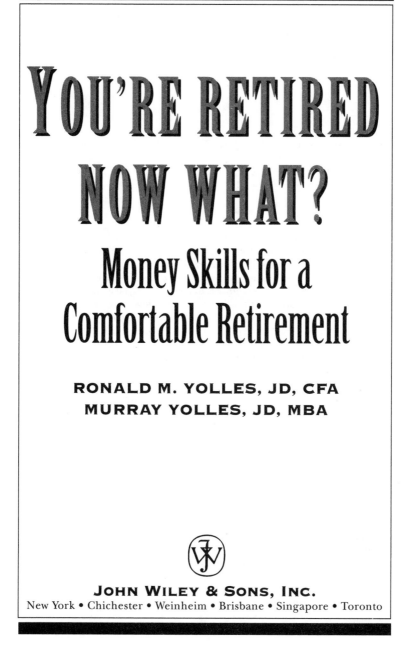

YOU'RE RETIRED NOW WHAT?

Money Skills for a Comfortable Retirement

RONALD M. YOLLES, JD, CFA
MURRAY YOLLES, JD, MBA

JOHN WILEY & SONS, INC.
New York • Chichester • Weinheim • Brisbane • Singapore • Toronto

Copyright © 1998 by Ronald M. Yolles and Murray Yolles. All rights reserved.
Published by John Wiley & Sons, Inc.

Published simultaneously in Canada.

This publication is designed to provide accurate and authoritative information in
regard to the subject matter covered. It is sold with the understanding that the
publisher is not engaged in rendering professional services. If professional advice
or other expert assistance is required, the services of a competent professional
person should be sought.

Library of Congress Cataloging-in-Publication Data:

Yolles, Ronald M.
    You're retired, now what? : money skills for a comfortable
retirement / Ronald M. Yolles and Murray Yolles.
        p.   cm.—(The Wiley personal finance solutions series)
    Includes bibliographical references and index.
    ISBN 0-471-24836-3 (paper : alk. paper)
    1. Retirees—Finance, Personal.   2. Retirement income—United
States. I. Yolles, Murray. II. Title. III. Series.
HG179.Y63   1998
332.024'0696—dc21   98–3802

Printed in the United States of America.

10 9 8 7 6 5 4 3 2

To Julie and Elinor, the heart of the Yolles family

CONTENTS

PART TWO   THE BEST INVESTMENT STRATEGY FOR YOUR RETIREMENT

FOREWORD

$

etirement. Few words in life create more confusion, fear, and anxiety. Will I have enough money? Will I need a part-time job? Do I have adequate health insurance? These are just a few of the many questions that one must address. These are concerns that are completely justified. After all, who can deny the uncertainty surrounding the future of Social Security and Medicare? Add in the volumes of information about investing, insurance, and estate planning and you begin to realize that there is much more to retirement than the media images of sandy beaches and green golf courses! Fortunately, you will not have to go it alone. This volume by Ron Yolles and Murray Yolles will provide you with the tools necessary to begin making some important decisions. Apply this wisdom and enjoy a safe and rewarding retirement.

ROBERT J. SANBORN, CFA
Portfolio Manager, The Oakmark Fund

PREFACE

T hough your friends, relatives, and kids tell you that you should be thrilled about entering this new stage in your life—*retirement*—you may well be too nervous to recognize the many choices now available.

Your daily routine has been dramatically altered. For the first time in 30 years, you have no job and no children around the house. How will you handle all this newfound free time? Can you do and see all of the people, places, and things that interest you? Most importantly, will your money last?

You may be uneasy about getting professional investment help, but even if you've never had to rely on anyone before, you will need advice on managing the complexities of a 20, 30, or even 40-year retirement.

This book breaks new ground by focusing on issues faced by individuals and couples *after* they retire. There are numerous books on the subject of *how* to save for retirement and *when* to retire. There are also books on estate and tax planning. But there are very few books that comprehensively focus on the issue of *what* to do once you are retired. That's how we arrived at the title, *You're Retired, Now What?*

Our goal for this book, which is designed to be a hands-on reference guide, is to provide you with an invaluable investment road map that will make your retirement journey smooth and comfortable.

The first step to successfully surviving your retirement is finding a source of objective information to help you evaluate, plan, and understand your courses of action. Unlike other critical issues in your life where you know whom to talk to about obtaining insightful advice, you may be confused about how to find reliable professional investment counsel. We hope that this book will be a significant resource and also clear up the confusion you may have about the investment world.

We believe that this book is unique in several ways. We feel very strongly that most of the information that retirees and preretirees receive is inappropriate for their specific financial circumstances. In addition to presenting detailed, objective, and well-documented advice and facts, we have devoted several chapters to outlining the problems that can result from conventional investment wisdom. We will show you alternative, more effective, ways to plan your overall investment and retirement program.

Perhaps more importantly, we hope to dispel myths about how retirees should "think" and "feel" about their financial planning. When you have finished this book, we hope that our faith in the well-researched and time-tested financial principles that we have discussed will help you overcome all or most of your fear of your upcoming retirement years.

Collectively, Ronald Yolles and Murray Yolles have been counseling clients, most of whom are retirees or preretirees, for more than 50 years. We like to say that we have been providing investment and financial counsel for over 150 years because we believe it is critical to understand, at least, the prior 100 years of investment and market history to provide well-informed investment counsel to our clients.

Over this long time frame, we have seen many clients who have implemented successful investment and retirement plans and also many people who have not been as lucky. We feel very strongly that one of the most valuable things that we can do in this book is to point out the numerous problems that people run into in their investment, financial, estate, and tax planning. Hopefully, by doing this, we can share our insights into the causes of these problems. It is our sincere hope that we can help you, the investor and retiree, to avoid these situations.

In the next 12 chapters, we will explore many key issues and provide critical topical and historical information pertaining to the world of finance. We will examine why certain behavioral traits perpetually lead investors to make emotional, hasty, and harmful investment revisions to what was a well-designed, long-term retirement plan. And we will look at other investors who have the personality characteristics to make productive investment decisions.

The single most critical issue for many retirees is how to achieve a growing and sustainable source of cash flow. We will examine the proper way, or what we call the optimal way, to broadly diversify a multimanager no-load mutual fund portfolio and achieve retirement investing success.

We feel that this book takes on a unique perspective. Not only do we enjoy a very close father (Murray Yolles) and son (Ronald Yolles) relationship, but we are currently business associates. At various times in our lives, we have each been a client of the other in his respective specialty. Murray Yolles has been a long-time client of Yolles Investment Management, Inc., with Ron Yolles as president and senior portfolio manager of his Southfield, Michigan–based firm. Ron Yolles has used Murray Yolles as his tax and estate planning attorney.

We believe that our different perspectives give us several

advantages in illuminating points emphasized in the book. Throughout, you will see several special boxes. One set of boxes will include case studies of our experiences with actual clients whose circumstances may be very similar to your own.

The book is organized into four parts with examples and case studies used throughout. Part I deals with issues faced by new retirees. Part II deals with the best investment strategies. Part III focuses on retirement plans, IRAs, pensions, and rollovers, and deals with health-related issues such as life, disability, and long-term care. Part IV focuses on estate and advisor issues, plus avoiding investment scams and understanding what protections are provided by the securities laws.

In our professional capacity as wealth managers, one critical observation that we have made is that retirement and retirement investing issues can be very upsetting and unnerving to many people who have spent a lifetime looking forward to retirement.

At Yolles Investment Management, Inc., we help our clients implement financial strategies that allow them to sleep soundly at night. With this book, we plan to dispel investment allegories and provide you with a level of comfort to be successful and confident enough to stick with your long-term retirement plan.

You're retired—*now* what? Read on and join us for what we hope will be a very important, insightful, and enlightening journey.

ACKNOWLEDGMENTS

$

This book was a team effort. Julie Yolles took our technical investment jargon and legalese and translated everything into "normal" English. She also deserves significant editing credit. Our colleagues at Yolles Investment Management, Inc., helped us with every aspect—from inception to production of the final manuscript. Darlene Hemker, with help from Sofia Subonj, orchestrated all of the typing and made sense of our dictation. Maria Bertolino and Tim Atkinson provided invaluable research and cite-checking help, while Sal Giacomazza held down the fort at our firm. Our clients at Yolles deserve special thanks for teaching us what retirement feels like. They are our living classroom. They ask the key questions.

Our colleagues in the Council of Independent Financial Advisors (CIFA)—Robert Rikoon, Ken Schapiro, Larry Waschka, and Stewart Welch III—have helped us define, and constantly redefine, what it means to operate a first-rate client-centered investment management firm. They will notice their input throughout the book.

Our editor, Debra Englander, had the insight that there were plenty of books out on how to save for retirement, but few, if any, objectively describe what to do upon retirement. She and senior editorial assistant Olga Herrera Moya have our gratitude for patiently and skillfully steering us through the writing, editing, and publishing process.

Research and technical help came from top firms and professionals including David Brief, Jacob Rosoff, and Dan Simon of Ennis, Knupp and Associates; Andre Mallegol and Douglas Ongaro of Pacific Investment Management Company (PIMCO); Michael Neary of The Oakmark Family of Funds; Timothy Radcliffe of Goldman Sachs; and Tom Bergh of Raymond & Prokop.

We would like to remember the late Marcus Plotkin, who defined what it meant to be a caring attorney in the context of dealing with the impact of estate planning on retirees and families and, in that same spirit, acknowledge the following attorneys: Milton Silverman, Richard Polk, Shel Lutz, Jon Lowe, Robert Goren, Ron Rothstein, Jack Schultz, Stuart Goldstein, Scott Moore, Robert Karbel, Sherwin Schreier, Jon Frank, Bob Siegel, Stan Weingarden, S. Lawrence Stein, Susan Feldstein, Jeff Robbins, Mark Landau, and Jay Schreier; and the following CPAs: Mark Pittman, Jim Boyes, Charles Kaye, Mark Hutton, Ed Schiff, Jeff Weiss, Ilene Beneson, Stuart Sakwa, Bert Stein, Catherine Fisher, Brad Wasserman, and Howard Morof.

RONALD YOLLES & MURRAY YOLLES

Southfield, Michigan
September 1998

INTRODUCTION

$

One of the most difficult situations faced by seasoned investment professionals is helping a client who has procrastinated and fails to seek our counsel early. This happened again recently when a friend (we'll call her Vera) visited our office shortly after her husband Samuel succumbed to lung cancer at age 72.

Although Sam worked right up until the year before his death, he and Vera neglected their retirement planning. Now, Vera, age 65, will have to pay the price—namely a lower standard of living and the necessity to return to work. Fortunately, though, we can still help Vera, using many of the same techniques we will present to you in this book.

Sam and Vera neglected all of the following areas of their investment planning:

1. They failed to invest their assets properly and missed nearly all of the benefits of investing in sound no-load mutual funds over the past 15 years.

2. They failed to evaluate sustainable withdrawal rates from their retirement accounts and therefore spent too much and saved too little.

3. Their estate plan was outdated, which caused Vera and their children needless probate and estate costs, hassles, and taxes.

4. They failed to evaluate and obtain long-term nursing care insurance, an omission that cost Vera $40,000 in caregiver costs.

5. Sam failed to involve Vera in financial decisions, which caused her utter confusion following his death.

6. Sam purchased a costly annuity that only provided income for his lifetime and left Vera with an income shortfall.

Sam and Vera's investment procrastination is one of the two most common problems that we see with retirees. The other common problem involves emotional as opposed to objective investing and decision making. This problem was exhibited by a new client (we will call her Samantha).

An edgy 65-year-old Samantha called us for help in March 1997. Although her 67-year-old husband, Darren, had a successful advertising business, they had failed to put away enough money for their retirement. They had lost money in almost every investment, including oil and gas limited partnerships, real estate partnerships, junk bonds, and a variety of investments in small stocks that were all supposed to become the next Microsoft.

Samantha made all of their investment decisions based on hearsay and emotion with a hope of striking it rich. She was envious of her younger sister June, who, along with June's husband, Ward, were in much better financial shape than Samantha and Darren even though Ward's lifetime earnings were lower.

June and Ward were long-time clients of Yolles Investment Management. We had put together a sensible long-term retirement program for them based on economic and financial *facts* rather than hearsay and emotion.

If you're looking for a comprehensive and objective source of information on how to structure and enjoy your financial life during retirement, this book is for you.

Too often, retirees or preretirees fail with their investments because they either do not receive truly objective financial counsel or they base their financial decisions on emotions or tips from friends, relatives, or even television or magazine gurus rather than facts.

In this book, we want to help you apply only those financial principles that have stood the test of time. Applying these *fact*-based principles, as opposed to *hearsay* and *emotion*, should give you the confidence to sleep at night and enjoy your retirement.

Among the issues covered in this book:

- How to avoid making emotional decisions by adopting a step-by-step framework for financial decision making.

- How to assemble a retirement plan that will allow you to sleep well at night.

- How the new tax law may affect when you should start taking Social Security distributions.

- A sensible and sustainable plan for making withdrawals from your retirement portfolio.

- How to avoid making "mental mistakes" that, in the past, have hindered you getting successful investment results.

- Why most index mutual funds should be avoided.

- Why no-load mutual funds are the safest and most cost-effective way to invest for anyone with less than a $25-million portfolio.

- Criteria for selecting the best and safest no-load mutual funds.

- Why value no-load funds are better in the long run than growth or momentum funds.

- Determining your "money personality" and how it impacts your investment choices.

- Assessing the smartest way for you to make withdrawals from your retirement plan accounts under the new tax law.

- How to designate your IRA beneficiary.

- Deciding at what age you should file for Social Security benefits.

- Determining whether you need a trust and, if so, what type.

- Evaluating your long-term nursing care insurance needs.

- How you can find a qualified independent investment advisor.

These and many other questions and issues will be answered and explored in depth in the pages that follow.

Part One

YOUR RETIREMENT MIND-SET

This part has three important introductory chapters. Chapter 1 provides a framework for how you should think about and organize your finances and your life during retirement. Included are work sheets and examples so you can plan properly for the significant effect even modest inflation will have on your retirement.

Chapter 2 teaches you to focus on cash flow, not income, during retirement and explores your nonportfolio sources of cash flow.

Finally, Chapter 3 shows how you can maximize your cash flow from your portfolio during retirement and still sleep at night.

CHAPTER ONE

Cost of Living and Other Financial Issues

IN THIS CHAPTER

This chapter focuses on several issues related to your spending and cost of living during retirement including:

1. How can you estimate what your cost of living will be during retirement?

2. Are your retirement spending needs similar to those of your peers?

3. How can you put together a retirement plan that will allow you to sleep at night?

4. How will inflation affect your retirement?

5. Will your children, or even your parents, need financial support during your retirement?

6. Can you avoid making emotional investment decisions and, instead, learn objective, systematic, and businesslike financial decision making?

W
e recently watched a 1985 videotape of a TV movie. On the tape was a commercial advertising a Mazda for $6,200. The same car would sell for $18,000 today. Many other items that you buy regularly (food, clothing, laundry detergent, travel, etc.) are significantly more expensive today than 10 or 12 years ago, even with the relatively mild inflation we have had since the 1980s. With just 4% annual inflation, a box of cereal costing $4 today will cost $8 in 18 years.

You're fooling yourself if you don't recognize and plan for inflation during your retirement.

ESTIMATING YOUR RETIREMENT COST OF LIVING

While planning your entire retirement spending needs over 20, 30, or 40 years is, at best, educated guesswork, you can accurately plan each year's expenses in an annual review with your investment and tax advisors. We have found this "annual checkup" approach to be more valuable, more flexible, and less costly than having an expensive leatherbound computerized financial plan. The challenge in an annual review is to estimate your spending needs both now and in the future.

Many people find that their cost of living is lower in retirement, while others find that their retirement costs are higher. If a substantial portion of your annual spending was devoted to your children, including education costs, then you will probably find that your cost of living is much lower during retirement, particularly if you do not have elderly parents to support. Additionally, if you trade down to a smaller house, condominium, or apartment during retirement, then your cost of living will be further reduced.

On the other hand, you could have a higher cost of living

RULE OF 72

The quick and easy Rule of 72 helps you determine how long it takes something to double in cost or value at a given rate of interest or inflation. You simply divide your interest or inflation rate into the number 72. At a 4% rate of inflation, the cost of our box of cereal would double from $4 to $8 in 18 years because 72 divided by 4% inflation = 18. Similarly, if you have a $300,000 investment portfolio that earns 9% per year, and don't make any deposits or withdrawals, your portfolio will double in value to $600,000 in 8 years: 72 divided by 9% = 8 years. The Rule of 72 can help focus your retirement thinking on rates of return, your portfolio's value, and inflationary costs.

during retirement, especially if your travel expenses increase. If you choose to purchase a vacation home during retirement, your costs could skyrocket. Also, with more time on your hands during retirement for visiting your family and friends, your travel expenses can greatly increase.

YOUR PERSONAL INFLATION RATE

The best approach is for you to accurately figure your likely retirement cost of living and your *personal inflation rate*. The government's *consumer price index* (CPI) has little relevance to you because it describes price increases of a basket of goods that the average consumer purchases. However, there is no such thing as the average consumer. You should focus on determining your own costs and needs during retirement. Following that, the rest of this book will be devoted to providing you with both the tools needed to objectively determine whether your assumptions are realistic and what's required to implement the best and safest strategy to achieve your goals.

A starting point to determine your capital needs during retirement is to take a look at your current standard of living in today's dollars. While some people find it necessary to make a very detailed budget of their current standard of living, others find it more productive to just estimate their costs and get a general idea of their capital needs. The following method is appropriate for those who do not want to prepare a detailed budget.

Figure 1.1 provides a quick and easy method for estimating your current standard of living. Using this work sheet, you can estimate what portion of your net after-tax income went to major saving and investment items. After these calculations, you can reasonably assume that you spent the remaining amount.

Take your adjusted gross income from your most recent tax return and subtract the total amount in taxes that you paid for the year. This is your after-tax net income, or what is more commonly called your take-home pay. Now, all you have to do is subtract the amount of net deposits you made during the year to your savings and/or investment accounts, and the remaining figure that you are left with is a good approximation of your cost of living.

FIGURE 1.1   DETERMINING YOUR COST OF LIVING (COL)—THE EASY WAY

	EXAMPLE	YOUR COL
Adjusted gross income	$100,000	
Federal income tax	(25,000)	
State income tax	(5,000)	
After-tax income	70,000	
Net investment deposits or withdrawals	(10,000)	
Net savings deposits or withdrawals	(4,000)	
Your cost of living	$ 56,000	

Let's look at our example: Say that you had $100,000 of income during a given year and that you paid $30,000 in taxes. This would leave $70,000 as your net after-tax income (or take-home pay). Now let us say further that you and your spouse made contributions of $10,000 to 401(k) and retirement plan accounts. This would reduce your figure to $60,000. Assume further that your savings account balance at the start of the year was $20,000 and at the end of the year this account balance was $25,000. Of this increase, only $1,000 could be attributed to interest accrued on the savings account. Therefore, you know that you deposited $4,000 to your savings account during the year. This $4,000 saved further reduces your figure to $56,000. That is a good approximation of your cost of living (i.e., what you spent) for the year.

Perhaps part of your $56,000 standard of living includes gifts to children or grandchildren. There also may have been some noncash deductions such as donations of personal property to charity, your mortgage interest deduction, and/or renter's credits that you were allowed that reduced your income, but the $56,000 is a reasonable approximation of your cost of living.

The challenge is to take your current cost of living, the $56,000, and determine whether your needs during retirement will be similar. Perhaps they'll be more. Or, perhaps your needs will be less.

In our experience, most people have slightly lower spending needs during retirement than while they are working because, for example, they no longer have children to support. Your challenge during retirement is to determine if your cost of living will change and to determine what your personal inflation rate will be.

No one can predict what inflation will be in the future, but we do have a hundred years of history that tell us that inflation has averaged about 3.7%. If there is no better evidence available at the time of calculation, this 3.7% should be your default figure when estimating inflation. However, we find that retirement costs are not always subject to the same ravages of inflation as costs during your working years. For example, even during inflationary times, most people have a fixed mortgage that is a large part of their cost of living. Their mortgage payment does not change with inflation. (For those of you who pay rent on an apartment, typically your cost of living *will* increase with inflation.)

Food, clothing, transportation, and other costs may creep gradually higher, but in our experience, these cost increases from normal inflation are often offset by certain obligations that you had during your working years that you no longer have to pay for during retirement. By the time you retire, in most cases your children are now independent and they, who constituted one of your most significant expenses during your working years, are no longer an expense. However, occasionally and with increasing frequency, your parents or your in-laws could become an expense if they need support during their later years.

No matter how carefully you plan, unexpected expenses can always arise. However, detailed planning gives you the best chance of being prepared for expected and unexpected retirement expenses.

TAKING AN INVENTORY

What we are asking you to do at this phase of your retirement planning is take an inventory. Make an educated guess of what your costs are likely to be in retirement, but make sure to approach the problem from all possibilities: How is your health? Do you have adequate insurance to cover any medical emergencies that could throw you off your plan? How are your parents' health? Do they have adequate insur-

THE MIDNIGHT PHONE CALL

These apocryphal stories come to us from Ed Olsen, a senior executive with the well-respected SoGen family of mutual funds in New York City. The stories deal with what happens after parents get a late-night call from their kids.

"Hi, Mom, it's me, Lucy, sorry to wake you. . . . Yes, everything is okay. . . . The kids are fine. I've decided to leave Charlie . . . uh-huh . . . uh-huh . . . yep . . . yes . . . well . . . I was hoping that the kids and I could come stay with you for a while."

SEVERAL YEARS LATER

"Hi, Dad, sorry to wake you. . . . We're all fine. . . . Now that Charlie and I have reconciled . . . we have another little problem, Dad. . . . We filed for bankruptcy . . . yeah . . . no . . . six months ago. . . . We didn't want to worry you and Mom. Well, we think the economy is much better in Boston where you guys are. . . . If we could move back in with you just till we're back on our feet. . . ."

ance, or might they be dependent on you? Are your children truly independent? Is it possible that they will be moving back into the household, or at least require some continuing support?

Take a look at what type of expenses you'll have during retirement: Do you want to travel more? Will you buy a motor home, boat, or time-share? Can you quantify an increase in expenses or at least make a reasonable guess?

In many ways, what we are doing with our clients, and what you should do when you make your retirement plan, is to take an inventory. This is similar to corporations preparing budgets—looking at sources and uses of cash flow. By making realistic projections, you will be able to make critical decisions and, most importantly, you'll acquire a sense of security, which is really what you are looking for.

No one wants to live beyond their means. Everyone wants to strike the proper balance between perhaps spending some capital during retirement years and not depleting one's nest egg. Only by taking a regular inventory the same way corporations closely watch their cash flow and income can you be on top of your retirement plan.

Figure 1.2 allows you to prepare a more detailed retirement budget and compare your cost of living to that of the median family in this country. Your costs may very well be less than these U.S. Department of Labor averages because you, as a retiree, do not have child care expenses.

By completing these retirement planning work sheets (Figures 1.1 and 1.2), you have taken an important first

FIGURE 1.2   YOUR COST OF LIVING—COMPARED TO THE AVERAGE FAMILY

EXPENDITURE PER YEAR	AVERAGE BUDGET	%	YOUR BUDGET	%
Food	$ 6,737	13		
House/rent payment	12,093	22		
Furnishings	3,436	6		
Auto	11,422	21		
Clothing	2,871	5		
Personal care	440	1		
Medical	1,809	4		
Contributions	2,181	4		
Family consumption and child care	4,062	8		
Savings	2,251	4		
Social Security	6,633	12		
Total spending for a median family in 1996	$53,935	(100)		

Source: Bureau of Labor Statistics.

step in understanding and quantifying your needs during retirement. Once you estimate your retirement spending needs, and in subsequent chapters gain an understanding of how to safely meet these needs, then you can begin to have confidence in your retirement planning and investment program.

Your level of comfort is necessary for your own enjoyment during retirement and also for the success of your retirement investment program. If you are comfortable with your plan, then you will stick to it even in bear markets, and sticking to this plan is critical for your long-term investment success.

Your stick-to-itiveness is critical, either as a do-it-yourselfer or as a client of an investment counseling firm. Despite the fact that the overall stock and bond markets have risen consistently over the past 70 years, somehow individual investors have managed to make very little money. Individuals have done poorly despite the fact that returns on stocks have averaged 10.8% over that 70-year period, bonds averaged 5.7%, and even cash investments averaged 4.1%.

STICK WITH A LONG-TERM PLAN

The following charts, which respectively show how the markets have done (Figure 1.3) and how individual investors have done (Figure 1.4), will demonstrate these investment cycles. A key to understanding why individuals tend to buy high and sell low comes from the study of the individual investor psychology and temperament. Most people when looking back on their own investment history can identify times when they clearly didn't act in their own best interests and often, in hindsight, can explain why they acted in a self-destructive manner—namely, they failed to follow a long-term plan.

FIGURE 1.3 STOCKS, BONDS, TREASURY BILLS, AND INFLATION (1926–1996)

INVESTMENT	ANNUAL RETURN	STANDARD DEVIATION
Common stocks	10.7%	20.30%
Small stocks	12.6%	34.19%
Government bonds	5.1%	9.29%
Treasury bills	3.7%	3.30%
Inflation	3.1%	4.50%

Source: Ibbotson Associates. Used with permission. Copyright © 1997 Ibbotson Associates, Inc. All rights reserved. (Certain portions of this work were derived from copyrighted works of Roger G. Ibbotson and Rex Sinquefield.)

FIGURE 1.4 SAD BUT TRUE: MARKETS RISE, BUT INVESTORS MISS THE BOAT (1984–1995)

Average S&P 500 Growth	████████████████	+15.4%
Average Investor's Results	█████	+6.2%

Source: Reprinted with permission from Dalbar, Inc.

By examining your own and others' emotional investment mistakes, we hope to be able to prevent you from making these and other common errors. We hope that the insights we share with you on irrational emotional investment behavior will give you the wherewithal and the determination to stick with a long-term retirement plan and not to succumb to your temporary feelings of either euphoria or panic. Investment decisions must be made in an unemotional, objective fashion.

$

CHAPTER TWO

Cash Flow and Nonportfolio Sources of Income

IN THIS CHAPTER

Here you will examine critical issues and questions related to your nonportfolio sources of income during retirement including:

1. Why you should focus on total return instead of chasing yield.

2. How to identify your nonportfolio sources of income.

3. When to begin taking your Social Security distributions.

4. How to determine whether it makes sense for you to tap into your equity in your home by taking out a mortgage and investing the proceeds to create needed cash flow.

Will it cost more or less to live during retirement maintaining the same standard of living you enjoyed before retirement? What impact will inflation have on your cost of living during retirement? The old school of thought is to examine your cost of living and personal inflation rate as discussed in Chapter 1. But, we think a still better way to address these issues is to work backward. A logical starting point for retirees and preretirees is to focus on what sources of income, or what we like to call cash flow, you will have during retirement.

Consider how much cash flow your resources can comfortably produce and then use that amount as a basis for focusing on your needs and your cost of living requirements during retirement. One of the greatest mistakes people make during retirement is to become obsessed with income rather than worrying about cash flow. Don't focus on one element of the retirement plan; look at the total return on your investments. Use Figure 2.1 to take an inventory of your expected sources of retirement income.

FIGURE 2.1   EXPECTED SOURCES OF RETIREMENT INCOME OTHER THAN YOUR INVESTMENT PORTFOLIO

SOURCE	$ AMOUNT
Pensions	
Social Security	
Work or consulting fees	
Real estate and land contracts	
Inheritances	
Other	
Total nonportfolio sources	

CONSIDER TOTAL RETURN

The smart investor focuses on total return, which includes appreciation to principal plus dividend income from any investment. Retirees who focus on only dividend income can easily be seduced by high-dividend-yield investments, such as junk bonds, which can pose risk of principal loss. Figure 2.2

FIGURE 2.2   STOCKS ARE ULTIMATELY A BETTER SOURCE OF INCOME THAN BONDS

	VANGUARD GNMA		LINDNER DIVIDEND		CD	
	PRINCIPAL	DIVIDENDS	PRINCIPAL	DIVIDENDS	PRINCIPAL	DIVIDENDS
1980	$100,000		$100,000		$100,000	
1981	93,000	$12,000	116,000	$10,000	100,000	$13,000
1982	109,740	13,020	141,520	10,440	100,000	8,900
1983	107,545	13,136	195,298	8,491	100,000	9,700
1984	109,696	12,905	212,874	11,718	100,000	8,300
1985	119,569	13,164	232,033	17,030	100,000	7,600
1986	121,960	11,957	259,877	20,883	100,000	6,300
1987	113,423	10,976	228,692	20,790	100,000	7,600
1988	113,423	10,208	262,996	20,582	100,000	9,400
1989	120,228	10,208	268,255	26,300	100,000	8,300
1990	121,430	10,821	228,017	21,460	100,000	8,100
1991	132,358	9,714	266,780	22,802	100,000	5,600
Total Dividends		$128,109		$190,496		$92,800

Note: Not only did Lindner Dividend, an equity-income fund, provide substantially more dividend income than Vanguard GNMA and a CD, but Lindner Dividend's principal also grew from $100,000 to $266,780 compared to $132,358 for Vanguard GNMA and $100,000 for the CD. Conclusion: Stocks should play a role in almost any retiree's investment mix.

Source: Yolles Investment Management.

illustrates how a total return investment such as an equity-income mutual fund (in this example the Lindner Dividend Fund) can, in the long run, produce both better growth *and* more income than an income-only investment such as the Vanguard GNMA Fund. We chose the 1980–1991 period for this illustration because it included both good and bad years for stocks, bonds, and CDs.

When you're taking an inventory of your expected sources of retirement income, first consider whether you or your spouse has a pension, either a lifetime pension or a pension for a series of years, that you will be able to draw from during retirement. Next, evaluate what your Social Security income will be during retirement. You can obtain this figure by calling 800-937-2000 (ask for Form 7004) or by searching under http://www.ssa.gov on the Internet. Other sources of information on Social Security and Medicare are listed in Figure 2.3.

WHEN TO TAKE YOUR SOCIAL SECURITY INCOME

A key decision that you should make early in your retirement is figuring out at what age you should take your Social Security income distributions. There are several choices.

You can elect to begin to collect Social Security at age 62, but the monthly payments to you will be greater if you postpone the election and will reach their maximum if you start collecting at age 70. If you continue to work after you begin receiving Social Security payments, the current payments may be reduced or eliminated. Beginning at age 70, you will collect your full Social Security payments regardless of how much you earned during the year.

The amount that you can earn annually while collecting all of your Social Security benefits increases each year. As of

FIGURE 2.3 SOCIAL SECURITY AND MEDICARE INFORMATION SOURCES

For most people, comprehensive retirement planning includes consideration of Social Security benefits. This necessitates understanding how the Social Security and Medicare benefit systems work.

The first place to look for information should be the Social Security Administration. Ask for the Request for Earnings and Benefit Estimate Statement. After sending this form to the Social Security Administration, you will receive a statement showing your Social Security earnings history, the amount paid in Social Security taxes, and an estimate of the Social Security benefits due to you when eligible.

The Social Security Administration offers numerous free short publications that describe its programs. Handbooks on Social Security and Medicare are also available for purchase from the U.S. Government Printing Office.

Commerce Clearing House is the best resource for an annual guide on Social Security and Medicare. This can be purchased through the publisher at the address listed.

Government Publications

These publications are available free from your local Social Security office or by calling 800-772-1213.

PAMPHLETS

Understanding the Benefits. A 40-page description of Social Security.

A Guide for Representatives. A 15-page description to help someone manage a recipient's money.

What Every Woman Should Know. A 17-page description for today's woman.

Working While Disabled: How We Can Help. A 28-page description available to the disabled.

SHORT BROCHURES AND FACT SHEETS

Your Social Security Number

Your Social Security Taxes: What They're Paying for and Where the Money Goes

How You Earn Credits

FIGURE 2.3 (CONTINUED)

SHORT BROCHURES AND FACT SHEETS

Your Earnings Record

Facts and Figures

Commerce Clearing House Paperbacks

These publications are available through the Cash Item Department, 4025 West Peterson Avenue, Chicago, IL 60646; 800-248-3248.

1997 Medicare Explained. Comprehensive coverage on all aspects of Medicare coverage. 192 pages; $22.

1997 Social Security Benefits (Including Medicare). Provides tax tables and benefit computation formulas and examples. 48 pages; $7.

1997 Social Security Explained. Provides a basic understanding of the Social Security system, including its laws, regulations, and rulings. Explains coverage, tax rates, and withholding. 320 pages; $26.

On Your Retirement: Tax and Benefit Considerations. Provides information on Social Security, Medicare, private health care, income tax, and private pensions. 192 pages; $15.

Source: Yolles Investment Management, Inc.

1997, if you are under 65, $1 of your Social Security benefits will be deducted for each $2 you earn above $8,640. If you are between 65 and 69, $1 in benefits will be deducted for each $3 you earn above $13,500. If your Social Security benefits were reduced while you were under 65, when you reach 65 your benefits will increase to take into account those months that your benefits were reduced. Also, if income you earn after you begin to collect Social Security increases your overall average earnings, then your subsequent monthly benefits may increase.

Since Social Security benefits are based on your date of birth and your earnings record, benefits will vary from person to person. Sometimes you and your family can qualify for additional amounts by choosing a particular *month* to start your retirement. Currently, many people receive maximum benefits with an application that becomes effective in January even if they expect to retire later in the year. Generally, it is a good idea to apply at least three months before you want to start receiving benefits.

Because the rules are complicated, we urge you to discuss your plans with a Social Security claims representative in the year prior to the year you plan to retire. You can discuss your alternatives with a Social Security representative at any time from 7 A.M. to 7 P.M. Monday through Friday (800-772-1213). For additional information on Social Security, see Chapter 8, Section II.

PART-TIME WORK AND OTHER SOURCES

Today, many people never completely retire. You may want to keep working at least part-time. Once you retire from your main career, you need to determine if you will be working at all during your retirement. Will you consult and/or work part-time? If so, estimate what income these activities will provide. You also need to evaluate whether any of your real or rental property or land contracts will produce income for you during retirement.

MORTGAGING YOUR PROPERTY FOR INVESTMENT FUNDS

As part of the planning process, you need to evaluate your overall financial situation. One concern is whether you own your home outright or are still paying off the mortgage. If you own your home free and clear in an area where real estate is not appreciating rapidly, then you are actually losing money, total return, and cash flow by not having a mortgage. You must accept that you are making an investment choice by having all or a sizable chunk of your capital tied up in your primary residence or a vacation home. This capital could be put to more productive use in a diversified portfolio of no-load funds.

This is one example whereby heeding conventional wisdom can be very detrimental in your investment planning. For most of the postwar era, the conventional wisdom was to own your home free and clear, thereby tying up a great deal of capital. This strategy worked very well for the World War II generation, and even an early part of the baby boom generation, as demand for housing greatly increased and housing prices went up at a rate faster than any other investment. However, things have since changed. Your house is not likely to be your best-performing asset in the years ahead because a baby bust followed the baby boom (see Figure 2.4).

FIGURE 2.4   BABY BUST

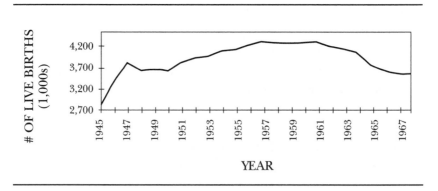

Sources: U.S. Bureau of the Census, *Statistical Abstract of the United States: 1996* (116th edition), Washington, DC, 1996; U.S. Bureau of the Census, *Historical Statistics of the United States, Colonial Times to 1970, Bicentennial Edition, Parts 1 & 2*, Washington, DC, 1975.

In the future, in most areas of the country there is strong economic and demographic evidence that your home is only very secondarily an investment. There are exceptions, like any other rule, and you will have to evaluate the long-term potential of the real estate market where you live and the likelihood of your home being a rapidly appreciating asset. The rate of appreciation may only keep up with the rate of inflation; it would be, therefore, a serious mistake to tie up a significant amount of your capital in a slowly appreciating asset.

In many cases, financial assets such as no-load stock, bond, and international mutual funds are likely to appreciate at a faster rate after taxes than your home will. Therefore, it may very well be prudent for you to take out a mortgage and free up capital for investment in these financial assets. Even if your home does appreciate, you are further ahead by having a mortgage; a mortgage provides a tax deduction for the mortgage interest paid, as long as the after-tax return on your investments is greater than your net-of-taxes mortgage cost. This is a safe assumption given the current low level of mortgage rates and the historical rates of return on stocks, bonds, and mutual funds.

In many cases, with mortgage interest rates in the low 7% range, your actual mortgage costs will be in the 5% to 5.5% range after deducting mortgage interest. Historical evidence supports that a well-diversified no-load mutual fund portfolio is likely to easily outdistance that 5.5% rate of return on an after-tax basis, net of all costs in the long run (i.e., over 15 years or more). (See Figure 2.5.)

Again, the conventional wisdom of paying off your mortgage may work against you, particularly in a retirement situation where cash flow could be very critical. There are only three nonmortgage ways to obtain cash flow from your primary or vacation residence and, in many cases, none of

FIGURE 2.5 WHEN INTEREST RATES ARE LOW, TAKE OUT YOUR MAXIMUM MORTGAGE

	Pay Off Your Mortgage? . . .			Not in Today's Interest Rate Environment!		
YEAR	HOME VALUE*	MORTGAGE	PORTFOLIO VALUE	HOME VALUE*	MORTGAGE†	NET PORTFOLIO VALUE
1998	$250,000	0	0	$250,000	$200,000	$200,000
2003	297,736	0	0	297,736	189,235	226,600
2008	354,586	0	0	354,586	173,590	256,738
2013	422,292	0	0	422,292	150,853	290,885
2018	502,926	0	0	502,926	117,810	329,573
2023	598,956	0	0	598,956	69,789	373,406
2028	713,322	0	0	713,322	0	423,070
	Ending net worth: $713,322			Ending net worth: $1,136,392		

Note: In the table above we have made a very complicated calculation, in which we make a number of assumptions about your standard versus itemized tax deductions. We have also assumed that your after-tax portfolio return will be 2.5% more than the new mortgage cost you have just assumed after taking into account that tax deduction that you receive for interest on this new mortgage.

*Assumes that your home will appreciate at about a 3.5% annual rate of inflation.
†Assumes a 30-year 7.5% mortgage.

these three alternative sources of cash flow will be appealing. You can sell the residence, rent out all or part of the residence, or, thirdly, take what is called a *reverse mortgage* on the residence, which in some unique cases may be prudent but often is an excessively costly alternative. (In a reverse mortgage, unlike a traditional mortgage where you pay the bank, the bank pays you every month for the right to own your home after you die.)

The example in Figure 2.5 assumes that a couple's single asset is their home and their only issue is whether to take out a mortgage and invest the proceeds. Because everyone's tax situation is different, we have made several assumptions in order to present this general example. You should seek tax, investment, and mortgage counsel to review your particular situation. Astute observers will notice that taking out a mortgage always makes sense if your portfolio grows at a rate greater than your true net mortgage cost regardless of the rate of appreciation on your home.

CHAPTER THREE

$

Maximizing
Cash Flow

IN THIS CHAPTER

In this chapter, you will learn:

1. A sensible and sustainable way safely to begin withdrawing your dividends, and even some principal, from your portfolio.

2. How your withdrawal rates should change during the three stages of retirement.

3. Open communication with both your spouse and professional advisors is the best approach to meet your joint investment goals and sleep at night.

4. Working with economic and market facts will produce better results than emotional investment decision making.

Often, the most important source of cash flow or income during retirement will come from your capital, or what we like to call your *investment portfolio*. Did you hear the one about the chicken farmer and the egg farmer? This useful analogy comes to us from James Garland, CFA, of The Jeffrey Company, a prominent investment counsel firm. We encourage our retiree clients to act like egg farmers instead of chicken farmers. Chicken farmers are really speculating on the price of their chickens. They raise chickens and frequently sell them in the open market every week hoping, or speculating, that the price of those chickens will go up. This behavior is similar to that of investors who are buying and selling stocks or mutual funds frequently (what we would call trading), speculating that the price of those stocks or funds will go up on a daily or weekly basis.

BE LIKE AN EGG FARMER
OR A LANDLORD

At our firm, we much prefer the mentality of the egg farmer. The egg farmer nurtures chickens to consistently and regularly produce eggs, which the farmer's family either consumes or sells in the market. They plan on living off those eggs for the course of their lifetime. This is similar to investors who live off their dividends or cash flow from their mutual funds or common stocks without having too much concern for short-term fluctuations in the price of those mutual funds or common stocks. Likewise, the egg farmer is not concerned with short-term fluctuations in the price of chickens as long as the egg production is consistent.

Another analogy we use with our clients is to encourage them to act like landlords instead of land speculators. The land speculator buys and sells property hoping the price of the property will go up for a profit when sold. The landlord owns high-quality property for the long run, and is just as concerned with the monthly income from his or her rental property and the fact that over time, the rent goes up to outpace the rate of inflation. Act like a landlord or an egg farmer. Don't act like a land speculator or a chicken farmer.

While we are examining using your capital or your investment portfolio as a source of cash flow during retirement, it is critical that we emphasize that there are other crucial aspects of your financial planning, such as medical or family emergencies that could deplete your capital base. It is absolutely essential that you have adequate health insurance, disability insurance, and long-term care insurance. You can have the perfect investment portfolio set up to produce a nice level of cash flow, but if you are not protected against a medical or other emergencies, then all of your diligent and intelligent investment planning is worthless. Protection from catastrophe or emergency is critical. Chapter 9 deals with insurance and health issues in detail.

Thus far we've looked at your nonportfolio retirement sources of cash flow including work, wages, Social Security, and pensions. We have also discussed unlocking hidden capital in your home by having a mortgage. Now we will shift gears slightly and explore what is probably your primary source of cash flow during retirement: your investment portfolio, or what we call your capital base. We will also look at how much sustainable cash flow your capital base will produce.

YOUR CAPITAL BASE: THE PRIMARY SOURCE OF INCOME—MAKING IT LAST DURING RETIREMENT

Take a careful look at the size of your capital base that you will be able to use during retirement. This is your so-called nest egg, which will fund the bulk of your retirement expenses. Nearly all clients who come into our office for advice concerning retirement planning face the same dilemma: how to enjoy their money effectively without depleting their capital too soon.

Most people have a hard time wrestling with this issue, and often do not spend as much or enjoy themselves as much as they could during retirement. We often see people leaving larger estates to their children and their heirs than they would anticipate.

Since the investment markets are unpredictable, there is no surefire formula for dictating the size of the withdrawals you will comfortably be able to make from your portfolio during retirement. However, in Chapter 5 we show you how much you can be withdrawing prudently each year from a broadly diversified retirement portfolio. At this point, however, we merely want to identify your capital base or sources of capital that you have working for you during retirement. In addition, we'll present some parameters that will give you an idea of what to expect as a minimum to withdraw from your capital without depleting your capital too soon.

Using Figure 3.1, you should take an inventory of your sources of retirement capital, including items in your portfolio, IRA, Keogh, pension and retirement plan, personal trust, and custodial accounts. In addition, as previously mentioned, you should consider other investments for your inventory such as real property, land contracts, and income-producing property, as well as hidden capital in your home that can be unlocked with a mortgage. As a rule of thumb we have provided Figure 3.2, which gives you an idea of how much you can be withdrawing from your capital during different stages of your retirement.

In Chapter 5 we explain in detail how to derive these sustainable portfolio withdrawal rates for retirees. By way of dis-

FIGURE 3.1 ASSET INVENTORY

	IN YOUR NAME OR TRUST	IN YOUR SPOUSE'S NAME OR TRUST	IN JOINT NAMES
Assets			
Your home (fair market value)	$	$	$
Other real estate			
Bank accounts			
Other savings accounts			
Stocks, bonds, and mutual funds			
Life insurance (face value)			
Business partnership interests			
Retirement plan accounts: IRA Keogh SEP Other (such as 401(k) or profit-sharing plans)			
Personal property (replacement value of jewelry, autos, household furnishings, etc.)			
Annuities, trusts, or other assets			
Collectibles (market value of fine art, precious metals, etc.)			
Total assets	$	$	$
Liabilities			
Mortgages	$	$	$
Life insurance loans			
Other loans or debts			
Total liabilities	$	$	$
Net estate (assets less liabilities)			

FIGURE 3.2   SUSTAINABLE PORTFOLIO WITHDRAWAL RATES FOR RETIREES

	AGE 55–65	AGE 66–75	AGE 76 AND UP
Primary objective	Save for retirement	Some income but also growth	A steady or growing income
Time horizon	30+ years	20+ years	10+ years
Projected return from a diversified portfolio	10%	9%	8%
Tax effect	(2%)	(2%)	(2%)
Inflation effect	(3%)	(3%)	(3%)
Real return	5%	4%	3%
Age adjustment	—	2.5%	6%
Sustainable portfolio withdrawal rate	5%	6.5%	9%

Source: Yolles Investment Management, Inc.

claimer, let us say that every investment environment is different; flexibility is required to be successful. Here we are giving broad guidelines that we believe will prove useful during the current environment.

THREE STAGES OF RETIREMENT

We also look at past historical periods to show how our guidelines would have held up under different conditions—periods of economic growth, economic recession, or economic inflation. During what we call the early retirement years ages 55 to 65, we feel that a 5% withdrawal rate is prudent and sustainable. During the mid-retirement years, ages 66 to 75, we feel that a 6.5% portfolio withdrawal rate is prudent and sustainable. During the later retirement years, ages 76 and over, we feel that as much as an 8%, 9%, or greater withdrawal rate can be sustainable, given your personal circumstances. See Figure 3.2.

Figure 3.2 suggests guidelines for withdrawing money from your investment portfolio. From ages 55 to 65, your portfolio must *at least* keep up with inflation and taxes. If your portfolio's total return (appreciation plus yield) is 10%, then you should withdraw only 5% annually (see Figure 3.2). After paying taxes, you will still see your portfolio grow fast enough to keep pace with inflation. For example, if you retire or semiretire at age 55 with a portfolio worth $500,000, then you can withdraw $2,083 per month and still see your portfolio grow in 10 years to $728,683 if you earn 10% annually (5% after taxes).

In Chapter 5, we will review different retirement scenarios and work through some case studies. But, as a starting point, these sustainable withdrawal rates are broad guidelines. If, for example, you and your spouse are both 63 years old and have a $600,000 capital base to retire on and are receiving $18,000 a year from Social Security as your only other source of retirement income, then using our guidelines, a 5% withdrawal on a $600,000 portfolio would provide $30,000 of additional retirement income to supplement your Social Security. This means that you could live comfortably on a $48,000 income ($30,000 + $18,000) during your retirement. Now we explain how you should recalibrate your annual portfolio withdrawal rate every five years and how you can recalibrate your portfolio withdrawal as you both age.

In our example, if you need substantially less than

$48,000 a year to live, then you have no worries whatsoever and your portfolio can comfortably sustain your standard of living. If you need close to $48,000 a year, then you will have to watch your capital closely and reevaluate your situation annually with the help of a competent financial advisor.

We firmly believe that everybody should have competent independent professionals including an independent highly qualified certified public accountant (CPA), a highly qualified attorney, a highly qualified independent insurance broker, and a highly qualified independent investment manager or advisor, preferably a chartered financial analyst (CFA). Chapter 12 will have more details about what the different financial designations and areas of training represent. Figure 3.3 illustrates the interdisciplinary nature of the financial planning process.

The following case studies may help illuminate different retirement issues that you are facing and/or retirement strategies that you are considering.

FIGURE 3.3   YOUR FINANCIAL TEAM

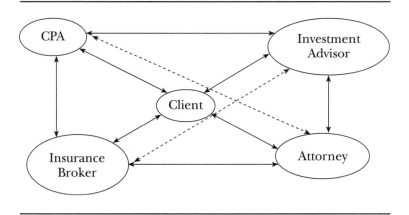

■$■ CASE STUDY 3.1—FRED AND WILMA

Our first case study involves Fred and Wilma. Fred worked as an attorney for 40 years. His law practice literally dried up, partly because eight years ago he thought that he could retire, so he stopped practicing law for two years. But then he realized that he needed more capital to fund his retirement. However, his return to the practice of law has not been very lucrative at all.

Fred and Wilma have always enjoyed a rather high standard of living. Fred has become very concerned about whether their capital will last during their retirement, while Wilma is more interested in enjoying retirement and continuing their lavish lifestyle, even hoping that they can buy a winter retirement home in Phoenix. Fred has developed insomnia, worrying about whether their lifestyle will be possible during retirement. In addition, most of Fred's and Wilma's close friends are financially better off than they are and are enjoying a very comfortable retirement lifestyle. For Fred and Wilma, emotional issues and pressures have been mounting, making it difficult to be comfortable participating in activities, vacation, travel, dining, and cultural events that they have always enjoyed with their friends, but now question whether they can afford.

In December of 1994, Fred and Wilma came to Yolles Investment Management, Inc., with these and other issues. Here's a look at how we helped the couple gain a feeling of control, organization, comfort, and safety in their financial lives.

In 1994, Fred turned 66 and Wilma 63. They had accumulated a portfolio including IRA accounts of $584,000. They were receiving $1,000 per month, which would continue through 1999, on a land contract from a piece of real estate that Fred had invested in. Their Social Security provided income of $16,700 a year. They owned their own home free and clear of mortgage debt and estimated that their home was worth $200,000, with very little appreciation potential. Fred was in very good health. Wilma was also in good health, although she did have diabetes. Their investment portfolio consisted entirely of cash and domestic common stocks and bonds that Fred had either selected himself or bought with the help of various brokers over the years. The portfolio was a hodgepodge, with little appropriate diversification. There was little coordination between Fred's holdings and different industry groups. For example, he had too many auto stocks and few holdings in other industry groups.

FIGURE 3.4   FRED AND WILMA'S MONTHLY DISTRIBUTIONS, 1994

BEFORE	AFTER
Stocks and bonds: $2,165 per month	Mutual fund portfolio: $3,222 per month

Since the bulk of Fred and Wilma's portfolio was in retirement accounts, we were able to immediately help them restructure their portfolio into a broadly diversified portfolio of no-load mutual funds. Not only were we able to substantially reduce the risk in Fred and Wilma's portfolio as measured by *standard deviation* (which we were able to cut in half), but we were also able to improve the expected return through broader diversification including international funds. Even the monthly dividend return improved on their portfolio by $1,057 per month, as shown in Figure 3.4.

$

$ CASE STUDY 3.2—ARCHIE AND EDITH VERSUS OZZIE AND HARRIET

Another case study involves the tale of two retired couples, Archie and Edith and their counterparts Ozzie and Harriet. By 1985, each family had accumulated $200,000 for retirement. Archie dominated his household and, against Edith's better judgment, insisted that all their retirement funds be put in certificates of deposit, which at that time were yielding 8%.

"Edith, even a meathead knows you puts your money in da bank," advised Archie.

In contrast, Ozzie and Harriet sought and received professional investment counsel from an advisor who advocated broadly diversifying their portfolio. It should be noted that both couples were 65 years old in 1985, in good health, and had just retired.

In the late 1980s and into the early and mid-1990s, Archie and Edith continued to roll over their CDs, and as inflation declined, the rate of interest on their CDs also declined sharply. Rates reached a trough in 1990 when the couple received only 4.5% on their CDs and they had to start dipping into their principal. (See Figure 3.5.)

Ozzie and Harriet, with their broadly diversified portfolio, thrived and were able to increase the amount of their biennial withdrawals while the value of their principal grew smartly over time. From 1985 to 1998, the difference in their standards of living and quality of life during their retirement has been nothing short of startling. Ozzie and Harriet's broadly diversified portfolio has averaged 13% a year and has grown in size to more than $600,000 over the 13-year period. They have made a grand total of $270,000 in withdrawals from their portfolio over that same 13-year period and have felt comfortable enough to make gifts to

FIGURE 3.5 ARCHIE AND EDITH VERSUS OZZIE AND HARRIET

	ARCHIE AND EDITH		OZZIE AND HARRIET	
YEAR	PRINCIPAL	WITHDRAWALS	PRINCIPAL	WITHDRAWALS
1985	$200,000.00		$200,000.00	
1986	216,000.00		226,000.00	
1987	233,280.00		255,380.00	
1988	251,942.40		288,579.40	
1989	272,097.79		326,094.72	
1990	253,981.70	–$29,000.00	368,487.04	
1991	236,140.97	–28,000.00	416,390.35	
1992	217,586.61	–28,000.00	470,521.10	
1993	198,290.08	–28,000.00	462,788.84	–$68,900.00
1994	178,221.68	–28,000.00	522,951.39	
1995	157,350.55	–28,000.00	509,835.07	–81,100.00
1996	135,644.57	–28,000.00	576,113.63	
1997	113,070.35	–28,000.00	531,008.40	–120,000.00
1998	117,593.16		600,039.49	
Totals		–$225,000.00		–$270,000.00

their grandchildren and also to two grown children who entered low-paying professions.

Archie and Edith have been forced to tap into their principal. Their portfolio size has declined steadily to about $117,000. If it wasn't for their son-in-law, who became a successful film director, the prospects for a very disastrous retirement and complete depletion of their capital by the time they are in their early 80s is and would be a very real threat.

$

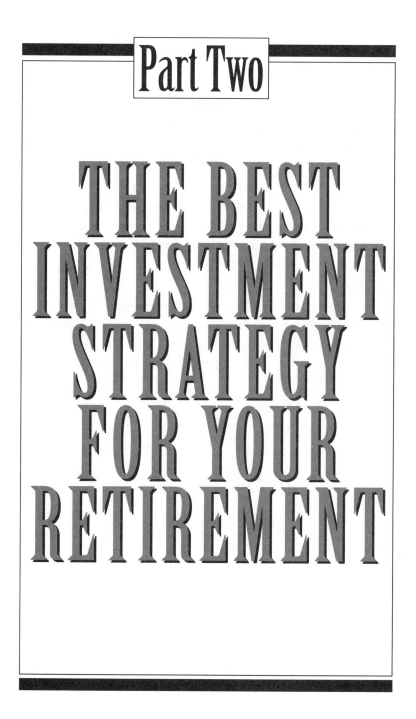

Part Two

THE BEST INVESTMENT STRATEGY FOR YOUR RETIREMENT

This part, which encompasses Chapters 4, 5, 6, and 7, covers the key subject of investing during retirement.

Chapter 4 deals with critical investment issues related to your investment temperament. In this chapter, we will teach you how to implement a retirement investment strategy that will let you sleep comfortably.

Chapter 5 provides an overview of investing concepts and focuses on the best overall approach to retirement.

In Chapters 6 and 7, we review specific investment strategies as well as recommendations for maintaining a comfortable portfolio during retirement.

CHAPTER FOUR

Identifying Your Money Personality

IN THIS CHAPTER

For many of you, this is the most important chapter in the entire book. The single greatest cause of investment failure and losses that we have seen is self-destructive behavior, including greed in search of wild returns or fear resulting in excessive caution. In this chapter we address the following topics:

1. What is your money personality? How might it hurt your investment results?

2. Learn how to make your money personality work for you so that you will earn the best possible return and be able to sleep at night.

3. Do "lifeboat drills" so that you know how to react when inevitable bear markets occur.

4. Discover your true tolerance for risk with our nine-question risk profile indicator, which will help you to structure a portfolio matching your temperament.

In the Introduction to this book, we told you about Samantha, who anxiously consulted us about whether she and her husband, Darren, could afford to retire. She was 65 years old and in good health. Her husband was 67 years old and in fair health. He was finding it increasingly difficult to run his advertising business. Unfortunately, Darren could not sell his company in order to have money to live on during retirement because his advertising clients depended entirely on him.

Samantha told us about her long list of investment failures—the ones she thought would be "home runs" but turned out to be "strikeouts." She felt that if she hit an investment home run, then she and Darren could retire comfortably.

We all have a bit of Samantha's batting streak in us. The challenge is to make objective decisions without allowing our human emotions to intrude. We are all subject to fear and greed. But, it's essential to learn to leave fear and greed out of our decisions. To do this, you must learn to recognize the telltale signs of fear and greed manifesting themselves in your investment behavior and personality.

Financial economics, which is the scholarly term for the study of investing and individual investor behavior, is a social science. Both bear and bull markets and individuals' behavior in those markets are explained by financial economics. Individual results in those markets are subject to influence by the vagaries of human behavior. Often, not only do fear and greed end up negatively influencing our individual portfolio results, but they also can have an influence on the overall market—at least in the short run. This was vividly seen in the October 1997 "Gray Monday" 554-point decline in the Dow Jones Index as investors reacted to economic turmoil in Hong Kong.

Psychologists and behavioral scientists have helped us to

understand how someone's emotions lead to suboptimal investment results, portfolio designs, and behavior. Amos Tversky, PhD, of Stanford University, and Meir Stateman, PhD, of Santa Clara University, have done innovative work on these topics in the field of behavioral finance.

In his pioneering research, Professor Tversky showed that individuals are actually more risk-averse than they should be when it comes to guaranteeing certain gain. Ironically, these investors are more willing to take risk when it comes to avoiding any nominal loss or when it comes to recouping a loss.

For example, Professor Tversky has shown that individuals prefer a sure $240 gain to a 25% chance of a $1,000 gain, even though this 25% chance of a $1,000 gain may produce more profit in the long run ($1,000 × .25 = $250). While this example may seem to be trivial, it merely serves as one instance where an individual's investment behavior may not be rational. Drawing on Professor Tversky's work, as financial advisors, once we have identified all of the areas where individuals are likely to behave irrationally, then we can begin to help you avoid these mistakes.

Let's return to our friend Samantha's daughter Tabitha, who worked for many years for the Bendix Corporation, which later became Unisys. Tabitha came to us in 1991 with a portfolio worth $270,000. Of this amount, $125,000 was in Unisys stock. Because she enjoyed her job and coworkers, Tabitha had an emotional attachment to the Unisys stock, even though there were neither economic nor safety reasons to hold onto the stock. In fact, Tabitha was taking 75% more risk in holding such a large position in this single stock as she would risk by holding a diversified portfolio (see Figure 4.1). Unfortunately for Tabitha, the Unisys stock stagnated and she cheated herself out of significant returns from 1991 through 1997 when she finally sold the Unisys stock for $12 per share.

FIGURE 4.1   WHAT IS YOUR THRESHOLD
FOR PAIN?: HOW DIVERSIFICATION REDUCES
NONMARKET RISK

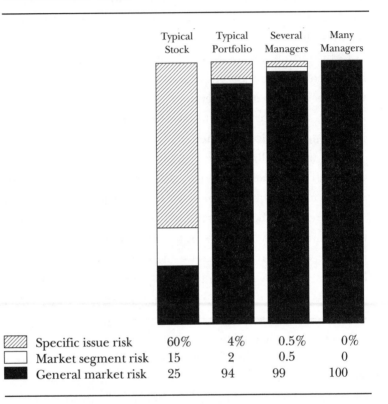

	Typical Stock	Typical Portfolio	Several Managers	Many Managers
Specific issue risk	60%	4%	0.5%	0%
Market segment risk	15	2	0.5	0
General market risk	25	94	99	100

Source: Reprinted with permission of The McGraw-Hill Companies from *Investment Policy—How to Win the Loser's Game, 2E,* by Charles Ellis. Copyright © 1993.

Tabitha had kept hoping that Unisys's stock price would return to the $24 per share that she originally paid. Tabitha was suffering from *mental accounting.* In this case, mental accounting meant that Tabitha set her buy and sell targets for her stock holding in Unisys based on her original purchase price. This is not rational. **A rational investor puts his or her capital to the best and safest use** *at all times* **with considera-**

tion given to the investor's required rate of return, toler- ance of risk, and need for safety. We like to say that money has no memory and the market does not remember the price at which you bought a given stock. It is much better for you to implement the proper portfolio today than to try to recoup old losses in an inferior investment.

Mental accounting takes on another form when a good portfolio of no-load mutual funds initially drops in value due to a decline in the overall market but then recovers as the market turns around. Too often investors will sell out when the market gets back to even and will sacrifice a per- fectly good and properly diversified portfolio. *Do not suc- cumb to this tendency.*

LIFEBOAT DRILLS

We use two techniques to help prevent investors from falling into mental accounting traps. One technique in- volves drafting a detailed portfolio policy statement (which we will discuss in Chapter 7). The second technique involves going through *lifeboat drills* to simulate how you will behave during predictable bear market conditions.

Figure 4.2 shows how different types of portfolios are likely to behave during market downturns of various severi- ties. Review your asset allocation and how your portfolio will likely behave during a downturn. Then use Figures 4.3 and 4.4 to test whether your portfolio fits into your comfort zone. You should do this so that you will not make unwise revisions to your solid long-term strategy based on short- term emotional pressures of a down market. We call this ex- ercise a lifeboat drill.

Figure 4.5 expands on the concepts illustrated in Figure 4.2. Here we show that all asset classes, and therefore all portfolios, become much less risky if held for the long

FIGURE 4.2   OPTIMAL PORTFOLIO ALLOCATIONS

(1971–1996)			
	CONSERVATIVE	MODERATE	AGGRESSIVE
Equity	0%	60%	100%
Fixed income	100%	40%	0%
Compound return (%)	9.2%	11.8%	13%
Annualized standard deviation	7.7%	11.8%	17.1%
Lowest annual return	–2.9%	–16.5%	–28.4%
Growth of $1	$9.04	$16.21	$21.09

Source: Ennis, Knupp & Associates, Chicago, IL. Used with permission.

term. If this table does not convince you to adopt a long-term investment discipline, then nothing will. *Please study it closely.*

REARVIEW MIRROR INVESTING

Another common problem our firm sees all too frequently is what we call rearview mirror investing. This mind-set manifests itself in investors having too much confidence that the future will resemble the immediate past. Investors too often succumb to the temptation of believing that mutual funds that have done well over the past 5 or 10 years will continue to do well over the next 5 or 10 years.

There are many examples of investors losing money by following this rearview mirror approach. For example, during the 1970s, the conventional wisdom was that hard assets such as gold, precious metals, energy, and real estate were the investment vehicles of choice. Unfortunately, during the 1980s financial assets such as stocks, bonds, and mutual

FIGURE 4.3   RISK/RETURN TRADE-OFF
IN THE SHORT RUN

Covering 65 One-Year Investment Periods, 1926–1996

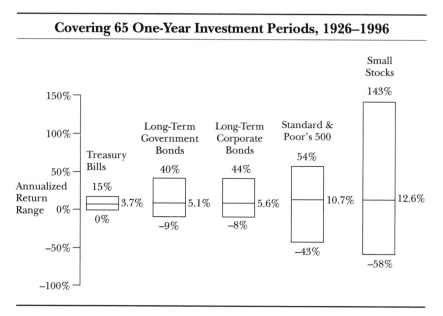

Note: Each bar shows the range of annual total returns for a different type of investment.

Source: Ibbotson Associates. Used with permission. Copyright © 1997 Ibbotson Associates, Inc. All rights reserved. (Certain portions of this work were derived from copyrighted works of Roger G. Ibbotson and Rex Sinquefield.)

funds prevailed. We say "unfortunately" because most investors waited until the beginning of the 1980s to go out and invest in the hard-asset type of vehicles that prospered during the 1970s.

In the late 1960s and early 1970s, the rearview conventional wisdom dictated investing in mutual funds that held all or most of the "Nifty 50" stocks, because they prospered tremendously. These stocks were termed one-decision stocks, because the only decision an investor had to make was to *buy* them.

Unfortunately, many of these stocks lost 80%, or even

FIGURE 4.4   RISK/RETURN TRADE-OFF IN THE LONG RUN

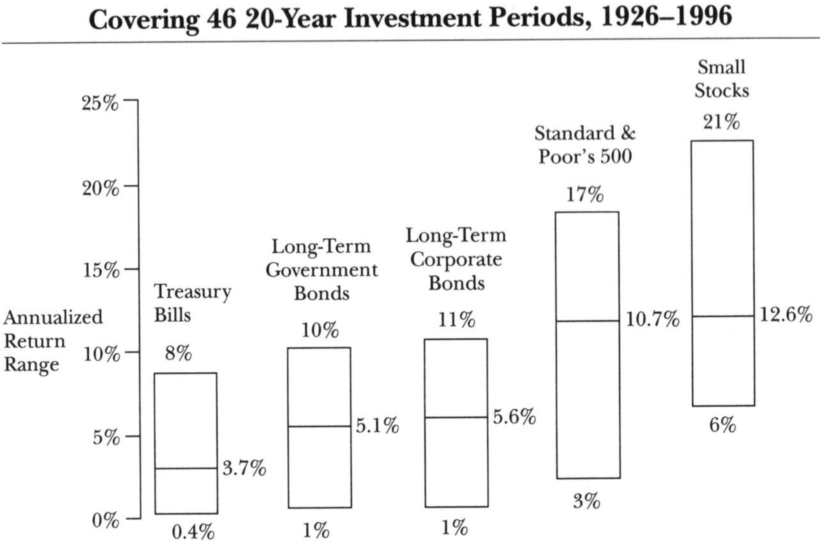

Covering 46 20-Year Investment Periods, 1926–1996

Note: Each bar shows the range of compound average annual total returns for a different type of investment.

Source: Ibbotson Associates. Used with permission. Copyright © 1997 Ibbotson Associates, Inc. All rights reserved. (Certain portions of this work were derived from copyrighted works of Roger G. Ibbotson and Rex Sinquefield.)

90%, of their value during the 1973–1974 bear market. In fact, even in the 1990s, many of them are just returning to their 1972 levels. The "Nifty 50" enthusiasm was a perfect example of both a stock mania or bubble, where stock prices were ridiculously inflated relative to the underlying economics of these 50 companies, and rearview investing, where a profitable strategy during one time period (1969–1972) proved disastrous during a subsequent period (1973–1974).

Similarly, in the current bull market, you see many popular blue-chip companies such as Coca-Cola, Gillette, and others selling for outrageous multiples of more than 40 times their companies' earnings. The prevailing logic would seem to be that you cannot go wrong by investing in these blue-chip stocks. But, history has shown us that you can pay too high a price for any stock, even the bluest of the blue chips. For this reason it is critical that each investor follow a diligent and rigorous analytical process to find reasonable values in his or her investments. Stories about stocks mean nothing! Psychologically, by following an informed process to find investments with reasonable valuations, you can have confidence that these investments will profit in the long run because they were purchased at a reasonable price.

YOUR RISK PROFILE

Figure 4.6 will help you understand how you will react under different market conditions. Over your lifetime, you should expect a variety of market conditions, including bear markets every three or four years, which may have very severe magnitude and duration. Like the true Rorschach test that helps psychologists develop a personality profile even when the patient gives standard answers to direct questions, our "investment Rorschach" helps us dig deeper into a new client's canned answer of "I want 15% growth, but I'm conservative and don't want risk."

Figure 4.7 shows nearly 100 years of investment history and should help you have a more comfortable feeling about bear markets. If you know how often bear markets occur, you can get a better sense of the nature of capital and investment markets and the merits of long-term investing, as long as you don't get too upset over the inevitable temporary declines. It is also critical that you not alter your strat-

Figure 4.5 Range of Returns: Maximum and Minimum Values of Returns for 1-, 5-, 10-, 15-, and 20-Year Holding Periods

SERIES	MAXIMUM VALUE		MINIMUM VALUE		TIMES POSITIVE	TIMES HIGHEST RETURNING ASSET
	RETURN*	YEAR(S)	RETURN*	YEAR(S)		
Annual Returns						
Large-company stocks	53.92	1933	–43.34	1931	51	14 (OUT OF 71 YEARS)
Small-company stocks	142.87	1933	–58.01	1937	50	31
Long-term corporate bonds	42.56	1982	–8.09	1969	55	6
Long-term government bonds	40.36	1982	–9.18	1967	51	6
Intermediate-term government bonds	29.10	1982	–5.14	1994	64	2
U.S. Treasury bills	14.71	1981	–0.02	1938	70	6
Inflation	18.16	1946	–10.30	1932	61	6
5-Year Rolling Period Returns						
Large-company stocks	23.92	1950–54	–12.47	1928–32	60	19 (OUT OF 67 OVERLAPPING 5-YEAR PERIODS)
Small-company stocks	45.90	1941–45	–27.54	1928–32	58	37

						7
Long-term corporate bonds	22.51	1982–86	–2.22	1965–69	64	7
Long-term government bonds	21.62	1982–86	–2.14	1965–69	61	1
Intermediate-term government bonds	16.98	1982–86	0.96	1955–59	67	2
U.S. Treasury bills	11.12	1979–83	0.07	1938–42	67	0
Inflation	10.06	1977–81	–5.42	1928–32	60	1

10-Year Rolling Period Returns

						(OUT OF 62 OVERLAPPING 10-YEAR PERIODS)
Large-company stocks	20.06	1949–58	–0.89	1929–38	60	17
Small-company stocks	30.38	1975–84	–5.70	1929–38	60	35
Long-term corporate bonds	16.32	1982–91	0.98	1947–56	62	6
Long-term government bonds	15.56	1982–91	–0.07	1950–59	61	0
Intermediate-term government bonds	13.13	1982–91	1.25	1947–56	62	2
U.S. Treasury bills	9.17	1978–87	0.15	1933–42/1934–43	62	1
Inflation	8.67	1973–82	–2.57	1926–35	56	1

*Compound annual rates of return in percent.

FIGURE 4.5 (CONTINUED)

15-Year Rolling Period Returns

SERIES	MAXIMUM VALUE RETURN*	YEAR(S)	MINIMUM VALUE RETURN*	YEAR(S)	TIMES POSITIVE	TIMES HIGHEST RETURNING ASSET (OUT OF 57 OVERLAPPING 15-YEAR PERIODS)
Large-company stocks	18.24	1942–56	0.64	1929–43	57	9
Small-company stocks	23.33	1975–89	–1.30	1927–41	54	44
Long-term corporate bonds	13.66	1982–96	1.02	1955–69	57	4
Long-term government bonds	13.53	1981–95	0.40	1955–69	57	0
Intermediate-term government bonds	11.27	1981–95	1.45	1945–59	57	0
U.S. Treasury bills	8.32	1977–91	0.22	1933–47	57	0
Inflation	7.30	1968–82	–1.59	1926–40	54	0

20-Year Rolling Period Returns

							(OUT OF 52 OVERLAPPING 20-YEAR PERIODS)
Large-company stocks	16.86	1942–61	3.11	1929–48	52	52	3
Small-company stocks	21.13	1942–61	5.74	1929–48	52	52	49
Long-term corporate bonds	10.58	1976–95	1.34	1950–69	52	52	0
Long-term government bonds	10.45	1976–95	0.69	1950–69	52	52	0
Intermediate-term government bonds	9.85	1974–93	1.58	1940–59	52	52	0
U.S. Treasury bills	7.72	1972–91	0.42	1931–50	52	52	0
Inflation	6.36	1966–85	0.07	1926–45	52	52	0

*Compound annual rates of return in percent.

Source: Ibbotson Associates. Used with permission. Copyright © 1997 Ibbotson Associates, Inc. All rights reserved. (Certain portions of this work were derived from copyrighted works of Roger G. Ibbotson and Rex Sinquefield.)

FIGURE 4.6   AN INVESTMENT RORSCHACH TEST: HELPING YOU FIND YOUR INVESTMENT TEMPERAMENT

Knowledge about your investment temperament can help you avoid unwise revisions to your well thought-out retirement plan.

This quiz should help you identify your investment temperament. Please choose the best answer to each question below—go with your first instinct.

1. In this table, which depicts actual investment data in the post–World War II era, choose the portfolio allocation between stocks and bonds that most closely matches your goals and temperament.

Finding Your Risk Tolerance

PORTFOLIO	% IN STOCKS	% IN BONDS	WORST YEAR	BEST YEAR	AVERAGE YEAR
1	100	0	−26.5	52.9	13.5
2	90	10	−23.4	48.1	12.7
3	80	20	−20.3	43.5	11.8
4	70	30	−17.2	39.0	11.0
5	60	40	−14.1	34.4	10.1
6	50	50	−11.1	31.8	9.3
7	40	60	−8.0	32.8	8.4
8	30	70	−6.1	34.7	7.8
9	20	80	−5.8	35.6	6.7
10	10	90	−5.0	36.9	5.9
11	0	100	−9.2	40.4	5.0

Source: Standard & Poor's.

2. On the golf course or at parties when others talk about their investing prowess . . .
   a. I listen closely because I don't want to miss out on a chance for big gains.
   b. I take everything with a grain of salt and always consider the source.

FIGURE 4.6 (CONTINUED)

3. Which statement best describes your investment approach?
   a. My instincts about people and investment opportunities are very good; I trust these instincts.
   b. I'm methodical; I research every decision. *Consumer Reports* is my favorite publication.
   c. There is such a thing as information overload. I gather relevant information, decide, and then don't look back.
   d. Decisions are tough. I often procrastinate—you can never be too careful.

4. In this graph, which depicts risk and return characteristics of 11 different portfolios, choose the portfolio number that most closely balances your return objective with your gut feeling as to how much risk you can tolerate. White bars show worst-case, hatched bars show best-case, and black bars show average scenarios.

Comfort Zones 1947–1990

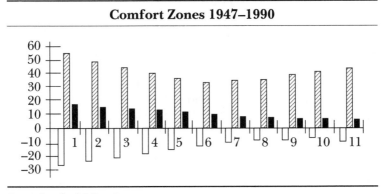

Source: Standard & Poor's.

5. Are you nervous about another stock market crash? If so, which of the following approaches to market risk feels best to you?
   a. A guaranteed 7% return would be sufficient to live on, and I'd take it.
   b. The best experts can consistently earn 20% per year; the challenge is to find them.
   c. The market always bounces back; I want to be aggressive and "buy on the dips."
   d. I'd like an expert to lay out an investment plan tailored to my needs; I don't know everything and believe in following the counsel of professionals in any field.

FIGURE 4.6 (CONTINUED)

---

6. If most of the television commentators and your friends were convinced that rapid inflation had returned and that cash and precious metals investments would work best, you would . . .
   a. Buy gold and CDs—this approach did well in the 1970s.
   b. Move some, but not all, of my portfolio into CDs and metals.
   c. Seek objective professional guidance.
   d. Stick to my existing long-term plan.

---

7. If these same friends and TV commentators felt that a depression or deep recession were about to occur and that government bonds were the only safe investment, you would . . .
   a. Buy government bonds.
   b. Move some, but not all, of my portfolio into government bonds.
   c. Seek objective professional guidance.
   d. Stick to my existing long-term plan.

---

8. In 1996, the stock market (S&P 500 Index) rose 37%. If your portfolio only made 15%, you would have been . . .
   a. Thrilled—that's all I need.
   b. Furious—I want to keep pace with the market.
   c. Disappointed—but I would stick with my long-term plan.
   d. Checking with my advisor to see what percentage of my portfolio was in stocks or no-load stock mutual funds, because I wouldn't expect my low-risk bonds and cash to keep up with the high-risk stock market.

---

9. During the furious bear market of 1987 (35% decline), the Saddam Hussein bear market of 1990 (20% decline), or the 11% market decline in October 1996, if your stock portfolio had declined nearly as much as the market at the time, you would have . . .
   a. Sold most of my holdings and bought safe CDs.
   b. Waited to get back to even and then sold everything.
   c. Added to my stock holdings to buy low.
   d. Done nothing, because I have only my long-term holdings in stocks or stock mutual funds and realize that stocks will fluctuate in the short run.

Answer Key

---

1. If you chose portfolio 1, 2, 3, or 4, score yourself 3 points; portfolio 5, 6, or 7, 2 points; portfolio 8, 9, 10, or 11, 1 point.

FIGURE 4.6 (CONTINUED)

2. Choice (b) scores 2 points; choice (a), 0 points.

3. Choice (c) scores 3 points; choice (b), 2 points; choices (a) and (d), 1 point.

4. Same scoring as question 1.

5. Choice (d) scores 3 points; choices (a) and (c), 1 point; choice (b), 0 points.

6. Choices (c) and (d) score 3 points; choice (b), 1 point; choice (a), 0 points.

7. Choices (c) and (d) score 3 points; choice (b), 1 point; choice (a), 0 points.

8. Choice (d) scores 3 points; choice (c), 2 points; choice (a), 1 point; choice (b), 0 points.

9. Choice (d) scores 3 points; choice (c), 2 points; choice (b), 1 point; choice (a), 0 points.

If your score is . . .
17 to 26 points—You have the "delegator" or "long-term investor" temperament necessary to succeed.

10 to 16 points—You have an "armchair quarterback" temperament that can work during calm market conditions, but could break down under severe market stress.

Less than 10 points—Your emotions could hurt you during severe market conditions. Several times a year, you should practice the "lifeboat drills" described earlier in this chapter. Also, you should seek the counsel of a seasoned investment professional whom you respect.

Source: 1990 Standard & Poor's Outlook. Used with permission.

egy based on emotional reactions when theses inevitable normal declines occur.

After completing Figure 4.6 and carefully reviewing Figure 4.7, you should walk yourself through a lifeboat drill. Look at different scenarios and the likely reaction of your portfolio during down market conditions; then test how you would react during those times. For example, if you have a $700,000 portfolio that declines to $600,000, will your intellect be able to outweigh your emotions? Will you stick with your long-term strategy, or will you abandon your well diversified portfolio and retreat to cash, thereby eliminating the benefit of long-term investing?

In our experience, a thorough understanding of investment history can help you do the proper thing when bear

FIGURE 4.7   LIKE SNOW IN WINTER, BEAR MARKETS ARE PREDICTABLE BUT ANNOYING

Here is a rundown on how frequently various types of stock market declines have occurred since 1900, how deep they have been, and how long they have lasted.

	ROUTINE DECLINE (5% OR MORE)	MODERATE CORRECTION (10% OR MORE)	SEVERE CORRECTION (15% OR MORE)	BEAR MARKET (20% OR MORE)
Number of times since 1900	318	106	50	29
How often to expect this	About 3 times/yr.	About once/yr.	About once/2 yrs.	About once/3 yrs.
Last time it happened	July 1996	August 1990	August 1990	October 1990
Average loss before decline ends	11%	19%	27%	35%
Average length	40 days	109 days	217 days	364 days
Chance of decline turning into a bear market	9%	27%	58%	100%

Note: Averages are means. Days are calendar days, including weekends.

Source: Ned Davis Research Inc.

FIGURE 4.7 (CONTINUED)

Down Markets 1946–1996 (Annual Basis)

YEAR	% LOSS	YEAR	YEARS TO MAKE UP LOSSES
1974	26.5	1973	3
1973	14.6	1946	2
1957	10.8	1969	2
1966	10.1	1977	2
1962	8.7	1953	1
1969	8.1	1957	1
1946	8.5	1962	1
1977	7.2	1966	1
1981	4.9	1974	1
1990	3.1	1981	1
1957	1.0	1990	1

Source: Reprinted with permission of the *Wall Street Journal.*

markets occur—namely, *do nothing.* At Yolles Investment Management, we've developed a humorous expression to describe how an investor should react to a bear market: "Don't just do something, sit there." In fact, if anything, bear markets are excellent times to add to your stock holdings. Remember: Buy low, sell high—always.

During a worst-case scenario, the returns you receive or losses you experience must fit within your tolerance for risk. This level of comfort will give you the best opportunity possible of realizing a solid rate of return by sticking with your long-term program. Figure 4.8 is a chart we use at Yolles Investment Management to help our clients understand the risk and return parameters of different portfolio approaches. While this chart is complicated, the *efficient market*

FIGURE 4.8 EFFICIENT MARKET LINE

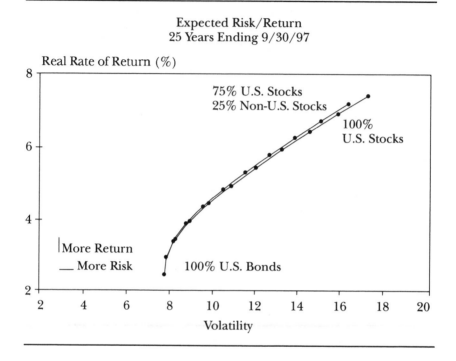

Expected Risk/Return
25 Years Ending 9/30/97

Real Rate of Return (%)

75% U.S. Stocks
25% Non-U.S. Stocks

100%
U.S. Stocks

More Return
— More Risk

100% U.S. Bonds

Volatility

Source: Ennis, Knupp & Associates, Chicago, IL. Used with permission.

line concept that it illustrates should make economic sense. Namely, if a portfolio contains more no-load stock funds, and a smaller allocation to bond funds, the portfolio will be more risky than a portfolio that has less exposure to the stock market. However, the greater the stock fund allocation, the greater the "real" (after inflation) return. The graph shows 11 optimal portfolios for different levels of risk. As the word *optimal* implies, these 11 portfolio designs are ideal for different investors depending on their return requirements and their risk tolerance. There is an ideal portfolio for every investor. **Our challenge is to help you find the ideal portfolio for you at different stages of your retirement.**

Also review Figure 4.2, which shows various optimal portfolio allocations for different investors and the amount of risk present in each of these portfolios. It is worth taking the extra time necessary to understand the exact nature of these portfolios, even though it may be difficult to understand the features of these portfolios at first glance. Stay with us, and you'll have a successful retirement.

CONCLUSION

This chapter on your money personality is probably worth rereading due to its importance and the complexity of the material. Investment success has nothing to do with your IQ, career, or station in life and everything to do with knowing yourself and your own limitations.

Investing During Retirement

As mentioned in Chapter 3, we counsel our clients and all retirement investors to act more like landlords than land speculators. The beauty of the successful landlord is that he or she receives a steady cash flow every month, and generally that cash flow increases at more than the rate of inflation. Many savvy parents and grandparents have started investing in real estate in college towns for their children or grandchildren. Their kids have a place to live, and the parents can collect rent from other students once their kids graduate and vacate the property.

INVEST TO BEAT INFLATION

We encourage retiree investors to adopt a similar attitude with their no-load mutual funds or high-quality common stock holdings, because stocks and stock mutual funds, along with real estate, are the only investments to beat inflation in the long run. Your attitude should be that, as long as your dividends are secure and gradually increasing over time, fluctuations in your principal are normal and expected. As long as the quality of your investments is high, fluctuations should not cause you undue worry. Since you are not a speculator and you're not dipping into your principal, you should not be concerned with short-term fluctuations in your portfolio value but, rather, with the consistency of your cash flow or dividend stream.

Retired investors most often fail by succumbing to either fear or greed. If you succumb to fear, you are likely to put too much of your portfolio in bonds or bond funds and barely keep up with inflation. If you succumb to greed, you will speculate on earning excess returns and unwittingly put your principal at risk. We want to present evidence that will encourage you to be a long-term investor rather than give in to greed by speculating on one extreme or fear by just buying bonds on the other extreme (we call these extremes lending or saving your money instead of investing).

Let's take this opportunity to summarize the investment world.

There are three things that you can do with your money: speculate, save, or invest. Speculation is for gamblers, and we refuse to devote more than one sentence of this book to the topic. Savers put their money in bank certificates of deposit or Treasury bills, both of which barely keep up with inflation, which is an inadequate approach for all but the wealthiest retirees. This book focuses on the third alternative: investing. Investing is not gambling but rather ownership. When you buy a share of stock in McDonald's, you are an owner, and your success or failure will be tied to the economic success or failure of McDonald's.

In the long run, the stock price of McDonald's, and any company, moves in direct proportion to the financial success of the company. As Figure 5.1 illustrates, the stock price of McDonald's over the past 33 years has moved in unison with the company's underlying earnings and dividends.

Figure 5.1 shows that while the earnings growth of McDonald's has been remarkably stable, its stock price, in the short run, has been much more volatile in reaction to world, economic, and market events. **But in the long run, stock price and company earnings always move in unison.** This economic fact should make sense to you; if not, please reread the previous few paragraphs—the concept is that critical.

Investing is not gambling. It's the essence of capitalism: Investors provide the liquidity for corporations like McDonald's to grow and hire more people and improve productivity. Everyone benefits. Investing—in stocks, mutual funds, and/or real estate—is the best way to stay ahead of inflation in the long run **if you can stick with your investment program**. The question is how can you stick with your program?

FIGURE 5.1   McDONALD'S STOCK PERFORMANCE

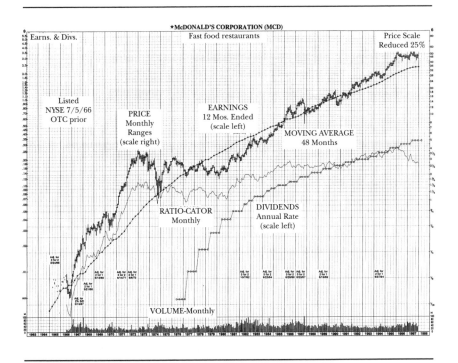

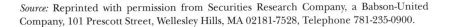

Source: Reprinted with permission from Securities Research Company, a Babson-United Company, 101 Prescott Street, Wellesley Hills, MA 02181-7528, Telephone 781-235-0900.

As mentioned earlier, adopting an attitude like a long-term landlord is paramount to becoming a successful investor. Stick with high-quality mutual funds or stocks through market ups and downs, just like landlords hold on to properties through the real estate market's ups and downs. And, as shown in history, you will be rewarded.

There is a saying that "knowledge is power" (Francis Bacon, 1597). A study of the stock market from 1926 to 1998 should provide you with this necessary faith in the superior long-term characteristics of high-quality stock and mutual fund investments to ride out market ups and downs. The next section clearly illustrates that you can earn the superior long-term stock market returns by adopting a reasonably safe, balanced approach.

INDEX INVESTING CAN BE HAZARDOUS TO YOUR WEALTH

No matter how wealthy they are, retirees and preretirees are perpetually worried about whether their money will last.

At Yolles Investment Management, Inc., we have developed a study of sustainable withdrawal rates for retirees. Our professionals found that most retirees are concerned with how much they can withdraw from their portfolios without depleting their principal. They generally rely on an IRA rollover account and their personal savings to supplement their Social Security during retirement. Some are fortunate enough to have a lifetime pension through their employers. Our clients often say, "We just need $80,000 a year from our investments to supplement our annual $18,000 from Social Security. Then we can maintain our living standard, including taxes." This experience led us to research different types of retirement portfolios and to develop guidelines for retirees.

Most investment professionals agree that the old conventional wisdom of retirees focusing on fixed-income instru-

STANDARD & POOR'S 500 INDEX FUND

An index fund replicates the performance of a given group of stocks and/or bonds. In this case, 500 of the largest industrial companies in the United States, including General Electric, General Motors, Microsoft, Intel, IBM, and Citicorp, are represented.

ments and certificates of deposit has been dispelled. There's now overwhelming research evidence that fixed-income-only portfolios don't work because of two factors: inflation and the fact that people are living longer and spending up to 30 years in retirement or semiretirement.

With this in mind, the question then becomes what type of balanced portfolio works best for retirees. As Figure 5.2 shows, a volatile portfolio like an S&P 500 Index fund will not accommodate a large withdrawal rate. Even though returns on the S&P 500 Index fund averaged 10.8% annually between 1965 and 1996, the Index fund would have accommodated only a 7% annual withdrawal rate. Figure 5.2 shows that a 7.2% withdrawal rate would have depleted this S&P 500 Index portfolio by 1994. Large down years in 1966, 1974, and 1977 were particularly detrimental to the S&P 500 Index portfolio relative to a more stable balanced portfolio.

Figure 5.2 shows that a balanced or blended portfolio worked out much better for retirees, even though this balanced portfolio also averaged a 10.8% return between 1965 and 1996. The greater stability in volatile years such as 1966, 1974, and 1977 allowed this blended portfolio to easily accommodate a 7.2% withdrawal rate and, in fact, grow from $100,000 to $514,293 by 1996. In fact, the blended portfolio would have accommodated an 8.8% withdrawal rate.

The technical term *dispersion* describes the stability or lack of stability in a given portfolio. Dispersion is the degree of scatter of returns around a given *average* return. For example, in Figure 5.2, both the S&P 500 Index and the balanced portfolio averaged approximately 10.8%; however, the balanced portfolio had a lower dispersion with a best return of 34% and a worst return of −16%, while the S&P 500's range was 37% to −26%. **All but the wealthiest retirees should take a low-dispersion investment approach.**

**FIGURE 5.2   RETIREMENT WITHDRAWAL
PROGRAM: GROWTH OF A $100,000 INVESTMENT**

YEAR	WITHDRAWALS	S&P 500 INDEX PORTFOLIO	BALANCED PORTFOLIO*
1965	$ 0	$100,000	$100,000
1966	7,200	82,965	89,154
1967	7,200	95,126	106,348
1968	7,200	97,854	124,883
1969	7,200	82,700	101,515
1970	7,200	77,830	89,487
1971	7,200	81,331	100,086
1972	7,200	88,853	104,806
1973	7,200	69,026	82,042
1974	7,200	44,500	61,801
1975	7,200	53,410	72,127
1976	7,200	58,338	84,217
1977	7,200	46,832	82,047
1978	7,200	42,378	82,458
1979	7,200	42,374	93,205
1980	7,200	47,610	110,476
1981	7,200	38,141	104,480
1982	7,200	37,616	121,621
1983	7,200	38,488	144,439
1984	7,200	33,153	134,542
1985	7,200	35,416	168,177
1986	7,200	34,562	190,848
1987	7,200	29,943	188,314
1988	7,200	27,219	213,475
1989	7,200	27,801	255,227

FIGURE 5.2   (CONTINUED)

YEAR	WITHDRAWALS	S&P 500 INDEX PORTFOLIO	BALANCED PORTFOLIO*
1990	$ 7,200	$19,608	$224,101
1991	7,200	17,576	292,273
1992	7,200	11,286	309,809
1993	7,200	4,914	364,980
1994	7,200	0[†]	352,856
1995	7,200	—	437,420
1996	5,400	—	514,293
Totals	$221,400	$ 0	$514,293
Average index return		10.77%	10.78%

*Lipper averages as follows: equity income 17%; fixed-income 30%; global 17%; high-yield 25%; small company 11%.
†Portfolio depleted by September 30, 1994.

Source: Reprinted with permission from Chase Global Data & Research, Investment View® Software, 73 Junction Square, Concord, MA 01742.

MYTH: S&P INDEX FUNDS ARE CONSERVATIVE

Any index will have as little or as much volatility as the stocks or bonds in the index. Although blue-chip stocks make up the S&P 500 Index, in many cases these stocks fluctuate more than many other mutual funds.

THE STORY OF BILL AND LIBBY

The volatile nature of the S&P portfolio, coupled with negative returns in 1966, 1974, and 1977—the early years for a 1965 retiree—led the professionals at Yolles Investment Management, Inc., to develop the hypothetical story of Bill and his "backward" sister Libby to illustrate the random nature of a volatile retirement approach. Figure 5.3 shows that Bill's retirement fund was wiped out due to poor returns in the early years, while "backward" Libby's portfolio, which earned identical returns but in reverse order, thrived because bad returns didn't occur until the later years.

The identical *rates* of return, but in a different *order*, can mean the difference between a comfortable retirement and a completely depleted retirement portfolio. Figure 5.3 shows that if a retiree's portfolio is faced with large losses during the early years of retirement (Bill's portfolio), the portfolio will never recover. The professionals at Yolles Investment Management, Inc., use this illustration to support the conclusion that a *balanced* approach to retirement, which eliminates large fluctuations, is probably best.

DIVERSIFY YOUR PORTFOLIO FOR STABILITY

As you can see from the prior examples, a broadly diversified portfolio that has a great deal of stability and little dispersion is a much sounder approach for retirees than an aggressive S&P 500 Index or other high-dispersion strategy.

A broadly diversified portfolio is also a much sounder approach than a fixed-income-only strategy. Recall the earlier information in Chapter 2 about how bonds and cash investments are clearly inferior to equity investments and broadly diversified portfolios that include international investments. Recall also the example in Chapter 3 of Archie and Edith, who stuck with their CD-only portfolio and barely made ends meet, versus Ozzie and Harriet, who broadly diversified and lived a very comfortable retirement.

Your broadly diversified investment strategy should be

FIGURE 5.3   A VOLATILE RETIREMENT PORTFOLIO LEAVES TOO MUCH TO CHANCE

	$100,000 Retirement Portfolio with a 7.2% Annual Withdrawal				
	BILL		**BILL'S AND LIBBY'S**	**LIBBY**	
YEAR	**RETURN (%)**	**PRINCIPAL**	**WITHDRAWALS**	**PRINCIPAL**	**RETURN (%)**
0	—	$100,000	$ 0	$100,000	—
1	30	126,000	7,200	140,000	40
2	–10	107,000	7,200	136,000	3
3	–33	71,000	7,200	145,000	11
4	14	73,000	7,200	159,000	14
5	–5	63,000	7,200	178,000	16
6	–14	48,000	7,200	199,000	15
7	23	52,000	7,200	228,000	17
8	11	50,000	7,200	320,000	37
9	4	45,000	7,200	300,000	–4
10	6	40,000	7,200	330,000	12
11	14	39,000	7,200	372,000	14
12	12	36,000	7,200	388,000	6
13	–4	27,000	7,200	396,000	4
14	37	31,000	7,200	434,000	11
15	17	28,000	7,200	538,000	23
16	15	25,000	7,200	460,000	–14
17	16	22,000	7,200	431,000	–5
18	14	18,000	7,200	487,000	14
19	11	12,000	7,200	342,000	–33
20	3	5,000	7,200	303,000	–10
21	40	0	7,200	399,077	30
Summary	8.22%*	0	$151,200	$399,077	8.22%*

*Annual return without withdrawals.

Source: Yolles Investment Management, Inc.

part of your well coordinated financial plan. The best way to make sure that all parts of your financial life are properly balanced is to go through an annual review checkup with your independent financial advisor. Steps for your financial checkup are highlighted in the accompanying box.

YOUR FINANCIAL REVIEW CHECKUP

Like your yearly physical with your doctor, your annual review with your financial advisor(s) should make sure that all aspects of your financial life are functioning in an effective and complementary fashion. At least all of the following should be checked:

1. *Cash flow:* Are your monthly and annual spending needs being met?

2. *Inflation protection:* Do you have enough growth investments to cover future inflationary increases in your cost of living?

3. *Overall diversification:* Have you minimized your dispersion of returns to secure the stable cash flow that you need?

4. *Your comfort level:* Do you understand all aspects of your retirement plan?

5. *Tax and estate plan:* Have you had an efficient plan created?

6. *Insurance protection:* Do you have enough insurance to protect you in case of extensive medical care or a long-term nursing home stay?

RETIREMENT INVESTING CASE STUDIES

$ CASE STUDY 5.1—GRANNY, THE 77-YEAR-OLD RETIREE

Granny came to Yolles Investment Management in 1990 with $400,000 entirely in Treasury bills and certificates of deposit. At that time, Treasury bills were yielding approximately 5.5% and

Granny was not spending all the interest her portfolio produced, because she was extremely frugal. The professionals at Yolles Investment Management analyzed her portfolio and took a careful look at her current and future cash flow needs. We also took a detailed look at all of her finances in order to make sure that her affairs were arranged to accomplish her financial objectives, including provisions for her two children and her grandchild.

Upon a detailed review, we found several glaring weaknesses in Granny's overall financial strategy, including a severe lack of inflation protection. As illustrated in Figure 5.4, we were able to assemble and manage a broadly diversified portfolio of no-load mutual funds that fit within Granny's tolerance for risk. The table shows, over time, how diversification significantly improved her cash flow from dividends, particularly as her principal grew. Providing her with extensive education became a key part in helping her understand the features and nature of each investment market. Any investor owes it to herself or himself to know what is and isn't possible for a given set of objectives (recall Figure 1.3 on page 12). We've found that these illustrations and graphs are excellent

FIGURE 5.4 CASE STUDY: GRANNY— AN INVESTMENT MAKEOVER

| YEAR | BEFORE (CD ONLY) | | AFTER (DIVERSIFIED) | |
	PRINCIPAL	WITHDRAWALS	PRINCIPAL	WITHDRAWALS
1990	$400,000	$14,712	$400,000	$14,712
1991	408,906	14,712	429,282	14,712
1992	408,541	14,712	436,009	14,712
1993	406,299	14,712	478,696	14,712
1994	409,363	14,712	458,131	14,712
1995	417,959	14,712	512,556	14,712
1996	424,331	14,712	563,492	14,712
1997	427,065	14,712	626,672	14,712
Current annual yield	$21,191		$42,300	
Dividend yield (%)			6.75%	

communication tools to help any investor understand what to expect under different market conditions. Once we were able to help Granny understand the benefit of conservative diversified no-load investing, she felt comfortable implementing the investment program.

With any investment program, you will gain more confidence over time as you see how your portfolio behaves in both good and bad market conditions. We feel it is crucial for you, ideally in conjunction with your seasoned independent advisor, to review alternative investment programs and scenarios in both present and past market conditions. We will cover this in detail in the next chapter.

As shown in Figure 5.4, through September 1997 Granny's portfolio had grown to $626,672 and her annual yield was $42,300. Alternatively, the annual yield from her CD portfolio would be $21,191 and her portfolio would be worth only $427,065. Over time, as this illustration shows, the equity and fixed-income markets work to outpace inflation.

Any investor must have a long-term horizon outlook and be willing to weather market ups and downs. Granny was fortunate that her investment horizon encompassed wonderful years for the markets. But the validity of a broadly diversified strategy has also been tested and proven successful during adverse market conditions.

There were other elements of her financial picture that also needed immediate attention. Granny was referred to a competent tax attorney, who was able to create some trusts and update her will, which helped Granny accomplish three objectives: First, she was able to make provisions for her asset distributions to her two grown sons, such as restricting how the assets would be passed to her younger son, who was less responsible and having marital difficulties. Second, Granny purchased long-term care insurance to prevent her assets from being depleted if at some point she required extended nursing-home or at-home care. We referred her to both an independent fee-for-service insurance consultant and the American Association of Retired Persons (AARP) to investigate low-cost alternatives in the long-term care area. Finally, a separate trust was drafted to provide money to Granny's only granddaughter, Ellie Mae, at appropriate ages to fund Ellie Mae's college education.

$

$ CASE STUDY 5.2—THE NERVOUS DOCTOR

A successful dentist was referred to Yolles Investment Management in November 1987 immediately after seeing his portfolio shrink from $1.2 million to $800,000 in the market crash of October 1987. He was 55 years old and in good health (at least before the crash of 1987). Worried about his investments, he was seriously considering putting all of his money in certificates of deposit and Treasury bills for the rest of his life; but he knew that the interest from these would not support his standard of living. Although not extravagant, he did require $120,000 per year to live. We estimated that the good dentist needed to accumulate $2 million in order to supplement the money he would receive from Social Security at retirement. If he averaged 10% a year (the historical return on an equity portfolio) he would have accumulated the necessary $2 million within nine years, by age 64.

Fortunately, the tail winds provided by the great bull market of the 1980s allowed our dentist—even with a conservative portfolio allocation of 55% in stock funds and 45% in bond funds—to average 14% a year and reach his retirement goal by age 62.

Any experienced investment advisor has to be a bit of an "investment therapist" in order to help clients feel reasonably comfortable with the capital markets so that they can enjoy the long-term returns that the markets provide. This is often much easier in hindsight than during the real world events when market declines can be terrifying, even to the calmest individuals. Fortunately, we were able to help our dentist through market ups and downs and provide enough stability and information so that he was able to stick with his long-term strategy and not react emotionally to normal market volatility.

In fact, the performance of the dentist's portfolio was so successful that we had to help him get appropriate tax counsel regarding potential excise and estate taxes if both his overall portfolio, and more specifically his retirement plan portfolio, grew too large at too early an age. These tax issues are detailed in Chapter 8. Suffice to say that our dentist was thrilled to have these solvable tax problems in exchange for the real danger of having an underfunded retirement that he faced after the market crash of 1987 and, more importantly, because of his own emotional fears regarding investments of any type.

$

▌$▐ CASE STUDY 5.3—THE SPENDTHRIFT PEDIATRICIAN AND HIS FRUGAL WIFE: FINDING A COMFORTABLE MIDDLE GROUND

In the movie *Hello Dolly*, Barbra Streisand stars as Dolly Levi, an eccentric, lovable woman with expensive taste. By movie's end, she has successfully bewildered, courted, and ultimately married Horace Vandergelder, played by Walter Matthau. Vandergelder is an extremely frugal man who, by the end of the film, is coaxed by Dolly into spreading his money around "like manure."

We had a similar husband-and-wife team come into our office in 1996, but this time the roles were reversed. At age 70, a pediatri-

FIGURE 5.5   A GIFT PROGRAM FOR "DOLLY AND HORACE" (9% ANNUAL RETURN)

YEAR	PORTFOLIO VALUE	WITHDRAWALS	GIFTS	YEAR-ENDING VALUE	HORACE'S AGE
1997	$800,000	$40,000	$8,000	$825,015	70
1998	825,015	40,000	8,000	852,376	71
1999	852,376	40,000	8,000	882,305	72
2000	882,305	40,000	8,000	915,041	73
2001	915,041	40,000	8,000	950,848	74
2002	950,848	40,000	8,000	977,506	75
2003	977,506	45,000	14,663	1,006,665	76
2004	1,006,665	45,000	14,663	1,038,559	77
2005	1,038,559	45,000	14,663	1,073,445	78
2006	1,073,445	45,000	14,663	1,111,604	79
2007	1,111,604	49,768	22,232	1,140,835	80

Note: This table is designed as an illustration of the gifting principle; in the real world, this couple would probably make larger gifts to reduce their taxable estate.

FIGURE 5.6   A GIFT PROGRAM FOR "DOLLY AND HORACE" (3% ANNUAL RETURN)

YEAR	PORTFOLIO VALUE	WITHDRAWALS	GIFTS	YEAR-ENDING VALUE	HORACE'S AGE
1997	$800,000	$40,000	$8,000	$775,667	70
1998	775,667	40,000	8,000	750,594	71
1999	750,594	40,000	8,000	724,759	72
2000	724,759	40,000	8,000	698,138	73
2001	698,138	40,000	8,000	670,707	74
2002	670,707	40,000	8,000	642,442	75
2003	642,442	40,000	8,000	613,317	76
2004	613,317	40,000	8,000	583,306	77
2005	583,306	40,000	8,000	552,382	78
2006	552,382	40,000	8,000	520,518	79
2007	520,518	40,000	8,000	487,684	80

Note: This example is shown as a contrast to example Figure 5.5. In real life, if the portfolio averages only 3% annually, then adjustments downward would be made to the annual withdrawal and gifting rate.

cian was much more a spendthrift than his 57-year-old wife, who was concerned about making their money last and enjoying their ultimate retirement. The wife worked with her husband in his medical practice.

The husband wanted to make gifts to his children and grandchildren while he was still young enough to enjoy them using these gifts. The wife's desire was to make sure that she and her husband would have a secure retirement. We presented them with illustrations and detailed spreadsheets that tracked different investment scenarios in both favorable (Figure 5.5) and unfavorable (Figure 5.6) investment climates. Through this education and changes we made to the couple's portfolio, we were able to help the couple find a happy middle ground.

Ultimately, a strategy was agreed upon whereby no more than 1% of their $800,000 portfolio ($8,000) would be used for gifts during any calendar year. When the husband reached age 75 this gifting percentage would be increased to 1.5%. At 80, it would be 2%. Figures 5.5 and 5.6 show how the husband and wife's gifting pattern would work at various ages with two different return assumptions.

$

$

CHAPTER SIX

Developing, Implementing, and Maintaining a Sensible Retirement Portfolio Strategy

IN THIS CHAPTER

This chapter focuses on detailed investment strategies. You will learn:

1. How to avoid chasing yield and putting your principal at risk.

2. How to assemble the proper mix of no-load stock and bond funds exactly tailored to your objectives.

3. How to select mutual funds that are likely to produce consistent, dependable results in the future.

4. How to determine your true tolerance for investment risk.

5. Top no-load mutual funds to consider during different stages of your retirement.

In our practice, investment planning is generally the area in which retirees make the most mistakes. Although many retirees get competent advice, there is still too much misinformation about investment strategy and planning.

Have you ever procrastinated and failed to implement a sound investment strategy? Too often we see retirees grasping for "guaranteed" investment vehicles or being seduced by various investment fads. Both of these traps almost always are detriments to maintaining a comfortable retirement in the long run.

You have now completed Chapters 1 through 5, which means you've taken an inventory of your sources of capital and your likely cost of living during retirement. Therefore, you now have an idea of what you will need to live comfortably during retirement. This should help you not succumb to the "guaranteed" investment trap.

DIVIDEND YIELD VERSUS CAPITAL APPRECIATION

Most people add up their sources of capital during retirement, including pensions and Social Security, and then have some idea of how much cash flow their financial portfolio will be required to produce to supplement these other sources. For example, if you felt that you needed $70,000 a year to live on and knew that Social Security would only provide $20,000 per year, then your portfolio would have to produce $50,000 per year. If the size of your portfolio is $500,000, then you could easily calculate that your portfolio would have to yield 10% annually to produce the required $50,000. This is a very normal case. Countless times every month, new clients come into our office and tell us that if they can just achieve a 10% annual *yield* from their portfolio, then all their spending needs during retirement will be covered. However, never in the 200-year history of investment markets has any vehicle consistently produced close to a 10% yield.

You will recall from the previous chapters that stocks have been the best-returning asset class, averaging close to an 11% total return annually. Still, only 4% of this 11% has come from dividend yield, and the remaining 7% annually has come from capital appreciation. The annual returns from stocks and mutual funds are very unpredictable.

Figure 6.1 shows a fairly representative period in the investment markets and illustrates the high volatility of stock returns. The 20-year period shown covers the years 1970–1989. The 1970s were a miserable decade for financial assets and a good decade for hard assets such as precious metals, real estate, oil, and energy. In the 1980s, the opposite occurred: It was a wonderful decade for financial assets such as stocks, bonds, and mutual funds holding stocks and bonds. You can see from Figure 6.1, column 2, that while stock returns averaged 11.55% for the period, the returns were extremely variable from year to year with a low return of –26% in 1974 and a high return of 37% in 1975. As a retiree making steady withdrawals for living expenses, you cannot tolerate this volatility since you would deplete your capital during large down years.

Recall our previous discussions of sustainable portfolio withdrawal rates for retirees. Figure 3.2 on page 29 is based on 200 years of data on reasonable returns from stocks, bonds, and cash equivalents such as certificates of deposit or Treasury bills. While many retirees would like to find an investment vehicle that would yield 10%, 12%, or 14% a year and from which they could make withdrawals, there are also many people who would like to find the Holy Grail.

If you don't familiarize yourself with various investment ve-

FIGURE 6.1 THE BENEFITS OF DIVERSIFICATION

YEAR	STOCKS*	BONDS†	60% STOCKS 40% BONDS	⅓ STOCKS ⅓ BONDS ⅓ CASH	BB&K INDEX‡
1970	4.01%	12.10%	7.52%	7.98%	4.7%
1971	14.31	13.23	14.14	10.83	13.7
1972	18.98	5.68	13.54	9.38	15.1
1973	–14.66	–1.11	–9.11	–3.03	–2.2
1974	–26.47	4.35	–14.88	–5.44	–6.6
1975	37.20	9.19	25.65	17.04	19.6
1976	23.84	16.75	21.18	15.19	11.5
1977	–7.18	–0.67	–4.57	–0.94	6.1
1978	6.56	–1.16	3.65	4.40	13.0
1979	18.44	–1.22	10.28	9.14	11.5
1980	32.42	–3.95	17.45	13.17	17.9
1981	–4.91	1.85	–1.99	4.06	6.4
1982	21.41	40.35	28.98	23.97	14.4
1983	22.51	0.68	13.43	10.52	15.4
1984	6.27	15.43	10.11	10.75	10.4
1985	32.16	30.97	31.85	23.38	25.4
1986	18.47	24.44	21.11	16.61	23.3
1987	5.23	–2.69	3.59	3.92	8.6
1988	16.81	9.67	13.97	11.01	13.2
1989	31.49	18.11	26.24	19.22	14.3
Compound annual return	11.55%	9.00%	10.89%	9.78%	11.54%

*Standard & Poor's 500 Index.
†Long-term Treasury bonds.
‡20% U.S. stocks, 20% bonds, 20% cash, 20% real estate, 20% foreign stocks.

Source: Reprinted by permission of the *Wall Street Journal*, Copyright ©1990 Dow Jones & Company, Inc. All Rights Reserved Worldwide.

hicles, then you are more likely to make a serious investment mistake while you're seeking higher yields. History is replete with examples of people investing hard-earned money in dubious investment vehicles that promise high yields but don't deliver. Many of these vehicles also cost people some or all of their principal. Unfortunately, there are plenty of unscrupulous investment salespeople out there who will seduce you with these too-good-to-be-true promises. Caveat emptor.

Some recent examples of "can't miss" investment opportunities that did miss—and missed in a big way—include real estate limited partnerships, oil and gas limited partnerships, junk bonds, various mortgage schemes, and on and on. We cannot emphasize enough the importance of understanding the capital markets and what is and is not possible on the return spectrum.

Two hundred years of historical data, and hopefully some common sense, show us that stock-type investments can return about 11% annually, bond-type investments can earn 6% or 7% annually, and cash-type investments can earn 4% annually over the long run. Stretching for returns beyond what has been historically possible will, in all likelihood, prove disastrous to your long-term retirement planning.

While investing is an essential part of capitalism, and an essential part of what our economic system is founded on, greed and speculation are not healthy. When you invest in a share of stock or the shares of a mutual fund that invests in numerous stocks, you are becoming an owner in the corporations from which you are buying stocks. As an owner, you will share in the success or failure of those corporations.

History has shown us that, over time, in developed countries, corporations do fairly well for their stockholders and produce excellent returns far superior to returns provided by instruments such as certificates of deposit, Treasury bills, or bonds. Here we emphasize *in the long run* stocks produced these types of returns. *In the short run*, stocks can be very volatile and can, and often will, lose you money.

If you will look back to Figure 6.1, which shows the benefits of diversification, and you look at the stocks column, you will see that in 4 of the 20 years shown stocks lost money. What conclusion can you draw from this example? If you need an immediate return of all your capital in a short period of time, such as a one-, two-, or three-year horizon, then your money does not belong in stock funds. On the other hand, if you have a fairly long time horizon and you don't need a return of your principal, but may only require some dividend income, then stocks are likely, though not guaranteed, to produce superior returns.

For retirees, the challenge lies in selecting the proper combination of stock and bond funds, because few retirees are in a position to have all of their assets in stock funds or all of their assets in bond funds. A further challenge comes in finding the specific stock, bond, and cash equivalent no-load funds for your individual situation. Remember that your situation will change as you get further into your retirement and you must from time to time adjust your asset allocation and mutual fund selections accordingly.

ASSET ALLOCATION

Like any recipe where the ingredients and proportions are critical, asset allocation describes how investable dollars are divided among the three major asset categories: stocks, bonds, and cash. Research shows that asset allocation determines 90% of any investor's results.

DIVERSIFY WITH FUNDS

For most retirees, there is what we call an *optimal portfolio.* This optimal portfolio contains the proper blend of different investment vehicles to meet a retiree's specific circumstances. On the simplest level, those who need growth will have more in stock funds, and those who need income will have more in bond funds. But, this is only the start of your optimal portfolio process. The investment vehicles used in your portfolio will include several different asset classes, including domestic stock funds, international stock funds, resource stock funds, domestic bond funds, high-yield bond funds, short-term bond funds, and international bond funds, as well as some cash equivalent funds.

To further achieve proper diversification, each category has to be divided into subcategories. For example, in the domestic stock fund category we would create the following divisions: large-cap stock funds, mid-cap stock funds, and small-cap stock funds. We would further break up each of these categories into value funds and growth funds. So, for example, you might have a large-cap value fund. Similarly, we would subdivide the different fixed-income categories and international categories. At this point on our way to achieving a proper broadly diversified portfolio, ironically, we are only about halfway done; even with these divisions, we need one further division among all categories, which is called *multimanager diversification.*

"Multimanager" means that we will use different money management firms in each category. To help clarify this complicated concept, let's take a look at an example. Two of the categories that we use are large-cap value funds and international value funds. However, it is unlikely that the same management organization will be best in both the large-cap *domestic* and the large-cap *international* value arenas. Therefore, we use different money management firms in each subspecialty: In the large-cap domestic value category, we like a fund called ICM Equity, which is managed by Investment Counselors of Maryland (hence ICM). In the international value category, we like a fund called Tweedy Browne Global Value Fund, managed by Tweedy Browne and Associates in New York.

So, our ultimate strategy encompasses not only multiasset classes but also multiple investment management firms. We call this a broadly diversified multimanager approach. Ultimately, an all-star team from different investment firms is put together; this is far safer than concentrating all of your investments with one mutual fund family such as Vanguard or Fidelity.

If you refer back to column 6 in Figure 6.1, you will see an example of a broadly diversified portfolio whose returns are

WHY NO-LOAD FUNDS?

For 99% of you, a properly diversified portfolio of quality no-load mutual funds will prove to be the best, safest, and most cost- and time-efficient investment strategy during retirement. This is true for several reasons:

1. A mutual fund pools money from thousands of shareholders to buy hundreds of stocks and/or bonds in a diversified and cost-efficient way, whereas any individual would probably have enough money to buy only 30 or 40 different stocks or bonds, with much higher commission rates and less diversification.

2. A no-load fund is bought directly. You eliminate the broker's 5% to 8% commission.

3. No-load funds are professionally managed. Do you have the time, training, temperament, and access to information to know what, and when, to buy or sell? Let pros do their job while you enjoy your retirement.

not quite as good as the returns produced by an all-stock portfolio, but still are very satisfactory and much more consistent. Most, if not all, retirees will value this consistency and will be willing to give up a few points of return for more stability.

DETERMINE YOUR OPTIMAL PORTFOLIO

Assembling an optimal portfolio is a very complex process, and includes mathematical formulas containing items such as correlation coefficients and standard deviations. For our purposes here, and for any retiree, the real value comes in having an understanding of different optimal portfolio investment alternatives. Many trained Chartered Financial Analysts (CFAs) and other investment professionals will be more than willing to help you review optimal investment alternatives.

You should think of the process of assembling an optimal portfolio as similar to implementing a recipe. For example, when baking a cake, you need the proper proportions of flour, sugar, baking powder, and eggs or your cake will neither be the correct consistency nor rise properly. Similarly, when assembling a portfolio you need the proper amount of stock, bond, cash-equivalents, international, and convertible bond funds or your portfolio will not perform properly. If you do not have an optimal, or ideal, portfolio design, then you are cheating yourself by taking too much risk and/or receiving too little return. An optimal portfolio design ensures that you will get the maximum return for the amount of risk that you are willing to take. Conversely, for the expected return that you wish to achieve, you will take no more risk than is necessary.

To carry our analogy one step further, just as you may want to add more sugar to your cake recipe, you may be tempted to concentrate your money in one hot mutual fund. You should resist this temptation, because both too much sugar and too much of one fund could make you sick and cause either tooth or portfolio "decay."

While the mathematical calculations of things like correlation coefficients and covariances are very complex when establishing optimal portfolio designs, the rationale behind optimal portfolios, and the rationale behind diversification, should be intuitively obvious. Different asset classes behave differently, so by holding various asset groups such as domestic and foreign stock, bond, convertible, cash, and resource funds, you are diversifying and spreading your risk. Figure 6.2 shows the risk and return characteristics of differ-

FIGURE 6.2   OPTIMAL PORTFOLIO (DOMESTIC HOLDINGS)

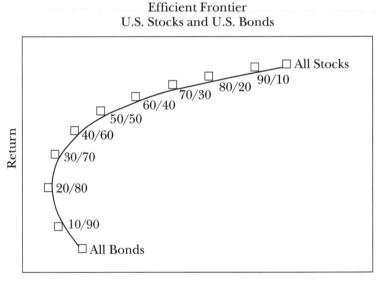

Efficient Frontier
U.S. Stocks and U.S. Bonds

Source: Ennis, Knupp & Associates, Chicago, IL. Reprinted with permission.

ent optimal portfolios of U.S. stocks and bonds, and Figure
6.3 shows how portfolios can be made better and safer by
adding international ("non-U.S.") funds.

Between the United States and other countries, we have
over 200 years of investment market data to use in studying
how different asset classes complement each other. These re-
lationships make economic sense. For example, when reviewing market history, we see that when United States stock and
bond markets are doing poorly the U.S. dollar is also doing
poorly. Not surprisingly, we often, but not always, see hard currencies in the low-inflation countries such as Switzerland, Germany, and Japan do well when the U.S. dollar is doing poorly.

FIGURE 6.3   OPTIMAL PORTFOLIO INCLUDING INTERNATIONAL HOLDINGS

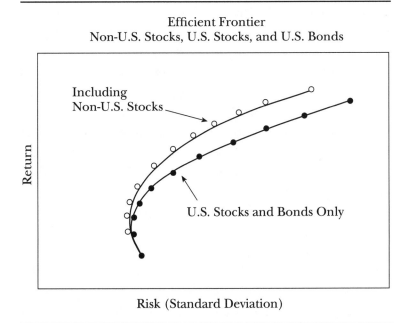

Efficient Frontier
Non-U.S. Stocks, U.S. Stocks, and U.S. Bonds

Source: Ennis, Knupp & Associates, Chicago, IL. Reprinted with permission.

Given this piece of historical data, it should not be surprising that a portfolio that includes both U.S. stocks and international bond funds, including bonds from Germany, Switzerland, Japan, and other foreign countries, should give a smoother, less volatile return than a less diversified portfolio that contains only U.S. stocks. In essence, the international bonds and U.S. stocks complement each other since they perform well at different times. This is the very essence of diversification. Figure 6.3 illustrates this phenomenon.

In Figure 6.4, we show a sample optimal portfolio for a moderate-risk investor. We define a moderate risk investor as someone who has a 12- to 16-year time horizon before he or she would consider withdrawing dividends. In addition, the investor should be able to tolerate a 15% dip in principal value during a bear market, while not allowing nerves to force a premature sale. Please note that this is what we would call the "technical definition" of the moderate-risk investor.

A moderate-risk investor could also describe the temperament of someone who has a much longer time horizon but is unwilling to take a great deal of risk. As you can see from Figure 6.4, our moderate-risk investor has approximately 53% of the assets in stock mutual funds and 47% in fixed-income funds for an optimal portfolio allocation. Based on historical data, we would expect that this optimal portfolio would return 9.25% compounded annually and have a standard deviation of 9.5%.

A standard deviation of 9.5% on a 9.25% expected return means that in a normal year, the returns on the moderate-risk portfolio would average 9.25% and fall within 9.5% above or below that 9.25% average. So, in a typical year, the return could range from –0.25% to 18.75%. (This is found by taking 9.25% and either adding or subtracting 9.5%.) For the statistically inclined, "normal" years mean seven out

FIGURE 6.4   OPTIMAL PORTFOLIO
FOR THE MODERATE-RISK INVESTOR

FUND	ALLOCATION
Domestic Stock Funds	
Growth	
Oakmark	10%
Selected American	9%
Value	
Mutual Discovery	10%
Third Avenue Value	9%
International Stock Funds	
Oakmark International	5%
SoGen Overseas	5%
Tweedy, Browne Global	5%
Fixed-Income Funds	
Northeast Trust (high-yield bond)	15%
PIMCo Foreign (international bond)	16%
PIMCo Total Return (domestic high-quality bond)	16%

Parameters

RETURN TARGET	RISK TOLERANCE	RISK AND RETURN RANGES
9.25%	–10% to –15% in a bear market	Normally (70% of the time) –0.25% to 18.75% Rarely (25% of the time) –9.75% to 28.25% Very rarely (5% of the time) < –9.75% or >28.25%

Note for Long-Term Investors: If you hold the portfolio for at least 10 years, your expected return is still 9.25%, but your range of returns should narrow to from 3% to 15.5%.

Source: Yolles Investment Management.

of 10 years. However, in the other three out of 10 years, history has shown that *abnormal* results are likely to occur on either the plus side or the minus side. Therefore, in three out of every 10 years, returns may be worse than –0.25% or better than 18.75%.

If you define yourself as a moderate-risk investor, then you have to feel comfortable with these parameters and rest assured that you will not alter your long-term strategy during market downturns or, for that matter, during outstanding market advances. Most often, either greed during those unusual advances or fear during those unusual declines throws investors off the track and spoils their long-term plans.

FIND YOUR RISK TOLERANCE

In working with clients, we try to take the emotion out of the portfolio management process in order to make sound business decisions. One tool we use is an objective questionnaire that helps our clients identify their true risk preferences. This questionnaire is outlined in Figure 6.5. (This risk tolerance test matches objectives with an ideal asset allocation. The investment Rorschach test in Figure 4.6 is an indicator of investment temperament.) In the United States today, risk taking is seen as a virtue, and in our experience, clients are likely to overestimate verbally their own ability to tolerate risk. Our test will help bring your true feelings and preferences to the surface.

A new client will often say, "I definitely want growth in my portfolio." But, the client will quickly go on to add, "Of course, I don't want to take a lot of risk." When we finally have these clients complete the objective questionnaire, it turns out that their risk tolerance is fairly low. After an education session or two, many of these people gain a better ap-

FIGURE 6.5   YOUR TRUE RISK TOLERANCE

These questions will help you both realistically identify your risk tolerance and investment time horizon and choose an asset allocation between stock and bond funds that fits your needs and objectives. Use your immediate reaction to choose your answers.

A. If the market declined 25%, you would . . .
   1. Sell immediately and buy CDs.
   2. Sell half of my stock holdings and wait for the other half to break even before selling.
   3. Stick to my long-term plan and, if anything, buy more when the market is depressed.

B. If you or your spouse had a medical emergency requiring a nursing home stay costing $40,000 . . .
   1. We would have to sell stocks to pay the nursing bills.
   2. We would take out a home equity loan to pay our nursing bills.
   3. We have sufficient cash reserves and/or a long-term nursing care insurance policy to cover this type of emergency.

C. If you have a big tax bill at year-end . . .
   1. We will sell stock shares to pay the bill.
   2. Our dividends are sufficient to pay a big tax bill and we are sure to reinvest the dividends we do not spend.
   3. We will reinvest all dividends and set aside sufficient cash for taxes.

D. Regarding leaving money to your children . . .
   1. We loved, cared for, and educated our children. We want to enjoy our money while we are relatively young—our kids are on their own.
   2. We'd like to leave a little something to our kids and grandkids to make their lives more enjoyable.
   3. Fortunately, we have sufficient wealth that we have provided for our kids and the charities that are important to us in our estate plan.

E. If a close friend with whom you play golf and who claims to have been been averaging 18% in aggressive mutual funds offers to help you invest, you . . .
   1. Probably would take my friend's advice and invest nearly all my money in the manner suggested.
   2. Invest half my money in my friend's recommendations.
   3. Stick with my investment plan that was returning only 9%, but was designed to meet my objectives.

FIGURE 6.5 (**CONTINUED**)

F. Which of the following investments would you prefer?
  1. An investment with a guaranteed 7% return.
  2. An investment with an 80% chance of returning 10% and a 20% chance of returning zero.
  3. An investment with an 80% chance of returning 20% and a 20% chance of *losing* 10%.

G. You will need income from your investment portfolio . . .
  1. Immediately, because our existing sources of retirement income are insufficient.
  2. Within three years as a supplement to our income from part-time work, Social Security, and/or pensions.
  3. In three or more years when our portfolio is large enough that we will need to draw only part of the dividend income that the portfolio produces.

H. Which of the following describes your feelings toward the stock market?
  1. The stock market is like Las Vegas; we've had friends or relatives lose all their money in the stock market.
  2. The stock market is risky but does offer good potential returns for part of our money. But, we do not believe in putting all of our eggs in one basket.
  3. The stock market is not gambling; rather, it allows investors ownership and participation in the growth of America's great companies, which is the core of capitalism. For example, buying a share of stock in McDonald's ties you to the success or failure of McDonald's.

I. You would describe your investment knowledge and experience as follows:
  1. We have always put our money in the bank because of safety considerations.
  2. We believe that there are better alternatives than bank certificates of deposit and we have faith that stocks, bonds, and mutual funds will produce better long-term returns.
  3. We are willing to ride out market ups and downs because we have faith that stocks, stock mutual funds, and real estate investments will stay ahead of inflation in the long run.

J. If you buy a stock or mutual fund that goes down in price you . . .
  1. Always wait to get back to even before selling.
  2. Normally sell because you should not throw good money after bad.

FIGURE 6.5 (CONTINUED)

3. Review the fundamentals of the given stock or mutual fund, and if the fundamentals are sound we would hold or add to our position, and if the fundamentals are no longer sound, then we would sell and find a better long-term holding.

K. Within the next two years how much annual income or cash flow will you need from your investment portfolio to supplement your Social Security, pension, and/or earned income?
   1. We will need to withdraw more than 8% annually from our investments, regardless of what these investments are earning.
   2. We will need to withdraw 6% annually from our investments an amount that we expect to be more than covered by the dividends that our investments produce.
   3. We will withdraw less than 4% annually from our portfolio regardless of earnings.

L. When do you intend to withdraw not only dividends from your portfolio, but also start to withdraw principal?
   1. We are already withdrawing principal from our portfolio because we either have no choice or have objectively developed a sustainable withdrawal plan.
   2. Within 5 to 10 years.
   3. We don't expect to need to touch our principal, at least not within the next 15 years.

Scoring Grid

Please record the number of your answer to each question in the appropriate space.

QUESTION	ANSWER	MULTIPLIER	POINTS
Example:	2	2	4

Temperament Dimension

QUESTION	ANSWER	MULTIPLIER	POINTS
A		1	
E		1	
F		1	
H		3	
I		1	
J		1	

FIGURE 6.5 (CONTINUED)

QUESTION	ANSWER	MULTIPLIER	POINTS
	Time Dimension		
B		1	
C		1	
D		1	
G		3	
K		3	
L		1	
		Total	

Scoring Chart

	TIME HORIZON	
TEMPERAMENT	SHORT-TERM (< 20)	LONG-TERM (23–30)
Growth-oriented (17–24 points)	50% equity 50% fixed-income	70% equity 30% fixed-income
Conservative (16 or fewer points)	30% equity 70% fixed-income	50% equity 50% fixed-income

preciation for what is, and isn't, possible in the investment markets and a better understanding of the strategy that will serve their long-term interests.

There is a saying that the stock market is an expensive place to find yourself in if you're not comfortable with your investment emotions. Nothing could be more true. You should not try to be someone you are not. You should be honest about your own temperament and your own tolerance for risk. If you can achieve this level of honesty, then you will be successful as an investor because your portfolio will be tailored to your comfort level. If you have a portfolio that does not match your comfort level in the long run, you will eventually come upon a day of reckoning and be ill-equipped to objectively execute the proper strategy at that time: Recall large recent declines in October 1987, 1990, and 1997 and the many emotional mistakes investors made during those down periods. Your score on our risk tolerance test should help you determine which of our optimal portfolios is most appropriate for you.

VALUE FUNDS AND GARP FUNDS

In referring back to our optimal portfolio for the moderate-risk investor in Figure 6.4, you will see that both the 53% in equity funds and the 47% in fixed-income funds are very carefully divided between subcategories within the major equity and fixed-income asset classes. Like the well executed recipe mentioned earlier, proper diversification with a fine attention to detail is critical for proper portfolio balance. In the equity category, we have included a 15% allocation to international equity funds, two 10% allocations to large-cap growth and value funds, and two 9% allocations to small-to-mid-cap growth and value funds. We feel this gives the proper balance to the portfolio.

Although the Morningstar rating service categorizes Selected American and Oakmark as value funds, we feel it is proper to classify these as *growth at a reasonable price* (GARP) funds, because those funds contain stocks in moderately growing companies. Rating services like Morningstar also classify only momentum funds that buy ultrafast-growing— we believe unsustainably fast-growing—companies as growth funds. We disagree, and you will notice that we have emphasized value funds and GARP funds instead of momentum funds. We do this consciously, because there is strong research evidence that value and GARP funds perform as well as, if not better than, momentum funds, and with less volatility. Figure 6.6 shows the value fund advan-

FIGURE 6.6   RATIO OF CUMULATIVE ANNUALIZED RETURNS

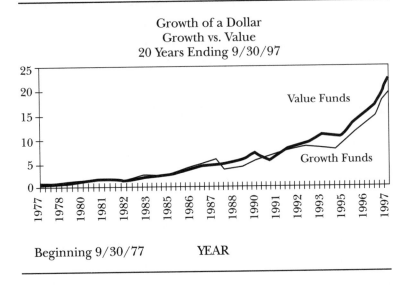

Growth of a Dollar
Growth vs. Value
20 Years Ending 9/30/97

Beginning 9/30/77   YEAR

Source: Ennis, Knupp & Associates, Chicago, IL. Reprinted with permission.

tage. We will discuss this more in depth in Chapter 7 when we talk about selecting good no-load mutual funds.

In Figure 6.6, you see that over the past 20 years, the value approach provided 25% more growth than the growth approach *and* incidentally the S&P 500 Index. What the chart does not show is that the value approach was also less volatile.

MODEL PORTFOLIOS

Figure 6.7 shows a recommended asset allocation for the growth-oriented investor. We define the growth-oriented investor as someone with a time horizon in excess of 16 years. This 16-year time horizon should allow the growth investor

FIGURE 6.7   OPTIMAL PORTFOLIO
FOR THE GROWTH-ORIENTED INVESTOR

FUND	ALLOCATION
Domestic Stock Funds	
Growth	
MAS Value (MCG)	9%
Oakmark Small-Cap (SCV)	10%
Selected American (LCV)	10%
Value	
Mutual Discovery (GV)	12%
Tweedy, Browne American (MCV)	10%
International Stock Funds	
Artisan International	6%
Ivy International	9%
Oakmark International	6%
Fixed-Income Funds	
Loomis Sayles Bond	7%
Northeast Trust	7%
PIMCo Foreign	7%
PIMCo Total Return	7%

Parameters

RETURN TARGET	RISK TOLERANCE	RISK AND RETURN RANGES
11%	−20% to −25% in a bear market	Normally (70% of the time) −1.9% to 23.9% Rarely (25% of the time) −14.8% to 36.8% Very rarely (5% of the time) < −14.8% or >36.8%

Note for Long-Term Investors: If you hold this portfolio for at least 10 years, your expected return is still 11.00%, but your range of returns should narrow to from 1% to 21%.

to go through at least four market cycles. A normal four-year market cycle will include both a bull and a bear market. The past 100 years of investment history show us that bear markets recur every three or four years, hence our calculation of at least four market cycles over a 16-year period. The long-term growth investor will not be withdrawing any dividends from the portfolio but, rather, will reinvest these dividends. This investor is looking strictly for long-term growth and is willing to tolerate a large amount of volatility.

We would expect the growth portfolio in the long run to average 11% compounded annually and have a standard deviation of approximately 12.9%. This means that in a normal year the portfolio's return would range between –1.9% (11% – 12.9%) on the low side and 23.9% (11% + 12.9%) on the high side. This range should cover normal market behavior that will likely occur in seven out of every 10 years; and as mentioned earlier, three out of every 10 years should be expected to be unusual and have returns either below –1.9% or above 23.9%.

Growth investors should have long-term faith that their portfolio, which is heavily weighted toward stock funds, will perform better than any alternative, although with a larger amount of volatility than more conservative portfolios. The growth investor should have faith that the historical relationship of stocks providing superior returns to bonds or cash equivalents will hold up in the future and that stocks in corporate America will do better than CD and bond alternatives.

We believe that this is a reasonable assumption given the vitality of the free-market economies in the developed world. In fact, we see many signs of increasing economic cooperation in the world, which should lead to better employment, productivity, and corporate profitability (i.e., higher long-term stock prices) worldwide.

Our growth allocation has 72% of the portfolio in stock funds and 28% of the portfolio in fixed-income funds. The stock fund allocation includes 21% allocated to international funds, a 12% allocation to a global value fund, 10% allocations to large-, mid-, and small-cap value funds as well as a 9% allocation to a mid-cap growth fund. The 28% allocation to fixed-income funds is divided about equally among international bond funds, high-yield bond funds, and high-quality domestic bond funds, which include government and high-grade corporate bonds.

Please note that some investors are in a position to have even more of their assets allocated to equity funds. This group could include very wealthy investors and families with little need for any dividend income during their lifetime, with the likelihood that they will be passing all of their mutual fund and stock holdings to their children, who will receive a stepped-up basis (estate taxes are discussed in detail in Chapter 10). This group would also include investors who have significant fixed-income holdings, which they cannot control through their retirement portfolio, and are looking to balance those fixed-income holdings with significant equity holdings. If this or some other reason dictates that you have more than 72% of your portfolio in equity funds, you should merely reduce the fixed-income proportions shown for our growth investor accordingly and divide the money among the stock categories shown in Figure 6.7, including international, in the same proportions that we have used.

Figure 6.8 shows the model portfolio for a conservative investor. You can see that the expected return for the conservative portfolio is 8.5% and, since the range of returns is 1.5% to 15.5%, that the standard deviation is 7%. This means that in a normal year the returns for our conservative investor will fall between 1.5% (8.5% − 7%) and 15.5%

FIGURE 6.8 OPTIMAL PORTFOLIO FOR THE CONSERVATIVE INVESTOR

FUND	ALLOCATION
Domestic Stock Funds	
Growth	
Clipper Fund	5%
Value	
FPA Crescent	6%
ICM Equity	6%
Mutual Beacon	6%
International Stock Funds	
SoGen International	6%
Tweedy, Browne Global	6%
Fixed-Income Funds	
FPA New Income	12.5%
Northeast Trust	12.5%
PIMCo Foreign	12.5%
PIMCo Total Return	15%
Strong Short Global	12.5%

Parameters

RETURN TARGET	RISK TOLERANCE	RISK AND RETURN RANGES
8.5%	–6% to –12% in a bear market	Normally (70% of the time) 1.5% to 15.5% Rarely (25% of the time) –5.5% to +22.5% Very rarely (5% of the time) < –5.5% or >22.5%

Note for Long-Term Investors: If you hold this portfolio for at least 10 years, your expected return is still 8.5%, but your range of returns should narrow to from 4.5% to 12.5%.

(8.5% + 7%). As mentioned earlier, this normal range of returns should be achieved in seven out of every 10 years, with three out of every 10 years producing unusual returns either less than 1.5% or more than 15.5%.

You can see that the allocation for our conservative investor focuses very heavily on fixed-income funds, with 65% of the portfolio allocated to fixed-income funds and only 35% to stock funds. Our stock fund allocation for the conservative investor includes 12% allocated to international funds, 6% allocated to each of small-, mid-, and large-cap value funds, and 5% allocated to a mid-cap growth fund. The 65% allocated to fixed-income funds is allocated almost equally among four categories of fixed-income funds, including international, short-term, high-yield, and domestic high-quality.

We hope that this broad framework of asset allocation guidelines for different types of investors is useful to you. For most of you, this asset allocation outline will prove to be the perfect starting point for shaping your retirement portfolio and creating a proper asset allocation. In one sense, the asset allocations that we have provided should be fairly intuitive. More aggressive investors have larger allocations to equity funds and more conservative investors have larger allocations to fixed-income funds.

The portfolio designs we have shown have assumed that a given investor has a tax-deferred portfolio such as an IRA or profit-sharing account, and we have consciously not used tax-free municipal bonds in any of our optimal allocations. If you are a taxable investor or you have a taxable portfolio, then merely substitute half of the asset allocation shown for domestic high-quality fixed-income funds with municipal funds. As an example, in Figure 6.9 we show an allocation for a taxable moderate-risk investor.

FIGURE 6.9   TAXABLE MODERATE-RISK
PORTFOLIO

FUND	ALLOCATION
Domestic Stock Funds	
Growth	
Oakmark	10%
Selected American	9%
Value	
Mutual Discovery	10%
Third Avenue Value	9%
International Stock Funds	
Oakmark International	5%
SoGen Overseas	5%
Tweedy, Browne Global	5%
Fixed-Income Funds	
Northeast Trust	15%
PIMCo Foreign	16%
PIMCo Total Return	8%
Vanguard Intermediate Muni	8%

TAX-FREE MUNICIPAL BONDS VERSUS STOCK FUNDS

Too often, investors who need income during retirement devote too much of their money to municipal bonds. This is another example where the conventional wisdom is often dead wrong. Investors who purchase municipal bonds almost entirely are ignoring diversification. They are subjecting themselves to an extremely high risk of not keeping up with inflation and they are, in all likelihood, cheating the next generation—namely their heirs. Accountants who encourage their clients to concentrate on tax-free investments put the cart before the horse in focusing strictly on the tax issue. They should focus on the investment merits of a properly diversified portfolio and the inflation protection that this diversified portfolio will provide.

The evidence is overwhelming that a broadly diversified portfolio works much better, even for income-oriented investors in any tax bracket. Figure 6.10 shows the effects of a municipal bond portfolio versus the effects of a more broadly diversified portfolio for investors. Note that the broadly diversified Vanguard Balanced Fund also takes a tax-efficient *low turnover* approach to investing.

Too often brokers, bankers, and certified public accountants (CPAs) oversell munis by saying a 5.5% muni is equivalent to a 9% stock fund. This is a grossly incorrect and misleading comparison. The correct comparison moves in the other direction by showing that a 90% tax-efficient, balanced fund averages 12% and produces a 10.8% after-tax return (12% × 90%) compared to the 5.5% municipal.

CONCLUSION

It is clear that the broadly diversified investor wins on all fronts. The investor wins with safety, diversification, and, ultimately, superior cash flow. It's a slam dunk. No contest. In Figure 6.10, the Vanguard Balanced Fund produced an

FIGURE 6.10   RETURN 1981–1996

FUND	PRETAX	POSTTAX
Vanguard Balanced	12.7%	11.1%
Vanguard Municipal	6.4%	6.1%

11.1% *after-tax* return compared to 6.1% for the Vanguard Municipal Fund. In Figure 2.2, we showed another example of how a diversified approach using some equities produces more income (cash flow) in the long run.

Figure 2.2 compares an equity-income fund (Lindner Dividend) with a bond fund (Vanguard GNMA) and a CD. The illustration shows the value of including some equities in a retiree's investment mix. Although not clear from Figure 2.2, in the long run equities provide *both* a larger *and* more stable (lower deviation) dividend stream than bonds and CDs. The period 1980–1991 was chosen because it includes good and bad years for all asset types.

$

CHAPTER SEVEN

How to Select and Assemble a Portfolio of the Best No-Load Mutual Funds

IN THIS CHAPTER

This chapter focuses on building a no-load mutual fund portfolio. You will learn:

1. How to select mutual funds which are likely to produce consistent, dependable results in the future.

2. A method for determining when to sell a mutual fund.

Many investors we see know that they need diversification in their portfolio but don't know how to go about selecting a good portfolio of no-load mutual funds. This is another area where conventional wisdom often does a great disservice to investors.

Much of the conventional wisdom recommends selecting your mutual funds based on a financial magazine's Top 50 Performers list. This rearview mirror approach is probably the worst way to invest in mutual funds. Generally, the funds that have done particularly well last year, or over the past couple of years, are not likely to do as well in the future. Figure 7.1 shows how dismally the top funds have performed in subsequent years. Figure 7.2 shows that only one of the top funds of recent decades retained that status the next decade.

DIVERSIFICATION AND OTHER FACTORS

We see well-meaning investors attempting to diversify a mutual fund portfolio who often end up buying funds that are substantially similar. For example, in August 1997 we received a call from a woman who was attempting to diversify her small IRA portfolio in which she held two mutual funds. The two funds that she held, Twentieth Century Ultra and Seligman Communications, were virtually the same; they both focused almost entirely on technology stocks. Ironically, the woman felt that she needed to purchase a third fund to achieve better diversification and the fund she was considering was the T. Rowe Price Science and Technology Fund, which would have merely duplicated her two existing holdings.

Assembling a well diversified portfolio is very similar to assembling an all-star baseball team. On an all-star baseball team, you want the best players at different positions including pitchers, catchers, infielders, outfielders, and hitters—

FIGURE 7.1 WHERE DID THEY RANK IN THE YEARS
THAT FOLLOWED?

FUND	1982	1983	1984	1985	1986	1987	1988	1989
Oppenheimer Target	1	136	606	216	779	1,160	25	768
Loomis Sayles Capital	2	318	529	22	75	71	1,386	788
New England Growth Fund	3	418	506	90	228	59	1,368	594
United Services Gold Shares	4	563	639	767	47	26	1,463	2
Strategic Investments	5	573	645	768	74	40	1,464	3
IDS Progressive	6	265	465	164	725	562	199	1,304
Fidelity Sel. Technology	7	3	602	740	931	1,123	1,402	847
Putnam Vista	8	329	554	250	188	307	480	414
Mass Financial Emerging Growth	9	50	514	360	549	1,099	477	412
Fidelity Precious Metals	10	599	632	769	55	17	1,461	175
Oppenheimer Regency		1	624	159	785	541	712	618
Java Growth		2	Fund may not exist					
Fidelity Sel. Technology		3	602	740	931	1,123	1,402	847
Alliance Technology		4	601	341	596	55	1,378	1,528
First Inv. Discovery		5	643	684	939	1,167	374	—
Strong Investment		6	175	582	265	755	846	1,281
Lindner Dividend		7	34	635	160	944	104	1,211
Royce Value Fund		8	382	287	821	694	110	894
Legg Mason Value Trust		9	84	155	745	1,036	83	679

FIGURE 7.1   (CONTINUED)

FUND	1983	1984	1985	1986	1987	1988	1989
Strong Total Return	10	159	376	176	237	435	1,585
Prudential-Bache Util.		1	117	59	1,066	132	95
Vanguard High Yield Stock		2	207	138	971	76	1,582
Copley Fund		3	387	271	1,057	225	795
SLH Amer. Telecomm		4	122	95	654	341	10
Franklin Utilities		5	462	108	994	678	408
Energy & Utility Shares		6	No trace of fund				
Fidelity Sel. Utilities		7	157	104	1083	381	67
Fidelity Qualified Dvd.		8	368	154	952	790	704
Windsor Fund		9	268	169	623	52	941
Sequoia Fund		10	274	508	197	713	317
Fidelity Overseas			1	7	60	931	848
Fidelity OTC			2	636	592	128	234
New England Zenith Capital Growth			3	1	4	1,434	221
Paine Webber Atlas			4	44	333	219	678
Putnam Intl. Equities			5	48	165	867	474
Alliance International			6	33	988	23	257
BT International			7	14	749	400	767
Hemisphere Fund			8	Does not exist			
Fidelity Sel. Health			9	136	780	881	42
GAM International			10	26	103	376	582
New England Zenith Capital Growth				1	4	1,434	221
Merrill Lynch Pacific				2	87	38	870
Nomura Pacific Basin				3	20	387	574
Tyndall-Newport Far East				4	527	542	1,296

FIGURE 7.1 (CONTINUED)

FUND	1986	1987	1988	1989
Financial Post-Pacific	5	138	119	680
GT Pacific Growth Fund	6	465	118	20
Fidelity Overseas	7	60	931	848
BBK International	8	435	666	1,020
T. Rowe Price Int'l	9	176	305	508
GT Japan Growth	10	6	161	4
Oppenheimer Ninety-Ten		1	1,418	1,548
DFA Japan Small Company		2	27	73
Oppenheimer Gold & SP Min.		3	919	127
New England Zenith Capital Growth		4	1,434	221
IDS Precious Metals		5	1,447	806
GT Japan Growth		6	161	4
DFA United Kingdom Sm. Co.		7	847	1,662
Franklin Gold Fund		8	1,438	46
Van Eck Gold/Resources		9	1,459	739
Colonial Adv. Str. Gold		10	1,440	1,108
Kaufmann Fund			1	22
Integrated Eq. Agg. Growth			2	544
Parnassus Fund			3	1,583
Columbia Special			4	183
Calvert Ariel Growth			5	446
Gabelli Growth			6	60
Fidelity Sel. Retail			7	258
Fidelity Sel. Trans.			8	296
Harbor Intern. Fund			9	98
Fidelity Capital Appreciation			10	366

FIGURE 7.2   TOP 15 FUNDS (LOAD AND NO-LOAD) FOR DIFFERENT 10-YEAR PERIODS

RANK	1968–1977	1978–1987	1988–1997
1.	Templeton Growth	Fidelity Magellan	Fidelity Sel: Home Finance
2.	Mutual Shares	Loomis Sayles Capital Dev.	Kaufmann Fund
3.	Amer. Insur. & Indust.	Twentieth Century Growth	Fidelity Sel: Electronics
4.	International Investors	International Investors	Fidelity Sel: Regional Bank
5.	Financial Ind. Inc.	Merrill Lynch Pacific	J. Hancock Regional Bank/B
6.	Paramount Mutual	Twentieth Century Select	Seligman Commun. & Info./A
7.	Security Investment	New England Growth	INVESCO Strat.: Financial Svc.
8.	Kemper Total Return	Weingarten Equity	T. Rowe Price Science & Tech.
9.	OTC Fund	Franklin Gold	INVESCO Strat.: Technology
10.	Founders Special	Phoenix Stock	Fidelity Adv. Eq. Growth/Inst.
11.	Pioneer	Phoenix Growth	INVESCO Strat.: Health Sci.
12.	Windsor	Lindner	Fidelity Sel.: Health Care
13.	Decatur Income	Amer. Capital Pace	Vista: Growth and Income/A
14.	Investors Selective	Quasar Associates	AIM: Aggressive Growth
15.	Eaton & Howard Incm.	AMEV Growth	Spectra Fund

each with a different specialty. Similarly, in a properly diversified portfolio, you want the best experts in different areas. Many factors go into choosing a well managed mutual fund. (See Figure 7.3.) We will describe in detail what factors to look for, and give examples of funds that we think you should consider adding to your portfolio.

FIGURE 7.3 QUANTITATIVE AND QUALITATIVE FACTORS FOR CHOOSING A GOOD NO-LOAD MUTUAL FUND

Quantitative Factors

1. Look for a manager with a solid track record in both good and bad market conditions either in private accounts or in a public mutual fund.

2. Look for a fund that has produced superior *risk-adjusted* returns relative to its fund peers.

3. The manager and/or fund must have a track record covering at least one significant bear market.

4. The no-load fund being examined should have an expense ratio below the average expense ratio for similar funds.

5. Portfolio turnover should be less than 50%, which means that the fund should hold its average stock for at least two years.

6. The manager who established the track record for the fund, or for the private accounts in question, should be managing the no-load fund at the time of review.

7. The manager should buy stocks selling at a 20% discount on a price-to-book-value basis relative to the price-to-book-value ratio of the Standard & Poor's 500 Index.

8. The manager should buy stocks with price-to-earnings ratios that are at least at a 10% discount to the price-to-earnings ratio of the S&P 500 Index.

Qualitative Factors

1. Look for a manager who owns part of the management company so there is little chance that the manager will leave to go to another mutual fund organization.

FIGURE 7.3 (CONTINUED)

2. Look for a single manager as opposed to management by committee.

3. Look for an eclectic manager who "puts a little different spin on the ball" than the Wall Street herd. In the investment profession, you have to be a maverick.

4. Look for a manager who "eats one's own cooking" by having a significant financial stake in his or her own mutual fund.

5. Look for a manager and research team with superior academic and professional credentials including the Chartered Financial Analyst designation (CFA), master's degrees or PhDs in finance or business administration from top-notch universities, as well as significant experience at first-rate investment or research organizations.

6. Your manager should have a written "discipline" for when he or she sells stocks.

Special Factors for Bond Funds

1. For domestic bond funds, look for an expense ratio of less than 0.5%.

2. Look for a domestic bond manager who has unconventional expertise for adding value in an area outside of garden-variety government bonds.

3. Look for a bond manager with the flexibility and expertise to move between different segments of the bond market as values present themselves.

4. Look for significant assets under management in excess of several billion dollars, because advantages in bond investing accrue with the largest firms, including economies of scale.

Figure 7.4 shows the 71 mutual funds that meet each of our seven tests of quality as of September 1, 1997: These tests were derived from work done by Nobel laureate Merton Miller. In the order in which they appear in the table, these tests include column by column reading from left to right: solid performance relative to peers and the Morningstar universe, solid risk-adjusted performance (Sharpe

FIGURE 7.4   HIGH-QUALITY MUTUAL FUNDS

Summary:	Page 1 of 2				Release Date: 10-31-97		

Primary Rank: ▲ Fund Name
Secondary Rank:

Fund Name	% Rank Cat 3 Yr	Mstar Avg Rating	Sharpe Ratio	P/E Ratio	P/B Ratio	Turnover Ratio	Expense Ratio
AIM High-Yield A	26	4.2	2.11	24.0	3.0	77	0.97
American Cent Inc & Growth	6	4.1	1.82	21.8	4.6	92	0.62
Aquinas Equity Income	30	4.1	1.81	19.6	3.1	40	1.37
BB&T Growth & Inc Stock Tr	24	4.0	1.91	19.5	3.9	20	0.86
Bond Fund of America	7	4.0	1.65	17.3	2.3	43	0.71
Capital World Growth & Inc	8	4.8	1.37	21.6	4.1	30	0.85
Centura Equity Growth C	19	4.0	1.71	24.1	4.1	46	1.04
Clipper	7	3.9	1.98	21.8	4.2	24	1.08
Compass Large Cap Val Instl	17	4.5	1.83	19.3	3.3	60	0.75
Compass Large Cap Val Svc	19	4.3	1.81	19.3	3.3	60	1.05
Davis Financial A	6	4.3	2.22	21.1	3.8	26	1.15
Davis NY Venture A	1	4.7	1.82	23.3	4.2	19	0.87
Delaware Decatur T/R Instl	26	4.3	1.67	23.2	4.4	87	0.81
Delaware Devon A	27	4.3	1.71	21.0	4.3	99	1.25
Delaware Devon Instl	23	5.0	1.73	21.0	4.3	99	0.95
DFA U.S. 6-10 Value II	27	4.0	1.56	22.0	2.0	15	0.85
Dodge & Cox Balanced	16	4.1	1.80	19.8	2.9	17	0.56
Dodge & Cox Stock	18	4.3	1.74	19.8	2.9	10	0.59
Dreyfus Core Value Instl	29	4.0	1.58	22.5	3.0	88	1.03
Dreyfus Core Value R	25	4.3	1.59	22.5	3.0	88	0.88
Dreyfus Disc Midcap Inv	4	4.3	1.61	24.0	4.6	71	1.35
Dreyfus Disc Midcap R	3	4.1	1.62	24.0	4.6	71	1.10
Dreyfus Premier Sm Co Stk R	26	4.0	1.38	23.7	3.7	49	1.25
Fidelity Destiny I	31	4.4	1.68	21.2	4.1	42	0.65
Fidelity Sel Regional Banks	20	4.1	1.79	19.9	3.0	43	1.45
Fidelity Sel Utilities Grth	5	3.9	1.39	24.1	3.5	31	1.46
First American Balanced C	17	4.0	1.97	20.6	4.1	73	0.80
First American Equity-Inc C	11	4.0	1.84	22.1	4.4	23	0.75
First American Stock C	12	5.0	1.85	20.6	4.1	40	0.80
Galaxy Small Cap Value Tr	11	4.1	1.81	24.0	3.6	39	1.05
Goldman Sachs Gr & Inc A	8	4.2	1.98	18.8	2.6	53	1.22
Greenspring	10	4.0	2.35	18.9	2.6	61	1.04
Griffin Growth & Income A	16	4.5	1.73	23.5	3.4	66	0.72
Griffin Growth & Income B	19	4.0	1.71	23.5	3.4	66	1.22
Hancock Regional Bank A	13	4.9	2.16	20.2	2.8	8	1.36
Heartland Value Plus	1	4.2	2.24	18.6	1.7	73	1.45
HighMark Val Momentum Fid	6	4.0	1.93	20.9	3.8	20	0.80
Invesco Total Return	16	3.9	1.93	20.8	4.0	10	0.89
* Loomis Sayles Bond Instl	1	5.0	1.71	14.8	2.0	42	0.75
* MAS Value Instl	7	3.9	1.98	16.3	2.7	53	0.60
Merrill Lynch Capital A	15	4.0	1.86	22.1	3.9	47	0.55
* Mutual Discovery Z	1	5.0	2.19	24.3	3.2	80	0.96

MORNINGSTAR Principia™ for Mutual Funds

Source: Reprinted with permission from Morningstar, Inc.

FIGURE 7.4 (CONTINUED)

Summary: Page 2 of 2   Release Date: 10-31-97

Primary Rank: ▲ Fund Name
Secondary Rank:

Fund Name	% Rank Cat 3 Yr	Mstar Avg Rating	Sharpe Ratio	P/E Ratio	P/B Ratio	Turnover Ratio	Expense Ratio
Neuberger&Berman Part	10	4.3	1.68	22.4	4.4	96	0.84
Neuberger&Berman Part Tr	11	4.1	1.67	22.4	4.4	96	0.94
Northeast Investors	8	4.2	2.29	17.1	2.0	32	0.66
*Oakmark	36	5.0	1.74	23.1	3.7	24	1.18
Performance Mid Cap Gr ConSv	6	4.4	1.87	21.5	4.1	28	1.23
Performance Mid Cap Gr Instl	5	4.7	1.88	21.5	4.1	28	0.98
PIMCo Value Instl	31	4.0	1.63	17.4	3.4	71	0.73
Prudential Utility B	13	4.1	1.35	17.7	2.3	17	1.61
Qualivest Small Comps Val Y	8	4.0	1.50	19.0	3.2	34	1.08
Scudder Value	19	4.3	1.83	18.2	3.6	91	1.25
*Selected American	1	3.9	1.91	23.7	4.3	29	1.03
Smith Barney High-Income A	28	4.3	2.06	8.0	1.7	72	1.10
Standish Equity	2	4.3	1.83	20.4	4.5	78	0.71
Strong Schafer Value	17	3.9	1.73	17.0	3.1	18	1.27
T. Rowe Price Dividend Grth	25	4.9	2.34	22.3	4.5	43	1.10
T. Rowe Price Small-Cap Val	35	4.0	1.98	20.2	2.8	15	0.94
*Third Avenue Value	2	4.9	1.78	23.5	2.2	14	1.21
Torray	1	4.3	2.21	24.4	4.1	21	1.25
*Tweedy, Browne American Val	9	5.0	1.94	18.4	3.8	16	1.39
*Tweedy, Browne Global Value	13	4.5	1.32	21.7	2.9	20	1.58
*UAM FPA Crescent Instl	2	4.5	3.13	20.6	2.4	100	1.59
*UAM ICM Equity	9	4.8	1.79	16.1	3.7	37	0.90
UAM NWQ Value Eqty Instl	23	4.0	1.59	22.2	3.4	25	1.00
USAA Growth & Income	35	4.2	1.78	24.4	3.5	15	0.89
Vanguard Index Value	20	4.1	1.66	20.3	2.9	29	0.20
Vanguard/Wellington	6	4.0	1.78	19.8	3.9	30	0.31
Wachovia Quantitative Eqty A	8	4.1	1.80	21.1	4.4	44	0.87
Wachovia Special Values A	4	4.6	2.35	23.4	2.4	38	1.21
Washington Mutual Investors	8	4.0	1.96	21.3	4.6	20	0.64

MORNINGSTAR Principia™ for Mutual Funds

Ratio—which shows that a manager can make money in the real world and is not just following statistical guidelines that may work), low price-to-earnings ratio, low price-to-book ratio, low turnover ratio, and low expense ratio. This allows for an apples versus apples comparison.

We have used this set of seven screens or tests to create what we call our short list of the highest-quality mutual funds on a risk-adjusted basis that have succeeded in the real world. We will highlight some of the best funds from this list and give our rationale for choosing these funds.

It's worth reminding you that the Securities and Exchange Commission (SEC) requires the magic words "past performance does not guarantee *future* performance" after all mutual fund performance advertising for a good reason, and you should do some of your own research in conjunction with your qualified advisor.

SOME ALL-STAR FUNDS

One fund that meets our tests is the Oakmark Fund, managed by Robert Sanborn, CFA. Bob Sanborn looks for stocks with moderate-to-good earnings growth, in sharp contrast to momentum growth funds, which look for stocks whose prices are rising rapidly and often have very rapidly increasing growth rates that cannot be sustained.

This is a good time to draw a distinction between growth funds and value funds. Both growth funds and value funds buy common stocks; however, they buy very different types of common stocks. As the name implies, growth funds buy growth stocks that are likely to experience rapid growth in their earnings. The prototypical growth stock in today's market is probably Microsoft, which has experienced steadily increasing earnings for more than the past 20 years.

Unlike growth fund managers, value fund managers believe that the stocks they invest in are bargains at current prices relative to some objective measure of the company's value—the company's earnings, book value, sales, cash flow, and/or dividends. Perhaps the useful way to think of the distinction between growth and value managers is that the value manager prefers "a bird in the hand" whereas the growth manager is looking for "two in the bush." As mentioned earlier, the historical evidence indicates that not only do value funds perform as well or slightly better than their growth counterparts, but value funds also experience significantly lower volatility.

If you refer again to Figure 7.4, you will see several funds that meet all of our tests. Another fund that we like on the list is Selected American Shares Fund, managed by Davis Selected Advisors. The Davis firm has a distinguished 30-year track record of success. For all 30 years, they have operated as a family firm, and their methods for choosing stocks have proven very effective over many different types of market conditions and cycles. The Davises follow the growth at a reasonable price (GARP) approach, similar to the one taken by Robert Sanborn at Oakmark in that the Davises look for moderate growers as opposed to rapidly growing companies.

The Davis firm suggests that they would rather hit a lot of singles and doubles than attempt to hit a home run and also run the risk of striking out.

We feel that this is a very appropriate choice of words for retirees. We rarely, if ever, meet a retiree looking for a home run in the investment world. Rather, we find people who have already hit a home run by saving a good amount of money in their careers and are looking for investment advice and help on preserving and safely growing the capital that they have accumulated over a lifetime. They are not looking for spectacular profits, but rather for reliability.

> *Do not look for investment advisors to be heroes,*
> *but rather look for consistent, dependable results.*

Selected American Shares is now managed by Christopher Davis, the third generation of the Davis family in their money management firm. Shelby Davis, Christopher's father, remains chairman of the board at Davis Selected Advisors. Further information on both the Oakmark Fund and Selected American Shares is shown in Figures 7.5 and 7.6. Particularly notice in these charts that both Oakmark and Selected American Shares display superior risk-adjusted characteristics relative to their peers, which is the apples versus apples comparison that matters. The risk-adjusted measures are identified with stars.

You should note that as managers both Bob Sanborn and Christopher Davis meet the qualitative checklist items for choosing a good no-load fund in Figure 7.3. Both Sanborn and Davis own significant shares in their respective management companies, take an eclectic approach to their investment decisions, and have carved out outstanding risk-adjusted track records.

We have placed asterisks in Figure 7.4 by those no-load funds that we think are particularly appropriate for our moderate-growth investor in different categories. In the international area we have highlighted the Tweedy, Browne Global Value Fund. In the mid-cap growth area we have highlighted the Oakmark Fund and Selected American Shares. In the different large-cap, mid-cap, and small-cap value categories, we have highlighted several funds including MAS Value Fund, Mutual Discovery Fund, and Third Avenue Value Fund.

In Figure 7.7, we put all these pieces together and show a sample model portfolio for the moderate-growth investor.

FIGURE 7.5   OAKMARK

Volume 31, Issue 1, August 29, 1997.

Oakmark

		Ticker	Load	NAV	Yield	SEC Yield	Total Assets	Mstar Category
		OAKMX	None	$40.89	0.8%	—	$5,767.0 mil	Large Value

Prospectus Objective: Growth

Oakmark Fund seeks long-term capital appreciation; income is a consideration.

The fund invests primarily in common stocks and convertibles. To select individual securities, the fund uses several qualitative and quantitative methods to determine economic value. The primary determinant of value is a company's ability to generate cash; other key factors include the quality of management and amount of managements' stock ownership. The fund especially seeks securities that are priced significantly lower than their long-term value. The fund may invest up to 25% of assets in foreign securities; it may invest up to 5% in emerging markets.

Historical Profile

Return	High
Risk	Below Avg
Rating	★★★★★ Highest

Portfolio Manager(s)

Robert J. Sanborn, CFA. Since 8-91. BA'80 Dartmouth C.; MBA'83 U. of Chicago. Sanborn is a portfolio manager and principal with Harris Associates, his employer since January 1988. From 1983 to 1987, he held a variety of positions with the State Teachers Retirement System of Ohio. He worked as a securities analyst and managed a $100 million venture-capital operation.

Performance 07-31-97

	1st Qtr	2nd Qtr	3rd Qtr	4th Qtr	Total
1993	7.95	2.71	7.45	9.54	30.50
1994	-4.18	2.92	6.86	-1.97	3.32
1995	9.19	6.18	8.37	6.98	34.42
1996	3.56	3.51	0.75	7.60	16.21
1997	3.99	15.22	—	—	—

Trailing	Total Return%	+/- S&P 500	+/- Wil Large Value	% Rank All Cat	Growth of $10,000
3 Mo	16.76	-2.89	-1.08	31 72	11,676
6 Mo	19.70	-2.84	0.50	14 42	11,970
1 Yr	45.13	-6.98	1.67	12 36	14,513
3 Yr Avg	26.79	-3.96	-0.18	11 30	20,381
5 Yr Avg	26.53	5.90	7.38	1 1	32,436
10 Yr Avg	—	—	—		—
15 Yr Avg	—	—	—		—

Tax Analysis	Tax-Adj Return %	% Pretax Return
3 Yr Avg	24.44	91.2
5 Yr Avg	24.65	92.9
10 Yr Avg	—	—

Potential Capital Gain Exposure: 31% of assets

Analysis by Michael Stout 08-15-97

What differentiates Oakmark Fund is its truly long-term perspective.

Most funds consider three to five years a long investment horizon, but Oakmark thinks in terms of 20 to 30 years when evaluating purchases. Manager Robert Sanborn grills company managements on their long-term strategic plans, and he and his staff try to discount cash flows far in the future. That can get very subjective, so they also pay attention to prices paid today for comparable businesses in buyouts. The goal is to find stocks selling for about 60% of their private-market values.

This long-term view explains a lot about the fund. Take its evolution from a mainly small-cap vehicle to a predominantly large-cap portfolio today (and hence its move to the large-cap value category this issue). Certainly its ballooning asset base was a big factor, but Sanborn says he's also convinced that large caps are best equipped for growth in the years ahead, given their access to the global

economy. A long-term focus also leads to the fund's low turnover and superb tax efficiency. And because it's easier for Sanborn to value companies in industries whose dynamics will stay stable for several years, there's no technology in this portfolio. The financial industry, which consumes 23% of assets, meets this criterion better.

A lack of technology stocks hasn't helped the fund so far this year, but it still places in the large-value group's top quartile. Over the long haul, Sanborn has led the fund to a 26.5% trailing five-year return—the second-best in the entire category.

Because Sanborn won't compromise his standards at a pricey market, the fund has accumulated a 16% cash position. That's a record high, but it provides a nice war chest for bargain-hunting if the market drops. And if that happens, this well-run fund—which has earned great risk scores—would probably hold up better than most.

Address:	Two N. LaSalle Street	Minimum Purchase:	$1000	Add: $100	IRA: $1000
	Chicago, IL 60602-3790	Min Auto Inv Plan:	$1000	Systematic Inv: $100	
	800-625-6275	Date of Inception:	08-05-91		
Advisor:	Harris Associates	Sales Fees:	No-load		
Subadvisor:	None	Management Fee:	1.00% max./0.85% min.		
Distributor:	Oakmark Fund	Actual Fees:	Mgt: 1.00% Dist: —		
States Available:	All plus PR,VI	Expense Projections:	3Yr: $37 5Yr: $65 10Yr: $143		
Report Grade:	A	Annual Brokerage Cost: 0.08%	Income Distrib: Annually		
NTF Plans:	Fidelity, Schwab, Jack White	Total Cost (relative to category):	Average		

	1986	1987	1988	1989	1990	1991	1992	1993	1994	1995	1996	07-97	History
							82%	91%	91%	93%	92%	92%	87%	Investment Style / Equity / Average Stock %
	—	—	—	—	—	13.02	19.13	23.93	22.97	29.75	32.35	40.89	NAV
	—	—	—	—	—	30.20	48.90	30.50	3.32	34.42	16.21	26.40	Total Return %
	—	—	—	—	—	20.32	41.28	20.45	2.00	-3.12	-6.74	-3.79	+/- S&P 500
	—	—	—	—	—	34.50	17.05	7.66	-9.06	-2.87	3.17	+/- Wilshire LV
	—	—	—	—	—	0.00	0.23	1.05	1.03	1.03	1.08	0.00	Income Return %
	—	—	—	—	—	30.20	48.67	29.45	2.28	33.39	15.12	26.40	Capital Return %
	—	—	—	—	—	1	11	37	85	24	Total Rtn % Rank Cat
	—	—	—	—	—	0.00	0.04	0.23	0.23	0.28	0.34	0.00	Income $
	—	—	—	—	—	0.00	0.21	0.77	1.47	0.84	1.87	0.00	Capital Gains $
	—	—	—	—	—	2.50	1.70	1.32	1.22	1.17	1.18	—	Expense Ratio %
	—	—	—	—	—	-0.66	-0.24	0.94	1.19	1.27	1.13	—	Income Ratio %
	—	—	—	—	—	34	18	29	18	24	—	Turnover Rate %
	—	—	—	—	—	8.3	328.8	1,214.1	1,626.9	3,301.6	4,195.0	5,767.0	Net Assets $mil

Risk Analysis

Time Period	Load-Adj Return %	Risk %Rank¹ All Cat	Morningstar Return Risk	Morningstar Risk-Adj Rating
1 Yr	45.13			
3 Yr	26.79	60 36	1.29 0.68	★★★★
5 Yr	26.53	52 12	2.08 0.65	★★★★★
Incept	31.51	—	—	

Average Historical Rating (36 months):   5.0★s

¹1=low, 100=high

Category Rating (3 Yr)

	Other Measures	Standard Index S&P 500	Best Fit Index S&P 500
	Alpha	-0.2	-0.2
	Beta	0.87	0.87
	R-Squared	83	83
Return	Above Avg	Standard Deviation	12.31
Risk	Average	Mean	24.45
		Sharpe Ratio	1.98

Portfolio Analysis 05-31-97

Share Chg (03-97) 000	Amount 000	Total Stocks: 46	Value $000	% Net Assets
		Total Fixed-Income: 0		
5,941	8,911	Philip Morris	392,093	7.31
0	7,096	First USA	351,252	6.55
0	3,607	Mellon Bank	315,573	5.89
297	6,947	Black & Decker	241,415	4.50
0	4,062	Polaroid	207,182	3.86
3,100	13,379	Tele-Comm TCI Group Cl A	202,360	3.77
167	10,085	US West Media Group	200,447	3.74
186	4,535	Knight-Ridder	195,555	3.65
665	6,641	Dun & Bradstreet	173,504	3.24
0	4,007	HJ Heinz	172,312	3.21
0	2,195	AMBAC	164,618	3.07
0	3,538	Anheuser-Busch	151,700	2.83
125	2,561	Fortune Brands	125,465	2.34
0	3,246	DeBeers Consolid Mines (ADR)	114,422	2.13
75	2,533	Fannie Mae	110,480	2.06
0	3,094	James River	108,680	2.03
0	1,125	Lockheed Martin	105,328	1.96
0	3,277	YPF (ADR)	98,295	1.83
0	2,422	Nabisco Holdings Cl A	95,976	1.79
1,335	3,149	Foundation Health Systems A	94,074	1.75
0	476	Unilever (NY)	92,225	1.72
200	2,749	Old Republic International	82,802	1.54
0	4,764	ACNielsen	80,393	1.50
0	3,658	Tele-Comm Liberty Media Cl A	79,384	1.49
0	1,220	McDonnell Douglas	78,538	1.46

Current Investment Style

	Stock Port Avg	Relative S&P 500 Current Hist	Rel Cat
Price/Earnings Ratio	23.5	0.88 1.0	1.05
Price/Book Ratio	4.0	0.63 0.8	0.98
Price/Cash Flow	13.0	0.79 0.8	1.04
3 Yr Earnings Gr%	29.9	1.36 0.9	1.47
1 Yr Earnings Est%	12.9	0.89 —	1.13
Debt % Total Cap	54.3	1.20 1.3	1.10
Med Mkt Cap $mil	6,498	0.2 0.3	0.46
Foreign %	7.0	—	1.08

Special Securities % of assets 05-31-97		Sector Weightings	% of Stocks	Rel S&P	5-Year High Low
O Restricted/Illiquid Secs	0	Utilities	0.0 0.0	5 0
O Emerging-Markets Secs	4	Energy	2.2 0.2	10 1
O Options/Futures/Warrants	No	Financials	23.1 1.4	26 15
		Ind Cycls	12.5 0.8	25 12
Composition % of assets 06-30-97	Market Cap	Cons Dur	11.3 2.9	12 2
Cash 15.9	Giant 14.6	Cons Stpls	24.7 2.2	27 5
Stocks 84.1	Large 42.6	Services	22.3 1.9	33 8
Bonds 0.0	Medium 37.3	Retail	0.7 0.1	6 0
Other 0.0	Small 5.5	Health	3.3 0.3	19 0
	Micro 0.0	Tech	0.0 0.0	8 0

M⊙RNINGSTAR Mutual Funds OnDemand

Source: Reprinted with permission from Morningstar, Inc.

FIGURE 7.6   SELECTED AMERICAN

Volume 31, Issue 1, August 29, 1997.

Selected American

	Ticker	Load	NAV	Yield	SEC Yield	Total Assets	Mstar Category
	SLASX	12b–1 only	$28.08	0.6%	0.68%	$2,055.0 mil	Large Value

Prospectus Objective: Growth and Income

Selected American Shares seeks growth of capital and income.
The fund normally invests at least 65% of assets in securities of U.S. companies, including common stocks, convertibles, fixed-income securities, and short-term instruments. It invests chiefly in blue-chip firms with market capitalizations in excess of $1 billion. The fund may invest up to 30% of assets in debt rated below investment-grade.
Selected Financial Services (formerly Prescott Asset Management) managed the fund from Jan. 1, 1983, to May 1, 1993.

Historical Profile

Return Above Avg
Risk   Average
Rating ★★★★
        Above Avg

Investment Style
Equity
Average Stock %

Growth of $10,000
— Investment Value $000 of Fund
— Investment Value $000 S&P 500
▽ Manager Change
▽ Partial Manager Change
► Mgr Unknown After
◄ Mgr Unknown Before

Performance Quartile (within Category)

	1986	1987	1988	1989	1990	1991	1992	1993	1994	1995	1996	07-97	History
	12.65	11.43	13.67	13.81	12.79	18.43	17.13	14.60	13.09	17.68	21.53	28.08	NAV
	17.15	0.24	22.04	20.07	–3.90	46.26	5.80	5.50	–3.26	38.09	30.74	33.16	Total Return %
	–1.53	–5.02	5.43	–11.61	–0.79	15.77	–1.82	–4.56	–4.58	0.56	7.79	2.97	+/- S&P 500
	–5.07	–3.36	–0.75	–5.07	3.69	20.62	–8.60	–7.96	1.08	–5.38	11.66	9.93	+/- Wilshire LV
	3.79	4.34	2.41	3.18	3.19	2.16	1.09	1.66	1.56	1.69	1.00	0.56	Income Return %
	13.36	–4.10	19.63	16.90	–7.09	44.10	4.71	3.83	–4.82	36.41	29.74	32.60	Capital Return %
	51	53	32	70	28	5	85	93	82	10	2	1	Total Rtn % Rank Cat
	0.48	0.58	0.26	0.45	0.43	0.24	0.19	0.26	0.22	0.22	0.18	0.12	Income $
	2.29	0.76	0.00	2.10	0.04	0.00	2.19	3.22	0.82	0.15	1.30	0.34	Capital Gains $
	0.85	1.11	1.11	1.08	1.35	1.19	1.17	1.01	1.26	1.09	1.03	—	Expense Ratio %
	3.07	2.38	2.07	3.06	2.04	1.41	0.95	1.37	1.42	1.42	0.87	—	Income Ratio %
	40	45	35	46	48	21	50	79	23	27	29	—	Turnover Rate %
	160.4	264.3	284.7	361.0	400.6	705.6	581.9	451.9	527.9	925.0	1,378.1	2,055.0	Net Assets $mil

Portfolio Manager(s)

Christopher C. Davis. Since 10-95. MA'87 U. of St. Andrews. Davis is a vice chairman with Davis Selected Advisers. He also serves as chairman of Shelby Cullom Davis Financial Consultants, Inc. and as a director at Rosenwald, Roditi & Co., an offshore investment management company. Previously, Davis worked for Tanaka Capital Mgmt. and as a portfolio accountant with State Street Bank and Trust Co.

Performance 07-31-97

	1st Qtr	2nd Qtr	3rd Qtr	4th Qtr	Total
1993	0.70	0.81	6.03	–2.00	5.50
1994	–3.79	–0.23	1.14	–0.36	–3.26
1995	10.09	10.87	9.53	3.30	38.09
1996	5.43	3.18	6.39	12.97	30.74
1997	1.90	18.11	—	—	—

Trailing	Total Return%	+/- S&P 500	+/- Wil Large Value	% Rank All Cat	Growth of $10,000
3 Mo	22.97	3.32	5.12	11 4	12,297
6 Mo	24.43	1.90	5.23	3 3	12,443
1 Yr	63.43	11.32	19.97	1 1	16,343
3 Yr Avg	33.23	2.48	6.26	2 1	23,647
5 Yr Avg	21.25	0.62	2.09	6 12	26,207
10 Yr Avg	15.91	0.96	1.47	6 9	43,788
15 Yr Avg	19.67	0.02	–0.72	5 11	147,802

Tax Analysis	Tax-Adj Return%	% Pretax Return
3 Yr Avg	30.80	92.7
5 Yr Avg	17.64	83.0
10 Yr Avg	13.06	82.1

Potential Capital Gain Exposure: 31% of assets

Analysis by Laura Lallos 08-15-97

Selected American Shares' continuing commitment to financials lends weight to the argument that the sector has further to go.

With value meisters such as David Dreman backing out of financials and growth managers eager to pick up their shares, one wonders where this traditional value sector is headed. After all, it has trended up, with a few minor corrections, ever since 1991.

Chris Davis is sticking to his outsized stake, however. Earlier this year, amid "euphoria" over the sector, he stopped buying and even did some selling. But a downturn in April enabled him to add to names like Wells Fargo, Bank One, and BankAmerica, without violating his value style. He finds that many of his favorites, including insurance and investment firms, still meet his main criterion, offering attractive after-tax earnings yield. Based on that same standard, he has also added to individual picks such as McDonald's and Hewlett-Packard this year.

Davis is using the strategy developed by his father Shelby (who still has a management role as chief investment officer of Davis Selected Advisers). Their search for well-managed firms with sustainable growth has earned marvelous results over the long term. The fund certainly isn't a trend-follower, as its turnover indicates. Nor is Davis oblivious to the market's heady valuations. Since the end of June, he has allowed cash to mount from almost nothing to more than 6%. He says he wants to be certain that newer shareholders have a long-term perspective. He doesn't want to have to sell into a downturn, and also wants cash for new purchases in such an event.

There's no doubt that the fund's sector concentration could cause steep short-term losses, but the fund's record speaks volumes. Given that record, other investors will likely take note that Davis is now building an energy stake, as he believes demand for oil is on a long-term upward trend.

Risk Analysis

Time Period	Load-Adj Return %	Risk %Rank¹ All Cat	Morningstar Return Risk	Morningstar Risk-Adj Rating
1 Yr	63.43			
3 Yr	33.23	69 80	1.77 0.78	★★★★★
5 Yr	21.25	77 94	1.43 0.97	★★★★
10 Yr	15.91	75 83	1.60 1.00	★★★★

Average Historical Rating (140 months): 3.9★s

¹1=low, 100=high

Category Rating (3 Yr)	Other Measures	Standard Index S&P 500	Best Fit Index S&P 500
	Alpha	0.2	0.2
	Beta	1.08	1.08
	R-Squared	90	90
Worst ... Best	Standard Deviation	15.54	
Return High	Mean	29.72	
Risk Above Avg	Sharpe Ratio	2.03	

Portfolio Analysis 06-30-97

Share Chg (03–97) 000	Amount 000	Total Stocks: 78 Total Fixed-Income: 0	Value $000	% Net Assets
85	930	American Express	69,285	3.81
380	740	IBM	66,739	3.67
295	1,108	Hewlett-Packard	62,048	3.41
848	1,387	Morgan St Dean Witter Discover	59,746	3.28
137	307	General Re	55,819	3.07
0	868	Travelers Group	54,731	3.01
480	1,130	McDonald's	54,593	3.00
30	184	Wells Fargo	49,697	2.73
720	1,055	Philip Morris	46,816	2.57
0	574	Halliburton	45,490	2.50
–50	305	Intel	43,253	2.38
50	355	Citicorp	42,856	2.36
0	583	Allstate	42,524	2.34
0	488	First Bank System	41,700	2.29
150	446	Burlington Northern Santa Fe	40,084	2.20
350	610	BankAmerica	39,383	2.17
0	1,100	FHLMC	37,813	2.08
0	770	SunAmerica	37,533	2.06
92	882	Masco	36,824	2.02
0	300	Pfizer	35,850	1.97
50	1,101	CenterPoint Properties	34,963	1.92
373	373	SmithKline Beecham (ADR)	34,158	1.88
0	225	American International Group	33,609	1.85
0	450	Chubb	30,121	1.66
0	407	Vornado Realty Trust	29,348	1.61

Current Investment Style		Stock Port Avg	Relative S&P 500 Current Hist	Rel Cat
Value Blnd Growth	Price/Earnings Ratio	24.4	0.92 0.9	1.09
	Price/Book Ratio	4.6	0.73 0.8	1.13
	Price/Cash Flow	16.0	0.97 1.0	1.29
	3 Yr Earnings Gr%	19.5	0.89 1.4	0.96
	1 Yr Earnings Est%	19.0	1.31 —	1.66
	Debt % Total Cap	40.3³	0.89 1.0	0.82
	Med Mkt Cap $mil	24,585	0.7 0.6	1.73
	Foreign %	3.5	— —	0.54

³figure is based on 50% or less of stocks

Special Securities	% of assets 06-30-97
● Restricted/Illiquid Secs	1
○ Emerging-Markets Secs	0
○ Options/Futures/Warrants	No

Composition	% of assets 06-30-97
Cash	0.3
Stocks	98.5
Bonds	0.0
Other	1.3

Market Cap	
Giant	49.0
Large	32.0
Medium	16.8
Small	2.1
Micro	0.0

Sector Weightings	% of Stocks	Rel S&P	5-Year High Low
Utilities	0.0	0.0	2 0
Energy	10.3	1.1	10 0
Financials	47.1	2.9	60 21
Ind Cycls	3.9	0.3	7 0
Cons Dur	1.2	0.3	4 0
Cons Stpls	5.3	0.5	36 5
Services	8.9	0.8	25 8
Retail	3.1	0.6	15 2
Health	7.4	0.7	18 4
Tech	13.0	0.9	14 0

Address:	P.O. Box 1688 Santa Fe, NM 87504 800–243–1575 / 505–983–4335
Advisor:	Davis Selected Advisers
Subadvisor:	None
Distributor:	Davis Selected Advisers
States Available:	All plus PR
Report Grade:	A
NTF Plans:	Fidelity , Schwab , Jack White

Minimum Purchase:	$1000	Add: $100	IRA: $250
Min Auto Inv Plan:	$100	Systematic Inv: $100	
Date of Inception:	02-20-33		
Sales Fees:	0.25%B		
Management Fee:	0.65% max./0.55% min.		
Actual Fees:	Mgt: 0.62%	Dist: 0.25%	
Expense Projections:	3Yr: $33	5Yr: $57	10Yr: $126
Annual Brokerage Cost: 0.12%		Income Distrib: Quarterly	

Total Cost (relative to category):   Below Avg

©1997 Morningstar, Inc. All rights reserved. 225 W. Wacker Dr., Chicago, IL 60606, 312–696–6000
Although data are gathered from reliable sources, Morningstar cannot guarantee completeness and accuracy.

M☉RNINGSTAR Mutual Funds OnDemand

Source: Reprinted with permission from Morningstar, Inc.

FIGURE 7.7 MODERATE-RISK PORTFOLIO DEVELOPER REPORT

| Snapshot | Page 1 of 1 | | Release Date: 12-31-97 | Snapshot Date: 12-31-97 | |

Moderate Risk Portfolio
Benchmark: Schwab Asset-Balanced Growth

Composition %

	Portfolio	Benchmark
● Cash	13.17	12.90
● Stocks*	43.96	56.70
● Bonds	40.57	30.30
○ Other	2.25	0.10
◎ *Foreign	41.57	27.40
(% of stocks)		

Performance Indicators

	12 Month		3 Year		5 Year		10 Year	
	Port	Bmark	Port	Bmark	Port	Bmark	Port	Bmark
Annlzed Ret %	17.77	17.76	20.3	———	16.36	———	13.26	———
Load-Adj Ret %	17.58	17.76		———	16.36	———	13.26	———
Potential Capital Gains Exposure							13.94 % of assets	
Overall Portfolio Expense Ratio							0.86 %	

Note: These hypothetical indicators reflect the current portfolio allocation. For each trailing time period, these indicators are calculated by weighting the average return of the underlying holdings. For performance based on an actual investment history, please refer to page 1 of Historical Detail Pages.

Sector Weightings %

		Portfolio	Benchmark	■ Portfolio ┃ Benchmark
♨	Utilities	0.75	3.60	
◑	Energy	4.20	8.40	
$	Financials	29.10	19.70	
⚙	Industrial Cyclicals	15.35	14.10	
▣	Consumer Durables	7.04	5.60	
♥	Consumer Staples	13.69	7.70	
⚒	Services	15.65	13.40	
🛒	Retail	2.81	5.40	
✚	Health	5.29	10.10	
▣	Technology	6.14	12.10	

(chart scale: 0 10 20 30 40 50 60 70 80 90)

Investment Style

Equity

Style

Value	Blend	Growth	
17			Large Size
14	8		Medium
5			Small

Fixed-Income

Maturity

Short	Interm	Long	
29			High Quality
			Medium
	10		Low

Portfolio Statistics

	Portfolio	Benchmark
Price/Earnings Ratio	21.95	28.30
Price/Book Ratio	2.98	5.20
Median Market Capitalization ($mil)	7146.82	33816.00
Average Weighted Price	98.93	
Average Weighted Coupon	8.10	
Average Weighted Maturity	8.14	
Average Credit-Quality Position	A	

Portfolio Holdings

Top 10 out of 10	$100.00
PIMCo Total Return Instl	16.00
PIMCo Foreign Bond Instl	16.00
Northeast Investors	15.00
Mutual Discovery Z	10.00
Oakmark	10.00
Selected American	9.00
Third Avenue Value	9.00
Oakmark International	5.00
Tweedy, Browne Global Value	5.00
SoGen Overseas	5.00

MORNINGSTAR Portfolio Developer for Principia™

Source: Reprinted with permission from Morningstar, Inc.

In this model portfolio you see a slight deviation from our asset allocation of Figure 6.4, with 44% of the portfolio in equity funds divided among many of the equity funds we have highlighted. The difference results from several equity managers holding more cash than normal.

Avoiding risky funds that may have had a period of spectacular performance is often a larger challenge for retirees than choosing sensible, consistently well performing funds. As humans, we are all susceptible to being seduced by the promise of extraordinarily high returns. If you keep in mind our tests or what professionals call *screens* for dependable funds, including the criteria listed in Figure 7.4 (e.g., low price-to-book ratio, solid risk-adjusted performance, and low price-to-earnings ratio), you will be able to steer clear of these ephemeral hot performers. They are like the meteorites that shine brightly for a brief period and then burn out. Certainly during your retirement you cannot afford to have investments that burn out; rather, you need consistent performers that will endure over many market cycles.

Figure 7.8 shows a number of these "hot" performing funds from the 1960s that burned out, never to be heard from again. Figure 7.9 shows current funds with many of the characteristics of hot performers.

Figure 7.3 on page 111 provides both quantitative and qualitative tests to choose mutual funds that are right for you. The checklist walks you through many of the steps that a professional investment management firm uses after developing a short list of funds (as we have done in Figure 7.4 on page 113), in order to make the final 10 or 12 no-load fund selections that will be used in your portfolio.

Once your portfolio is established and you have implemented the asset allocation that fits your temperament as well as your investment and income needs, you should plan on holding all of your no-load funds for the long run. Only

FIGURE 7.8 "HOT" PERFORMING FUNDS: "WHERE ARE THEY NOW?"

Go-Go Funds of the 1960s—
Mutual Fund Performance 1970–1974

FUND	VALUE OF $10,000	% CHANGE 1970–1974
Eaton & Howard Growth	$4,949	−50.5
Enterprise	4,714	−52.9
Fidelity Trend	5,887	−41.1
Growth Fund of America	4,990	−50.1
Hartwell Growth	4,694	−53.1
Manhattan	2,888	−71.1
Mates Investment	1,961	−80.4
Mathers	5,895	−41.1
Midamerica Mutual	5,063	−49.4
Nicholas Fund	5,634	−43.7
Pennsylvania Mutual	1,312	−86.9
Pilgrim Fund	5,299	−47.0
Price New Horizons	5,890	−41.1
Scudder Stevens Common Stock	6,048	−39.5
Selected American Shares	6,024	−39.8
State Farm Growth	5,899	−41.0
20th Century Growth	6,353	−36.5
Value Line Fund	4,930	−50.7
Vanguard	2,224	−77.8
Average for all funds	$5,641	−43.6
DJIA price change	$7,694	−23.1
S&P 500 price change	$7,445	−25.5

Source: Standard & Poor's and Growth Stock Outlook 1970–1974. Reprinted by permission of Standard & Poor's, a division of The McGraw-Hill Companies.

FIGURE 7.9   TODAY'S GO-GO FUNDS

FUND	P/E	CURRENT ASSETS (MIL.)	% ASSET GROWTH
Smith Barney Spec. Equities	52	$447	45
Govett Smaller Cos.	49	440	–15
IAI Emerging Growth	49	763	25
John Hancock Special Equities	49	1,675	41
Stein Rowe Cap. Oppor.	48	1,010	235
PBHG Emerging Growth	48	841	32
TCW/Dean Witter Small-Cap	48	215	62
PBHG Growth	47	4,063	100
Putnam OTC Emer. Growth	45	2,000	56
BT Investment Small Cap	45	245	51

Source: Reprinted with permission from Morningstar, Inc.

an extraordinary event should prompt you to sell one of your funds. The following are some of the instances in which you should sell:

1. A change of managers occurs where the new manager is inexperienced.

2. A fund either raises its expense ratio or initiates an onerous 12b-1 fee program.

3. A fund superior to a fund you own becomes available for the first time on a no-load basis.

4. A change in your personal circumstances requires a greater allocation to either equity funds or fixed-income funds.

5. A fund consistently underperforms in its peer group for an extended period of time with no reasonable explanation.

6. A fund becomes too large and unwieldy to execute its management style effectively.

MUTUAL FUND FEES

Since no one works for free in the investment industry, your challenge is to avoid excessive costs.

1. All mutual funds charge an annual management fee of approximately 0.5% for bond funds, 1% for domestic stock funds, and 1.4% for international stock funds.

2. Avoid any fund that charges either a front- or a back-end load. These are used to pay the stockbroker, financial planner, or insurance agent who sells a given fund. You are better off buying no-load funds either directly or through a discount brokerage firm like Charles Schwab & Company.

3. A 12b-1 fee is an extra fee of approximately 0.25% charged by some funds for distribution and marketing. In general, avoid funds with 12b-1 fees unless that fund's overall expense ratio is low.

THE REBALANCING AND PORTFOLIO REVIEW AND MONITORING PROCESS

Thus far we have discussed several elements of the portfolio management process. We have explained the critical need for you to focus on your objectives. Ask yourself what you're trying to accomplish from your portfolio. Do you need a consistent monthly income? Are you funding charitable obligations? Are you supporting your children or an elderly parent? Are you living off a pension and planning on passing this money on to your heirs?

We also have examined issues relating to your personal risk tolerance. The stage of your retirement will influence both the amount of risk you can take and the amount of your portfolio that you can afford to have allocated to equity funds. These funds should produce a higher return but are more volatile.

We've also shown that risk tolerance is a function of your temperament. You may be able financially to take significant risk but, if you're not comfortable doing so, you can give up several points on the return side for more stability. It's worth repeating that the investment markets can be dangerous, and you need to know your comfort tolerance.

We have discussed how to establish your proper asset allocation, your optimal portfolio design, and the specifics of selecting no-load funds. Now it is time to move on to the process of managing your portfolio on an ongoing basis and reviewing your individual holdings and personal circumstances that might require a change in your portfolio.

In consultation with your investment advisor, you should have a written investment policy statement that specifies the objectives for your portfolio and the review process. (A sample investment policy is shown in Figure 7.10.) This policy statement should set out your broad asset allocation guidelines. At least quarterly or semiannually, you should review your portfolio with your advisor to make sure that your portfolio has stayed within these guidelines.

For example, there will be periods when either the domestic equity funds or the international equity funds in your portfolio dramatically increase in value. The equity funds would then represent a larger portion of your entire portfolio than your initial allocation dictated. All things being equal, you may want to consider what is called *rebalancing* your portfolio at this time by reducing some of your holdings in these appreciated funds and adding to segments of your portfolio that have not appreciated. To a certain extent, this is counterintuitive; however, history shows us that this discipline will in fact force you to buy low and sell high. Normally, you do not want to rebalance too often because this activity may create a taxable event. Only when your portfolio gets significantly out of balance—by, say, 5%—should you rebalance.

FIGURE 7.10 MODERATE POLICY

Portfolio Policies for Mr. & Mrs. John Q. Smith
December 1997

Objectives

> **Return Requirements:** Growth to stay ahead of inflation. At retirement, a *growing* cash flow to maintain the Smiths' purchasing power.
>
> **Risk Tolerance:** Average relative to other investors.

Constraints

> **Time Horizon:** At least a 30-year joint life expectancy.
>
> **Liquidity:** Only for emergencies and $200,000 per year for the Smiths to live on in today's dollars.
>
> **Regulations:** IRA withdrawal rules.
>
> **Taxes:** Retirement accounts are tax-deferred.
>
> **Unique Needs:** Mr. Smith wants to keep between $.3 and $1.0 million in his outside brokerage account for speculative purposes.

Strategy and Asset Allocation

An allocation that emphasizes moderate growth investments and broad portfolio diversification will best meet the Smiths' objectives. The portfolio should have 38–48% in domestic equities—preferably moderate-risk no-load funds; 18–22% in conservative international funds; 4–7% in conservative resource and REIT funds; 20–28% in domestic bond funds; 6–10% in international bonds; and 3–7% in short-term bond funds. This mix hedges inflation and deflation risk.

A long-term investment policy is critical to prevent unwise revisions based on short-term pressures. No-load funds can best provide diversification, low cost, professional management, and liquidity.

We have included descriptions of recommended no-load and closed-end funds and institutional trusts.

LESSONS FROM INVESTMENT HISTORY

To invest successfully over your lifetime, you must be a student of investment history. The philosopher George Santayana counseled that "those who cannot remember the past are condemned to repeat it." Similarly, investors who do not study financial market history are condemned to repeat the mistakes that other investors have made.

Investment history teaches us that:

1. The twin demons of fear and greed have cost people fortunes over the centuries.

2. If something appears too good to be true, it is.

3. Over the past 200 years, *in the long run,* relative and nominal investment returns from stocks, bonds, and cash equivalents have been remarkably stable and remarkably predictable.

History is replete with examples of fear and/or greed leading investors astray. We will start with examples of greed because they're more dramatic.

In his classic book, *Extraordinary Popular Delusions and the Madness of Crowds,* Charles Mackay identified many investment bubbles where people allowed greed to lead them to pay ridiculous prices for certain types of investment. Needless to say, like the story about the emperor with no clothes, these relatively worthless investments turned out to be "barely" worth anything at all.

We will recount a few of these bubbles by way of illustration, so you can see the warning signs of investment types and investment attitudes to avoid. In Holland in the 1700s, there was a tulip bulb mania, with Dutch citizens paying ridiculously inflated prices for particularly colorful tulip bulbs, all because speculators whipped up a frenzy among tulip buyers. In the end, this tulip mania subsided and tulip bulbs that at one point sold for double the price of a house ultimately sold for the equivalent of the price of a glass of water.

A recent mania in the United States was the "Nifty 50" stock bubble in the 1960s and early 1970s. At that time, investors bid up the price of the 50 most popular blue-chip stocks in the United States to ridiculous levels. Some of these stocks were bid up to 50, 100, or even 150 times their annual earnings. The average stock sells for about 14 times earnings, and history has shown that it is rarely a good idea to pay more than 20 times earnings for a given stock.

The final bubble we will look at occurred in Japan in the 1980s, when Japan was called "Japan, Inc." and its markets were thought to be invincible. Suffice it to say that both common stocks and real estate in Japan are selling for less than half the price today that similar assets sold for 10 years ago. No investment is invincible.

These three situations show that greed has led investors to try to earn unrealistic returns. Now, let's look at the opposite circumstances, where investors have been overly fearful and exercised excessive caution.

Perhaps the most painful example of investor overcaution occurred in the post–World War II era when many invested almost exclusively in government and corporate bonds. This strategy, in many cases, was an overreaction to losses from the Great Crash and the Depression and the conventional wisdom at the time that common stock investments were excessively risky. Unfortunately, as shown in Figure 7.11, the 1948 government bond investor had lost 90% of the bonds' purchasing power 32 years later because of rapidly increasing inflation in the 1960s and 1970s.

In our practice at Yolles Investment Management, we witnessed similar symptoms of overcaution in the mid-1980s

FIGURE 7.11   BOND RETURNS VERSUS INFLATION

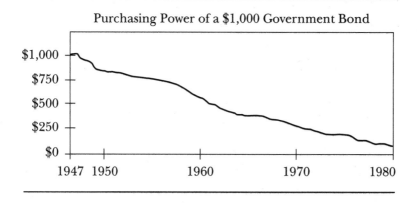

Purchasing Power of a $1,000 Government Bond

and again after the market crash of 1987. Some investors limited themselves to fixed-income vehicles like certificates of deposit, which had very low returns that did not keep up with inflation on an after-tax basis. More importantly, they cheated themselves out of the only investment that historically has outpaced inflation—sensible common stock or stock fund investments.

COMMON INVESTMENT MISTAKES TO AVOID

If we analyze all of the mistakes we've seen investors make over the years, these errors can be grouped into three general categories:

1. Allowing emotions to overrule intellect.

2. Getting caught up in an investment fad.

3. Not getting professional, objective advice.

As an example, in our era much of the conventional wisdom dictates that index funds are the investment vehicle of choice.

Unfortunately, the people who are now getting caught up in the index fad are much more likely to get burned than the people who invested in index funds 15 years ago when such funds were at bargain prices. Large-cap index funds have done particularly well from 1982 through 1997. However, funds based on the Standard & Poor's 500 Index and Dow Jones index did poorly from 1966 to 1982 when both of these popular indexes did not appreciate at all. The bulk of mutual funds did substantially better than these indexes during that 16-year flat period, as did the majority of private money managers.

Similarly, many who invested in real estate limited partnerships in the late 1980s lost a great deal of money. These partnerships were popular during the late 1970s and early 1980s when hard assets such as real estate did well and there were plentiful tax benefits. However, the 1986 Tax Reform Act eliminated many benefits from these partnerships and signaled the beginning of a long bear market in real estate.

Rather than trying to anticipate each and every investment fad (this "timing" is commonly referred to as "the loser's game"), investors are better off drafting and sticking

INDEX FUNDS

A stock or bond index tracks and measures the value and performance of a given group of stocks and/or bonds. For example, the popular Standard & Poor's 500 Index tracks the performance of the 500 largest companies in the United States—blue-chip companies like Merck, Johnson & Johnson, Microsoft, General Electric, and General Motors. Similarly, the Dow Jones Industrial Average tracks the performance of 30 large industrial companies, and the Lehman Government Bond Index tracks the performance of government bonds. An index fund replicates the performance and specific holdings of an index.

to a sensible long-term investment policy. Earlier in this chapter we provided a format for drafting your own investment policy and setting out a plan of action for achieving your goals. Reviewing this policy can remind you of your objectives during times when your emotions may lead you astray because of short-term concerns that cause greed and/or fear.

THE TORTOISE WINS THE RETIREMENT RACE

This chapter has detailed ways in which a consistent and dependable investment approach proves superior to a high-flying investment approach. While investors may look for a magic formula or the Holy Grail of the investment world, there are no shortcuts to investment success. Figure 5.2 on page 66 illustrates the beauty of the broadly diversified multimanager no-load type of investing that we have detailed in this chapter. Our broad diversification is contrasted with the current investment indexing fad represented by funds based on the Standard & Poor's 500 Index. This broadly diversified approach has a safe low dispersion of returns; this is critical to retirees who cannot take the risk of a steep decline inherent in indexing approaches.

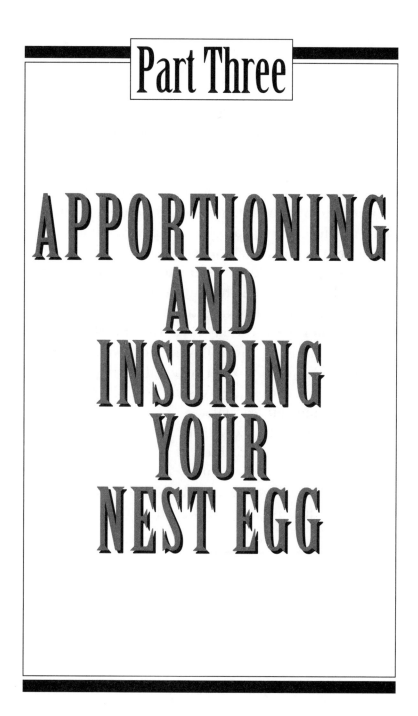

Part Three

APPORTIONING AND INSURING YOUR NEST EGG

In Part I we explored your capital needs during retirement as well as your various sources of cash flow to meet these capital needs.

Part II covered the world of investing and your investment temperament. You now have the tools to design an investment program that will meet your retirement needs and allow you to sleep comfortably.

This section explores various events and decisions that could derail even the most carefully constructed and soundly researched investment program.

In Chapter 8 we review savvy withdrawal strategies for IRAs, pensions, and rollovers. Following the right strategy is essential in order to avoid paying too much in income and/or estate taxes, or possibly even drastically depleting your capital.

Chapter 9 reviews key insurance issues. The best investment plan is worthless if unexpected medical expenses deplete your capital. Your financial life involves a series of intertwined decisions which must be coordinated; any weak link will cause the entire chain to collapse.

$

CHAPTER EIGHT

Withdrawal Strategies Using IRAs, Pensions, Rollovers, and Social Security

IN THIS CHAPTER

This chapter will help you determine a withdrawal strategy and how to coordinate the various sources of funds including IRAs, other qualified retirement plans, and Social Security.

Section I provides you with an overview of withdrawal planning that takes into account all of your resources.

Section II summarizes withdrawal planning using qualified retirement plan accounts.

Section III reviews withdrawal options under Social Security retirement income benefit programs and other programs administered by the Social Security Administration.

SECTION I—WITHDRAWAL PLANNING

The first step in planning withdrawals is to determine how much money is needed in order to retire. Many investors arrive at this amount by using a schedule from a broker's brochure or financial magazine similar to the one shown in Figure 8.1. Since most people ignore qualifiers or descriptions of limitations that appear below the table ("For illustrative purposes only" in small print is not enough to deter people from making dangerous assumptions), we have added our own warning: "DO NOT USE."

Tony and Cleo are in their late 50s and need $100,000 a year to live on at 1998 prices. They will receive $30,000 per year in combined Social Security and pension benefits, leaving $70,000 per year to be provided by their investment portfolio. Since their portfolio totals $660,000, $70,000 would be about 10.6% of this sum (10.6 is the factor given

FIGURE 8.1   WITHDRAWAL RATES

DO NOT USE*	DO NOT USE*					DO NOT USE*
NUMBER OF YEARS FOR PORTFOLIO TO LAST	**AVERAGE ANNUAL RETURN**					
	6%	**7%**	**8%**	**9%**	**10%**	**11%**
10	13.4%	14.0%	14.8%	15.5%	16.2%	16.9%
15	10.2	10.9	11.6	12.3	12.7	13.8
20	8.6	9.3	10.0	10.9	11.7	12.6
25	7.7	8.4	9.3	10.1	11.0	11.8
30	7.2	8.0	8.8	9.5	10.6	11.5

*"For illustrative purposes only" is not enough to protect the reader from relying on this type of table to his or her detriment.

DO NOT USE*   DO NOT USE*   DO NOT USE*

in Figure 8.1 for 30 years of withdrawals from a portfolio with an average annual return of 10%). Since an average annual return of 10.8% per year for common stocks was achieved during the 1926 to 1996 period, their position would seem secure. This is not so. *The volatility of the annual returns must be taken into account.* As Figure 5.2 on page 66 shows, for the 1965 to 1994 period a $100,000 portfolio with an average annual return of 10.77% but matching the S&P 500 Index's performance for that period could not survive a withdrawal rate of even 7.2% of $100,000 ($7,200 per year).

A different approach is shown in Figure 8.2. It starts with several portfolio mixes of stocks and bonds. Here, Tony and Cleo would look for the withdrawal rate for 30 years of retirement with a portfolio of 50% stocks and 50% bonds. The table indicates that 6% can be withdrawn the first year, or

FIGURE 8.2 WITHDRAWAL RATES—SECOND VERSION

DO NOT USE	DO NOT USE			DO NOT USE	
	YEARS IN RETIREMENT				
PORTFOLIO	**10**	**15**	**20**	**25**	**30**
70% stocks/30% bonds	12.7%*	9.6%*	8.1%*	7.3%*	6.7%*
60% stocks/40% bonds	12.4	9.3	7.8	6.9	6.3
50% stocks/50% bonds	12.2	9.0	7.4	6.5	6.0
40% stocks/60% bonds	11.9	8.7	7.1	6.2	5.6
30% stocks/70% bonds	11.6	8.4	6.8	5.8	5.2
20% stocks/80% bonds	11.3	8.1	6.4	5.5	4.9

Source: T. Rowe Price Associates.

Note: An accompanying article in the *Wall Street Journal* pointed out the limitations involved.

*The percentage shown is for the first annual withdrawal. From then on you increase your withdrawal annually by the inflation rate.

$60,000 on a million-dollar portfolio. (If the inflation rate is 4%, then $62,400 could be withdrawn in the second year, and so on.) Can we trust this table any more than Figure 8.1?

An article in the *Wall Street Journal* on February 14, 1997, cautioned that tables like Figure 8.2 should be used only "with great care. If you live five years longer than you expect while earning returns that are maybe half a percentage point

SOMETIMES, MISLEADING INFORMATION IS NOT IN THE FORM OF A TABLE

On October 12, 1997, The Detroit News *carried a Dow Jones News Service article that quoted an actuary who recommended a formula calling for:*

> *...savings equal to seven years of preretirement income. For those earning $35,000 a year, that would be about $250,000, a sum far less intimidating than $1 million or more. For someone earning $100,000, the target would be $700,000. With seven years of pay saved, retirees could count on an annual income that's half of what they made while working. That might put high earners on a tight budget, so [the actuary] figures they might want to save eight years of pay. Since the seven-year formula allows most retirees to protect their principal investment and live off income, it's a good number to start with.*

(Reprinted by permission of the Wall Street Journal, *© 1997 Dow Jones & Company, Inc. All Rights Reserved Worldwide.)*

Comment: *This formula will be far off the mark for many retirees because we believe that it cannot be a "good number to start with" if you are not able to finish with a number that is useful.* **Do not rely on this type of advice: Note its limitations!**

a year below the historical averages, the suggested withdrawal rates could be too high by 20% or more." (Reprinted
by permission of the *Wall Street Journal,* © 1997 Dow Jones &
Company, Inc. All Rights Reserved Worldwide.) Even a detailed warning like this will often be overlooked. Reliance on
tables of this sort can be very dangerous.

In this chapter, we are evaluating what is a sustainable
rate for someone who is contemplating retirement. In
Chapter 3, there is a discussion on increasing the withdrawal rate as a retiree gets older. The examples used in the
two chapters may not seem consistent. This planning is an
exercise in dealing with probabilities, not certainties. Con-
tinual fine-tuning and adjusting is essential. As noted above,
being off slightly (by as little as 0.5%) in an estimated annual withdrawal rate can create a serious problem. Still, you
can handle this situation by continually making adjustments. Often, there will not be one unchanging sustainable
rate of withdrawal for long periods of time.

This chapter and, for that matter, a good part of this
book, is based on learning from experience; that is, what
has happened before gives us guidance on what will happen
in the future. The theory is usually helpful, but not always
so. We do not know what economic conditions will be like
during the next 10, 20, 30, or more years that will encom-
pass your retirement years. We also do not know what personal events will happen to you that will affect your financial
condition. A basic principle involved in this planning, or in
planning in any field where the records of the past are re-
garded as significant to predicting future performance, is *regression to the mean*—the idea that things will basically return
to normal. If a baseball player has a batting average for the
prior five years of .250, but for the past 10 games the batting
average is .550, regression to the mean dictates that trend-

ing toward .250 rather than maintaining .550 is more indicative of future performance.

Sir Francis Galton, who lived more than 100 years ago and is credited as being one of the fathers of fingerprint identification, was an eccentric but also an astute observer. He once measured the heights of 928 adults and noted that the children whose parents were taller than 68.5 inches were on average shorter than their parents. In addition, he found that the children of parents who were shorter than 68.5 inches were on average taller than their parents. So those of us who are taller than our parents and whose children are even taller will probably not have seven-foot great-grandchildren destined to become basketball millionaires. Regression to the mean will usually operate.

You will have to frequently examine and adjust your portfolio to determine suitable withdrawal rates during retirement. You should not rely too heavily on regression to the mean. For example, for the past 25 years, long-term interest rates have averaged almost half of what they averaged for the 150 years prior to 1970. Will regression to the mean take over or will this be an exception? For portfolios with a time horizon of 20 years or less that are adequately diversified, it won't matter much. Regression to the mean can give us some guidance, but the shorter the time frame, the less you should rely on it. Without substantial reliance on regression to the mean, there would be a flood of optimists thinking that they had a sufficient portfolio at age 50, and a torrent of pessimists believing that they still did not have a sufficient portfolio at age 80. While not a perfect tool, it is the best one that we have; probability is as close to certainty as we can get.

In the October 1997 issue of *Worth* magazine, personal finance columnist Scott Burns summarizes conclusions from an unpublished paper prepared by three researchers at

Trinity University in San Antonio, Texas, relating to managing money during retirement. The study includes calculating probabilities of being able to maintain various withdrawal rates under different circumstances.

Some of the conclusions of the Trinity study as described by Scott Burns are:

[1.] Except for short periods, withdrawal rates over 7% are hazardous. . . . A 100% stock portfolio . . . has only an 86% chance of surviving a 10% withdrawal rate for 15 years, and the chances that the same portfolio would survive a 10% withdrawal rate for 30 years are little better than 50–50.

[2.] Although they post lower returns than stocks, bonds can improve a portfolio's odds of success at lower withdrawal rates. . . . At withdrawal rates of up to 6% a year for 30 years, a portfolio of 25% stocks and 75% bonds had a 100% success rate in every period since 1926 (through 1995). . . . Generally speaking, at moderate withdrawal rates—anything up to 6% a year—bond holdings of 25% to 50% produce a higher success rate than 100% stocks. [*Note:* This is another way of pointing out that long-term average annual returns can be misleading. A portfolio with 100% in stocks will give higher long-term average annual returns, but the degree of volatility is extremely important.]

[3.] You can live reasonably well during retirement and still pass something on to your children, but the size of the estate will vary greatly. It's all a matter of chance. . . . A portfolio consisting of 75% stocks and 25% bonds could support a 6% per year withdrawal rate for 15 years but, again basing the probabilities on past performance for the 1926 through 1995 period, the size of the remaining estate could range from 5% to 540% of the initial wealth. . . . In other words, a starting nest egg of $100,000 could dwindle to as little as $5,000 or swell to as much as $540,000. The median estate size would be $200,000.

Frequent reviews of performance are necessary so that adjustments can be made. Also, as you get older, different allocations of investments will become advisable. Age, health, market performance, unforeseen events, and inflation are factors that can affect both withdrawal rates and asset allocation. Diversifying broadly using stocks and bonds—both U.S. and international—greatly increases the probability that you will have enough capital to sustain you comfortably through retirement. However, unforeseen factors such as being sued and held liable for damages or having to help loved ones in financial trouble are examples of unexpected challenges.

By analyzing your withdrawal program realistically, postponing retirement, or cutting back to working on a part-time basis for a brief period can greatly increase the probability of a secure retirement. In 1995, my wife and I calculated that we would have enough to last us about 27 years. I was 63 and my wife was 56. We estimated that if I worked for four more years and she worked part-time during that period and our portfolio would hold its own, that she would be financially secure to age 90 or so.

We both happened to change jobs at that time, and after two years, we came up with an unexpected bonus—we each enjoy what we're doing much more than before, although we make less than we previously did. If our portfolios hit some potholes, either or both of us could undo at least part of the damage by extending the part-time employment for a short period. In fact, if I am still in good health, I may cut back a little more and continue to age 69 or so.

If you no longer enjoy your job you may find that you can change positions and meet your financial goals with less stress. A former law client who was one of three partners in a service business dreaded the pressures of work. At age 64, he sold his business interest, invested the proceeds, and obtained a job at the township golf course working nine months a year. He is completing his fourth year with the parks and recreation department with no thought of quit-ting. Working several years for $25,000 per year and enjoy-ing it rather than working one or two years for $150,000 per year and being miserable will make sense for many people. After age 60, this kind of math can work.

Continuing to work on a part-time basis can make invest-ment setbacks in your retirement years less of a burden. The added period of less stressful employment also gives you an opportunity to more accurately assess your finan-cial needs—to confirm that you have enough or to reveal that you may need more while you are in a position to do something about it. If your retirement is a comfortable one—replacing cars regularly, taking vacations, making substantial gifts to loved ones, maintaining a vacation home or boat—you have the ability to cut back to some de-gree if necessary. If you have substantial equity in your home, you may consider selling it and moving into a smaller home or apartment. By tacking on a year or two of less stressful employment, you may not only keep your portfolio from disappearing but keep yourself around a lit-tle longer, too.

A *reverse mortgage* is a possibility in some cases. Instead of paying the bank, the bank sends you a check monthly. The amount is determined by the value of your home, interest rates, and your age. The mortgage loan is generally repaid when you move or upon death. The availability of a reverse mortgage at some future time can serve as a psychological safety net. There are a number of variations, so you should shop carefully. Generally, the best terms are found in *home equity conversion* mortgages sponsored by the Federal Hous-ing Administration (FHA) or in reverse mortgages sup-ported by the Federal National Mortgage Association (FNMA or "Fannie Mae").

SECTION II—WITHDRAWALS FROM QUALIFIED RETIREMENT ACCOUNTS

There are a number of different types of *qualified* retirement programs. Many corporations offer 401(k), profit sharing, and pension plans to their employees. Governmental agencies offer 403(b) plans. Other plans are established by employers, the self-employed, or the participants themselves. Some examples are: IRA, Keogh, SEP, Simple IRA, Simple 401(k), and Roth IRA. "Qualified" refers to compliance with complex governmental rules resulting in favorable tax treatment, such as tax-deductible contributions and tax-free accumulation prior to withdrawal. In this section we are concentrating on the withdrawals from the accounts. It is important for you and your advisor to review the literature about the plan or plans in which you participate. The employer, broker, or bank that is the sponsor may have included provisions that are unique to that particular plan.

Withdrawals from these plans prior to age $59\frac{1}{2}$ are usually penalized, and certain minimum distributions must be taken once age $70\frac{1}{2}$ is reached. Someone who is about to retire, or who has retired, must fit these rules into the overall withdrawal-during-retirement strategy. The following case histories will illustrate common problems and solutions. Since most retirement plan accounts are IRAs, including those accounts that were initially other types of retirement plan accounts and were rolled over or transferred into IRA accounts, they are emphasized. Other types of retirement plans have similar rules in some instances, and very different rules in others. The policy behind different treatment is often unclear. Again, the objective of this chapter is to make you more knowledgeable so that you can work with your tax advisor—not replace him or her. These rules are not only complex but are constantly changing.

$ CASE STUDY 8.1—MARK

Mark was 54 when he decided to retire early from his management position and teach part-time at the local community college. He asked the trustee of the company pension plan to send him a check for the $350,000 balance in his retirement plan account. Instead, he was sent information about his options. He then realized how great a mistake he could have made. He learned that he could have his money rolled over into his personal IRA and avoid paying a 20% withholding tax, plus an 11% additional federal income tax (he was in the 31% bracket) and a 4.5% state income tax. There is generally also an additional 10% penalty tax on withdrawals from a qualified plan before $59\frac{1}{2}$ years of age. But, if Mark waits until he is 55 and terminates his employment, withdrawal of his account would not then be subject to the 10% penalty tax.

What Could Have Happened to Mark

Retirement plan account balance	$350,000
20% withholding for federal income tax	–$70,000
11% balance of federal income tax	–$38,500
4.5% state income tax	–$15,750
10% penalty for early withdrawal	–$35,000
Balance after taxes	$190,750

By establishing an IRA account and rolling over the entire $350,000 balance, no taxes or penalties would be assessed until Mark withdrew amounts from the IRA, and then only to the amounts withdrawn. The remaining monies could continue to accumulate tax-free. The penalty tax would apply to only amounts withdrawn before age $59\frac{1}{2}$, and this penalty would be avoided if "substantially equal periodic payments" over Mark's life expectancy or over the joint life expectancy of Mark and a beneficiary were made. Avoiding the penalty requires utilizing Section 72(t)(A)(iv) of the Internal Revenue Code, and professional guidance should be secured. This payment schedule could be revised or discontinued after five years or when Mark turns $59\frac{1}{2}$, whichever period is longer.

Mark could establish his rollover IRA account through either a direct or an indirect rollover. If he uses a *direct rollover*, the transfer would be made directly into an IRA account that he would have his broker establish for him beforehand. The trustee of his prior employer's plan would transfer Mark's account balance directly to this new IRA rollover account. It is important to have the plan administrator issue the check directly payable to the broker for the benefit of the IRA. (This procedure is also used when a plan participant changes employers and the retirement plan account from the prior employer is transferred to the participant's plan account with the new employer.)

An *indirect rollover* is a payout made to the participant. Under this procedure, for tax purposes Mark would have 60 days to roll it over into an IRA or a qualified plan of a new employer. In this case, 20% would be withheld from the distribution made to Mark (even if it is eventually rolled over). Thus, Mark would have to dip into his own funds to make up for the 20% withheld by his prior plan if he wanted to roll over his entire balance within the 60-day period. (See Figure 8.3.)

If Mark were at least $59\frac{1}{2}$, he could have qualified for a *forward averaging formula*, which would reduce the federal income tax exposure on a lump-sum distribution. Under the forward averaging formula, the tax is paid in one year but is calculated as if the distribution had been made evenly over 5 or 10 years. To qualify for this treatment:

1. The distribution must include the employee's entire balance from all qualified plans of his or her employer.

2. The total balance must be received within one calendar year.

3. The employee must be at least $59\frac{1}{2}$ (10-year averaging is limited to people born before 1936; 5-year averaging is phasing out in 1999).

4. The employee must have been a plan participant for a minimum of five years.

5. The distribution must have been made because of death, disability, or termination of employment.

6. The employee can use forward averaging only once.

In some instances, if the employee was born before 1936 and was a plan participant before 1974, a portion of the distribution would be taxed at a 20% rate with the balance subject to forward averaging. In Mark's case, and in most cases, a rollover into an IRA or other qualified plan is preferable to forward averaging as long as the funds aren't needed immediately.

$

FIGURE 8.3   COMPARING DIRECT AND INDIRECT ROLLOVERS OF AN IRA

Direct Rollover

1. If $350,000 is in the retirement account, the entire $350,000 is transferred to the new IRA.

Retirement Plan Account   IRA Account

```
┌──────────────┐          ┌──────────────┐
│   $350,000   │ ──────▶  │   $350,000   │
└──────────────┘          └──────────────┘
```

Net Effect:

1. Full balance is transferred—no reduction.

2. Additional tax and penalty cost: 0.

3. Entire balance of $350,000 can continue to accumulate tax-free.

Indirect Rollover

1. Amount withheld from rollover for federal taxes: $350,000 × 20% = $70,000

2. Since the $70,000 withheld is deemed to be a "taxable distribution," it is taxed at distributee's tax rate—assuming 31%: $70,000 × 31% = $21,700

3. Penalty of 10% on $70,000 taxable distribution: $70,000 × 10% = $7,000

4. Depending on state tax law, about 4.5% levied by state on taxable distribution: $70,000 × 4.5% = $3,150

Net Effect:

1. Instead of $350,000 in the IRA account, there is $280,000 ($350,000 – $70,000).

2. Additional tax and penalty cost: $21,700 + $7,000 + $3,150 = $31,850

LESSON: It is better to go with the direct rollover.

$ CASE STUDY 8.2—CLARK

Mark's friend Clark is 55 and works for Bubbly Cola, a Fortune 500 company. Clark wants to take early retirement and work part-time as a football coach at his son's high school. Mark has alerted Clark to the benefits of a direct rollover. Clark intends to execute a direct rollover of his $400,000 retirement plan account to an IRA that his broker is opening. Clark is discussing his plans one Saturday morning at the barbershop when Kent, another customer, overhears the story and asks Clark if he has Bubbly Cola stock in his plan account. (Actually, $50,000 of his account is in Bubbly Cola stock.) Kent urges Clark to consider keeping the stock out of the IRA. This is a choice that one has with regard to company stock only.

This is good advice in Clark's case since the value of the stock was $3,000 when it was added to his account. If Clark were under age 55 when his employment terminated, the 10% excise tax would apply only to the $3,000 *cost basis* of the stock, not its $50,000 value. The stock can continue to appreciate tax-free until sold. Dividends would be taxable (they would not be taxable if the stock were held in an IRA), but generally this would be a minor negative in deciding to keep the stock out of an IRA.

Let's assume that Clark continues to hold the Bubbly Cola stock until he dies 30 years from now. By then, the stock is worth $700,000. Clark's heirs get a stepped-up basis for the stock (equal to its fair market value as of the date of Clark's death) and are able to sell it for $700,000 and pay no capital gain tax. On the other hand, if the stock were in his IRA, Clark would probably have liquidated all or most of it to take required taxable distributions from the IRA beginning at age $70\frac{1}{2}$. To the extent that the stock is still in the IRA, it would be taxable for income tax purposes to his heirs. (The stock would be included in Clark's estate for federal estate tax purposes regardless of whether it was held in an IRA.)

$

$ CASE STUDY 8.3—ROSE

Rose is 52 and is leaving her job to open up her own consulting business. She has $500,000 in her retirement plan account. She doesn't need much capital to start the business but does need a

SOME RETIREMENT PLAN TRANSFER CONSIDERATIONS

If you are planning to change jobs or retire, you will have to repay amounts borrowed from the retirement plan or pay taxes and possibly an additional 10% penalty tax. If you are rolling over your balance to a new employer's plan that allows loans, you may be able to repay the old loan and then borrow from the new plan. If you are going to roll over the account or transfer it to an IRA, you can't borrow from the IRA *nor can you use your account as collateral for a loan.* You can withdraw funds and reinvest in an IRA account within 60 days without paying income tax or penalties.

If you are planning to withdraw part of your retirement plan account to start a new business or another project, note that there is a difference between withdrawing the money from the retirement plan account before rolling it over to an IRA and withdrawing money after it is rolled over into an IRA. Either way, the withdrawal is taxable. But if you are 55 or older, the 10% penalty tax won't apply if the withdrawal is made from the retirement plan after separation from service. To make a withdrawal from an IRA before age $59\frac{1}{2}$, the penalty tax will apply unless you qualify under certain emergency situations discussed in the next section. Also, if you follow rules requiring "substantially equal periodic payments" figured over your life expectancy and you keep up with these withdrawals for five years or until age $59\frac{1}{2}$, the penalty tax will not apply. (See Case Study 8.3.)

steady income flow until the business is established. If she elects to receive "substantially equal periodic payments" to avoid the 10% penalty for withdrawals before age $59\frac{1}{2}$, she would have more taxable income than necessary once the business is established. Her portfolio manager advises splitting the retirement account among several IRAs and taking "substantially equal periodic payments" from one of them. The additional IRAs provide flexibility.

$

$ CASE STUDY 8.4—LOU AND LULU

Lou has several IRAs that have a $300,000 total balance as of December 31, 1997. He is required to start taking a minimum distribution when he reaches 70½. If he doesn't take the minimum distribution each year, a penalty equal to 50% of the shortfall will be assessed. Lou was born in May 1927 and turned 70½ in November 1997. His first required minimum distribution (RMD) must be made by April 1 of the year following the year he turned 70½ (i.e., by April 1, 1998). All subsequent distributions must be made by December 31 of each calendar year. Thus, by December 31, 1998, he has to take his next RMD. For 1998, he will have to take two distributions, although he could have taken his first distribution during November or December 1997 after he reached 70½.

There are several planning alternatives that a tax advisor could clarify. Lou needs to decide whether he should utilize his own life expectancy or his joint life expectancy with his 67-year-old wife, Lulu. She is the beneficiary of his IRAs. On the joint life expectancy table authorized by the IRS (IRS Publication 590, Individual Retirement Arrangements; call the IRS at 800-829-3676 to order), their joint life expectancy is 22 years. To calculate the first required minimum distribution, he divides his IRA balance of $300,000 by 22 years for an RMD of $13,636. This amount is calculated on the basis of all of Lou's IRAs and qualified plan accounts. Each year, reference must be made to the joint life expectancy table. (See Figure 8.4.) To locate the joint life expectancy, you find where "70" and "67" meet. Find "67" on the top of the chart and run down the left column to where "70" is, and 22.0 is the factor. Or, you can locate "70" at the top of the chart and run down the left column to where "67" is, and again 22.0 is the factor. Now try it for the ages of you and your spouse.

Upon Lou's death, Lulu has the option of treating his IRA as her own. She can name new beneficiaries, choose a new minimum distribution schedule, and, if she's under 70½, make additional contributions. Different rules apply if the beneficiary is not the spouse. Certain trusts can also efficiently act as recipients of distributions. If Lou had named his son or anyone other than his spouse as a beneficiary and given that person or persons complete control of the account after his death then:

- If Lou died *before* the required beginning date (April 1, 1998), either (1) the entire account must be distributed to the beneficiary by December 31 of the calendar year that includes the

FIGURE 8.4   EXCERPT FROM IRS TABLES OF EXPECTED RETURN MULTIPLES

Ordinary Joint Life and Last Survivor Annuities Two Lives—Expected Return Multiples									
AGE	65	66	67	68	69	70	71	72	73	74
65	25.0	24.6	24.2	23.8	23.4	23.1	22.8	22.5	22.2	22.0
66	24.6	24.1	23.7	23.3	22.9	22.5	22.2	21.9	21.6	21.4
67	24.2	23.7	23.2	22.8	22.4	22.0	21.7	21.3	21.0	20.8
68	23.8	23.3	22.8	22.3	21.9	21.5	21.2	20.8	20.5	20.2
69	23.4	22.9	22.4	21.9	21.5	21.1	20.7	20.3	20.0	19.6
70	23.1	22.5	22.0	21.5	21.1	20.6	20.2	19.8	19.4	19.1
71	22.8	22.2	21.7	21.2	20.7	20.2	19.8	19.4	19.0	18.6
72	22.5	21.9	21.3	20.8	20.3	19.8	19.4	18.9	18.5	18.2
73	22.2	21.6	21.0	20.5	20.0	19.4	19.0	18.5	18.1	17.7
74	22.0	21.4	20.8	20.2	19.6	19.1	18.6	18.2	17.7	17.3
75	21.8	21.1	20.5	19.9	19.3	18.8	18.3	17.8	17.3	16.9
76	21.6	20.9	20.3	19.7	19.1	18.5	18.0	17.5	17.0	16.5
77	21.4	20.7	20.1	19.4	18.8	18.3	17.7	17.2	16.7	16.2
78	21.2	20.5	19.9	19.2	18.6	18.0	17.5	16.9	16.4	15.9
79	21.1	20.4	19.7	19.0	18.4	17.8	17.2	16.7	16.1	15.6
80	21.0	20.2	19.5	18.9	18.2	17.6	17.0	16.4	15.9	15.4
81	20.8	20.1	19.4	18.7	18.1	17.4	16.8	16.2	15.7	15.1
82	20.7	20.0	19.3	18.6	17.9	17.3	16.6	16.0	15.5	14.9
83	20.6	19.9	19.2	18.5	17.8	17.1	16.5	15.9	15.3	14.7
84	20.5	19.8	19.1	18.4	17.7	17.0	16.3	15.7	15.1	14.5
85	20.5	19.7	19.0	18.3	17.6	16.9	16.2	15.6	15.0	14.4
86	20.4	19.6	18.9	18.2	17.5	16.8	16.1	15.5	14.8	14.2
87	20.4	19.6	18.8	18.1	17.4	16.7	16.0	15.4	14.7	14.1

FIGURE 8.4 (CONTINUED)

AGE	65	66	67	68	69	70	71	72	73	74
88	20.3	19.5	18.8	18.0	17.3	16.6	15.9	15.3	14.6	14.0
89	20.3	19.5	18.7	18.0	17.2	16.5	15.8	15.2	14.5	13.9
90	20.2	19.4	18.7	17.9	17.2	16.5	15.8	15.1	14.5	13.8
91	20.2	19.4	18.6	17.9	17.1	16.4	15.7	15.0	14.4	13.7
92	20.2	19.4	18.6	17.8	17.1	16.4	15.7	15.0	14.3	13.7
93	20.1	19.3	18.6	17.8	17.1	16.3	15.6	14.9	14.3	13.6
94	20.1	19.3	18.5	17.8	17.0	16.3	15.6	14.9	14.2	13.6
95	20.1	19.3	18.5	17.8	17.0	16.3	15.6	14.9	14.2	13.5
96	20.1	19.3	18.5	17.7	17.0	16.2	15.5	14.8	14.2	13.5
97	20.1	19.3	18.5	17.7	17.0	16.2	15.5	14.8	14.1	13.5
98	20.1	19.3	18.5	17.7	16.9	16.2	15.5	14.8	14.1	13.4
99	20.0	19.2	18.5	17.7	16.9	16.2	15.5	14.7	14.1	13.4
100	20.0	19.2	18.4	17.7	16.9	16.2	15.4	14.7	14.0	13.4
101	20.0	19.2	18.4	17.7	16.9	16.1	15.4	14.7	14.0	13.3
102	20.0	19.2	18.4	17.6	16.9	16.1	15.4	14.7	14.0	13.3
103	20.0	19.2	18.4	17.6	16.9	16.1	15.4	14.7	14.0	13.3
104	20.0	19.2	18.4	17.6	16.9	16.1	15.4	14.7	14.0	13.3
105	20.0	19.2	18.4	17.6	16.8	16.1	15.4	14.6	13.9	13.3
106	20.0	19.2	18.4	17.6	16.8	16.1	15.3	14.6	13.9	13.3
107	20.0	19.2	18.4	17.6	16.8	16.1	15.3	14.6	13.9	13.2
108	20.0	19.2	18.4	17.6	16.8	16.1	15.3	14.6	13.9	13.2
109	20.0	19.2	18.4	17.6	16.8	16.1	15.3	14.6	13.9	13.2
110	20.0	19.2	18.4	17.6	16.8	16.1	15.3	14.6	13.9	13.2
111	20.0	19.2	18.4	17.6	16.8	16.0	15.3	14.6	13.9	13.2

FIGURE 8.4 (CONTINUED)

AGE	65	66	67	68	69	70	71	72	73	74
112	20.0	19.2	18.4	17.6	16.8	16.0	15.3	14.6	13.9	13.2
113	20.0	19.2	18.4	17.6	16.8	16.0	15.3	14.6	13.9	13.2
114	20.0	19.2	18.4	17.6	16.8	16.0	15.3	14.6	13.9	13.2
115	20.0	19.2	18.4	17.6	16.8	16.0	15.3	14.6	13.9	13.2

fifth anniversary of Lou's death, or (2) the beneficiary can take the distributions based on his or her life expectancy so long as they begin before the end of the calendar year after the year that Lou died.

- A nonspouse beneficiary may not roll over Lou's retirement account into his or her own IRA account.
- If Lou died *after* the required beginning date, distributions must continue at least as quickly as the payout period selected by Lou. The joint life expectancy table cannot be used to the extent that a nonspouse beneficiary is more than 10 years younger than Lou. After Lou dies, the actual life expectancy of the beneficiary can be utilized.

$

In all of these life expectancy calculations, either the recalculation method or the reduce-by-one method is used and, once selected, can't be changed. Again, you will probably want to consult a professional advisor. Generally, the attorney who prepared your estate plan or your CPA is the best one to talk to if you have a substantial portfolio in IRA or retirement plan accounts. Also, it is most important to have the advisor review the retirement plan's agreement— particularly the terms of distributions. Because IRA and retirement plan accounts have their own rules, estate planners should pay particular attention to the choice of beneficiary for these accounts. To give you a glimpse of some of the complexities in this area—particularly how IRA beneficiary designations interact with estate planning—here are some subtopics from an article written for tax lawyers by an expert:

- Features to include in a trust designated as an IRA beneficiary
- Irrevocable retirement plan payment trusts
- Post-death channeling to the decedent's IRA
- Loss of the marital deduction when a QTIP marital trust is the designated beneficiary
- Problems when reduce-to-zero marital trusts are designated as beneficiaries

The following eight types of distributions from regular IRAs are not subject to the 10% penalty tax (the premature distribution penalty), although these distributions are taxable:

1. "Substantially equal periodic payments" as described earlier
2. Distributions taken in order to pay for higher education expenses
3. Qualified first-home purchase distributions
4. Distributions to a beneficiary after the death of the participant
5. Withdrawals made upon the disability of the participant as determined under IRS guidelines
6. Distributions taken in order to pay medical expenses exceeding 7.5% of the participant's adjusted gross income
7. Withdrawals made in order to pay health insurance premiums after the participant is separated from employment, has received unemployment compensation under

federal or state law for at least 12 consecutive weeks, and meets other requirements

8. Distributions after the participant is 59½

Before age 59½, penalty-free withdrawals from other types of plans such as Keoghs, 401(k) plans, and 403(b) plans are subject to special rules. You can seek guidance from your employer or the administrator of the plan. Generally, versions of the regular IRA exceptions for medical expenses, higher education expenses for certain family members, or purchase of a home are available. In addition, most of these plans, *but not IRAs*, allow borrowing of up to the lesser of $50,000 or 50% of the participant's vested account balance, usually subject to repayment within five years.

A new type of IRA—the Roth IRA—became effective in 1998. A couple with an annual adjusted gross income of up to $150,000 (and an unmarried individual with income of up to $95,000) may deposit $2,000 each annually to his or her Roth IRA account. Although these contributions are not income tax deductible, they are not taxed as they grow nor upon withdrawal. Since withdrawals may begin as soon as five years later if you are then at least age 59½ (or to use the money to buy your first home), Roth IRAs may even be of interest to those who will retire shortly who may be reluctant to have the money unavailable for too long.

$ CASE STUDY 8.5—BILL BATSON

Bill Batson is 60 and has been making annual contributions to his Roth IRA for five years. He could begin making withdrawals but doesn't. At 70½ he has to begin withdrawals from his deductible IRA but does not have to withdraw any amount from his Roth IRA, which can continue to grow tax-free. In fact, being 70½ does not even prevent him from making further contributions.

$

It is possible to convert a regular IRA, deductible or nondeductible, SEP or SARSEP IRA, or Simple IRA into a Roth IRA if an individual's *adjusted gross income is less than $100,000*. To do so, you must pay income tax on all prior contributions and earnings that were not taxed. If the conversion takes place before 1999, you can spread the tax bill over four years. Is it worth converting? Here are four factors for you and your advisor to consider:

1. What is today's deduction worth versus the tax rate you can expect to pay in retirement?

2. What growth are you likely to achieve in the account that will eventually be withdrawn tax-free?

3. Can you pay the income tax on converting without making a taxable withdrawal from the IRA to pay the tax?

4. What are the state and local income tax consequences?

The following five rules should be noted relative to the Roth IRA:

1. Only upon death are distributions required.

2. The maximum contribution to the Roth IRA is coordinated with the contribution to the regular IRA so that the maximum annual IRA contribution level is not exceeded.

3. Just as with regular IRAs, there can be a rollover between Roth IRAs only once in 12 months.

4. No transfer can be made from a Roth IRA to a regular IRA, qualified plan, 403(b), Simple IRA, or Education IRA.

5. There cannot be a rollover from a qualified plan or 403(b) arrangement to a Roth IRA.

Currently there are: regular IRAs, Simple IRAs, Education IRAs, SEP-IRAs, and Roth IRAs. SARSEP IRAs still exist for those who adopted them before 1997. The Medical Savings Account (MSA) has some IRA-like features but should not be considered an IRA. There is a new type of MSA, designed for senior citizens and available in 1999, described in Chapter 9. Because of differences in rules relative to contributions, transfers, rollovers, and distributions, none of these categories should be commingled. This is an area where Congress has made changes in the rules and is likely to continue to do so. Since many rules have changed recently and further changes are likely, decisions regarding your retirement program should be made only with the assistance of a professional advisor.

Here is the last case history in Section II of this chapter. Its message should be clear.

$ CASE STUDY 8.6—JIM, JUNIOR, AND JANE

Jim, a widower, died in 1998. His son, Junior, was the beneficiary of his IRA with a balance of $250,000. Jim's daughter, Jane, was his joint owner with rights of survivorship of his house, his only other asset. The value of the equity in the house was $250,000. At first, it seemed that Jim's plan for equal bequests would work out. There was no federal estate tax since the total estate was under $625,000, the maximum credit exclusion equivalent in the year of death. However, Junior's lawyer told him that Jane could sell the house with no income tax liability while Junior would eventually have to pay income tax on the entire $250,000 from the IRA—which would leave him with substantially less than what his father intended.

$

SECTION III—SOCIAL SECURITY DISTRIBUTIONS

In this section, we will concentrate on the Social Security retirement income distributions that will supplement the amounts that you will withdraw from your investment accounts. Much of the information in this part is contained in various Social Security pamphlets. This section brings the information together in an overview. You can check with Social Security and your advisors for updated details in areas of special concern.

To qualify for retirement benefits, the first reference is made to your date of birth. For those born after 1928, 40 credits are needed. Generally, 4 credits are earned for every year of work. One less credit is needed for every year of birth before 1929 (39 credits for those born in 1928, 38 credits for 1927, and so on). Most people earn many more credits than are required to qualify for benefits. But earning the required credits is only the beginning.

The more income that you earn while working increases your benefits. You may request a personalized estimate of benefits by filling out a Request for Earnings Benefit Estimate obtained by calling 800-772-1213. After you complete and send the form back, Social Security will send you your earnings history and estimates of retirement benefits. To aid your planning, the estimates will be for "early benefits" (as early as age 62), "full retirement" (as early as 65), and "maximum benefits" (age 70). There are automatic cost of living increases that will supplement these estimates. Full retirement age is increased for those who are born after 1937 as shown in Figure 8.5.

If you were born after 1937, you can qualify for benefits as early as age 62 but your benefit will be about 70% of the full

NOTE: *It is important to sign up for Medicare at age 65 even if you do not retire, because medical insurance may cost more if you apply for it later. Medicare covers people age 65 or older, disabled people, and people with permanent kidney failure. For more information call Social Security and ask for the pamphlet "Medicare" (Publication #05-10043).*

FIGURE 8.5   AGE TO RECEIVE FULL
SOCIAL SECURITY BENEFITS

YEAR OF BIRTH	FULL RETIREMENT AGE
1937 or earlier	65
1938	65 and 2 months
1939	65 and 4 months
1940	65 and 6 months
1941	65 and 8 months
1942	65 and 10 months
1943–1954	66
1955	66 and 2 months
1956	66 and 4 months
1957	66 and 6 months
1958	66 and 8 months
1959	66 and 10 months
1960 and later	67

benefit. For those born before 1938, the early benefit at age 62 will be about 80% of the full benefit. The law's objective is to provide about the same total Social Security benefits over one's entire lifetime even if one retires early. For every year before age 65, your benefit level is reduced by a little more than 6%.

If poor health causes your early retirement, contact Social Security about the Supplemental Security Income (SSI) program that Social Security administers, although it is a separately funded program. The Supplemental Security Income program provides payments to low-income individuals age 65 and over, blind persons, and the disabled. Widows and children of workers who have died, including those who have died before retirement, may receive Social Security survivor's benefits. Disability benefits under the Social Security Act may be paid to disabled workers before their retirement, and their dependents.

Spouses of retired workers are entitled to one-half of a retired worker's benefits unless the spouse begins collecting before age 65, in which case the spouse's benefit is permanently reduced by an amount that depends on how many months before he or she will be age 65.

There has been some confusion as to whether a spouse is eligible for retirement benefits based on his or her own employment apart from spouse's benefits. Social Security pays a person's retirement benefits first, and if the spouse's benefit would be higher, an additional amount equal to the shortfall is paid so the spouse gets a combination of benefits.

The Social Security booklet "Retirement Benefits" provides an example:

> Mary Ann qualifies for a (monthly) retirement benefit of $250 and a wife's (monthly) benefit of $400. At age 65, she will receive her own $250 retirement benefit and [Social Security] will add $150 from her wife's benefit for a total of $400. If she takes her retirement benefit at any time before she turns 65, the payments will be reduced.

Under certain circumstances, a divorced spouse may be able to get benefits based on a former husband or wife's record. Benefit payments to a divorced spouse do not reduce the amount of benefits for which the current spouse can qualify. In order for a divorced spouse to qualify for these benefits, their marriage must have lasted for at least 10 years and the divorced spouse must be currently unmarried and age 62 or older. In addition, they must have been divorced for at least two years and the worker must also be 62 or older with enough credits to qualify for benefits.

If you are 70 or over, you collect your full Social Security benefits regardless of how much you earn during the year. Before age 70, earnings may reduce or eliminate Social Security benefits. Workers who are under 65 will have $1 in benefits held back for every $2 in earnings above the earnings limit set for that year. If you are 65 through 69, $1 of Social Security will be withheld for every $3 in earnings above the limit. The limit is increased every year. In 1998, the limit on earnings is $9,120 for workers under 65 and $14,500 for workers 65 through 69. For additional information on retaining benefits while working, call Social Security and order a copy of the pamphlet "How Work Affects Your Benefits" (Publication #05-10069).

For those who are self-employed, the amount earned is not the only factor. Generally, if you are engaged in self-employment activities for more than 45 hours a month, you are considered not retired. But you are retired if you work fewer than 15 hours a month. The rules get a little more technical if you are engaged between 15 and 45 hours per month in self-employment. If your business is sizable, or you are considered to be in an occupation requiring a lot of skill, working between 15 and 45 hours a month will probably mean that you are not retired.

Being self-employed, your earnings are considered for Social Security purposes when received by you rather than when you earned them. An exception is made for amounts earned before you became entitled to Social Security but received afterward. If you are self-employed and want further information on determining such questions as to whether your work is considered substantial, call Social Security and ask for the fact sheet "When You Retire from Your Own Business: What Social Security Needs to Know" (Publication #05-10038).

There are retirees receiving Social Security who now live in another country. A number of Americans have chosen to

REPORTING NONQUALIFIED PLAN EARNINGS

Unlike self-employment, wages are counted for Social Security purposes when they are earned rather then when they are received. For example, you cannot expect to qualify for Social Security while working before you are age 70 by postponing receipt of these earnings until after you reach 70. This type of deferral is categorized as *nonqualified plan* earnings and is required to be reported on the W-2 form in the year earned.

retire to Mexico because it offers a lifestyle that is appealing for what appear to be lower prices. (*Caution:* Be careful about dealing with foreign currencies and foreign institutions. A few years ago, there was a devaluation of the Mexican currency that adversely affected a number of Americans living in Mexico with bank accounts in Mexican banks.) Others retire to their native lands. If you are not a U.S. citizen, or if you work outside of the United States, different rules apply in determining your qualification for Social Security.

If you are a U.S. citizen you can receive your Social Security checks in most countries except Cambodia, Cuba, North Korea, Vietnam, and some of the former Soviet Republics. For more information on receiving Social Security while living in foreign countries, request the booklet "Your Social Security Payments While You Are Outside of the United States" (Publication #05-10137).

The Social Security Administration has a number of pamphlets that you can request related to such items as retirement benefits, Medicare, and the Supplemental Security Income program. The key telephone number is 800-772-1213 and the toll-free fax line is 888-475-7000. Sometimes you can get an answer to a fairly simple question by calling the 800 number. Otherwise, you should try to obtain the telephone number of your local office and, if necessary, schedule a face-to-face meeting with a claims representative.

There may be a Social Security office closer than the one you are initially referred to, so be sure to discuss location options. If you are still not satisfied after meeting with a claims representative, refer to your state office on aging. A schedule of telephone numbers of state offices on aging appears in Chapter 9. Other helpful sources may be the National Committee to Preserve Social Security and Medicare (800-966-1935) or the office of your Senator or Congressman. Your Senator or Congressman has a staffer assigned to help constituents who are having problems with Social Security or other federal programs.

If you disagree with any decision that Social Security makes in your case, you have a right to request reconsideration. Your request must be in writing and filed with any Social Security office within 60 days of the date that you receive a letter with an adverse finding. There are further steps in the review process and they are explained in the fact sheet "The Appeals Process" (Publication #05-10041). If the matter is serious enough for you to seek the assistance of a lawyer or other representative, refer to the fact sheet "Your Right to Representation" (Publication #05-10075).

CHAPTER NINE

Insuring Your Investment Portfolio

IN THIS CHAPTER

As we have discussed in other parts of this book, we look to the past to determine such probabilities as likely expected rates of return under certain conditions and maintainable withdrawal rates during the retirement years. With probabilities there is the possibility of not realizing one's expectations. In this chapter we consider areas where an individual may decide not to "self-insure" the entire risk. For example, with regard to long-term care, some people will determine that half or some other fraction of the potential long-term care costs will be covered by insurance and the balance will be "self-insured." Health insurance, Medicare, long-term care, and life insurance coverages all relate to physical well-being. In this chapter we also cover: (1) viatical settlements of life insurance policies—a relatively new development to aid the terminally ill—and (2) economic protective developments such as personal umbrella liability insurance, as well as a noninsurance development—the use of legal devices such as offshore trusts to protect someone's net worth including his or her investment portfolio.

Because of changing laws, much of what is in this chapter is not old hat. There are decisions that you will make about insurance after 1997 that were not under consideration before. This chapter should give you a head start with those decisions.

HEALTH INSURANCE

The high cost of health care makes health insurance a necessity for most people. Medical expenses can destroy or severely damage most retirement portfolios. Health care costs have risen faster than the overall inflation rate for the past 15 years or longer. As a consequence, the cost of health insurance has also risen substantially.

When you buy health insurance, adding a substantial deductible feature (such as $1,000 instead of $200) will substantially reduce annual premiums. A comprehensive major medical policy should cover at least 80% of medical bills that are over and above the deductible. The policy should be guaranteed renewable and noncancelable.

Other possibilities are managed care plans such as health maintenance organizations (HMOs) and preferred provider organizations (PPOs). HMOs are supposed to control medical costs by adopting measures including dictating whom the insured and other family members may see for medical care. A PPO is usually formed by an insurer or a large business that negotiates with a group of doctors and hospitals to provide medical services at reduced prices. If the insured goes to an approved physician, the entire bill is paid for, but only a portion is paid if an outside physician is seen. Choosing an HMO or a PPO is much like selecting any health insurer. The following suggestions for those who are over 65 and considering Medigap insurance will also apply if you're considering an HMO or a PPO.

Many employers still provide group health insurance. With group coverage the insurance premium will cover each individual. Group coverage is estimated to be about 15% less expensive then the cost of purchasing the same coverage individually. Also, with group insurance, individuals who have serious chronic problems usually are not excluded. Sometimes professional organizations and fraternal groups provide group insurance. Check with any organizations and groups that you belong to about group coverage. It may even be worth joining a group for this coverage alone.

If you retire or are laid off, you can continue group coverage for at least another 18 months, according to federal law. You may be charged up to 102% of what the coverage costs the employer, but the cost is still less than an individual policy with the same coverage. If you are a dependent of a covered employee and are in danger of losing health coverage because the covered employee has died, is divorcing or separating from you, or has become eligible for Medicare, you can buy coverage for yourself through that covered employee's group for up to three years. These provisions are contained in the Consolidated Omnibus Budget Reconciliation Act (COBRA). There are exceptions, such as when a company terminates the entire plan.

NEW MEDICAL SAVINGS ACCOUNT

Another development scheduled to be available in 1999 is a new version of the Medical Savings Account (MSA). Initially, this new version will be available for up to 390,000 senior citizens. The federal government will provide a tax-free cash allowance for these Medical Savings Accounts based on age and other factors such as the cost of living. These cash allowances will cover premiums for a health insurance policy with a high deductible amount as well as fund part of the deductible. To the extent that an individual's premiums and medical expenses do not use up this account, it accumulates. Once it reaches 60% of the deductible, the amount over that figure may be withdrawn and retained by the individual. The principal concern is that if you have substantial medical expenses, they could far exceed the balance that you have available to meet them.

MEDICARE, MEDICAID, AND MEDIGAP COVERAGE

Medicare and Medicaid are government programs that provide medical insurance. Medicare coverage is available for those 65 or over who qualify for Social Security retirement benefits. Medicare benefits consist of Part A, basic hospital insurance, and Part B, supplementary medical insurance. Basic hospital insurance includes in-patient hospital care, some skilled nursing home care, and, under certain circumstances, hospice care. Supplementary medical insurance covers physician services, outpatient hospital care, physical therapy, medical equipment, and certain other services not covered by basic hospital insurance. The participant pays only nominal monthly premiums with the major cost subsidized by the federal government. Supplementary medical insurance, Part B, is optional.

For those who receive Social Security benefits, Medicare (Part A) starts automatically at age 65. If you are not getting Social Security, you should sign up for Medicare as you approach your 65th birthday, even if you are not ready to retire. For those with limited resources, some states will pay the Medicare premiums and certain other out-of-pocket Medicare expenses. Your state determines if you qualify under this low-income Medicare beneficiary program. For more information, contact Social Security (800-772-1213) and request a copy of "Medicare Savings for Qualified Beneficiaries—HCFA" (Publication #02184). Medicare does not cover prescription drugs and certain other medical costs. Also, Medicare often reimburses health care providers at rates below those charged to a patient. A number of HMOs cater to Medicare patients by offering broad coverage for an annual fee plus nominal copayments.

Since uncovered costs may be substantial, many retirees purchase Medicare supplemental insurance, also known as Medigap. This is insurance that pays for expenses not covered by Medicare such as deductibles and copayments. Medigap policies do not extend the coverage beyond the limits provided by Medicare. By law, insurance companies are required to offer Medigap policies in 10 different categories ranging from "A" (basic) through "J," which is the most comprehensive.

New Medicare regulations went into effect in October 1997, so the following information may not appear in earlier editions of Social Security's Medicare booklet. There will be additional health plans owned and operated by doctors and hospitals that may be superior to the plans of some of the insurers, but we will have to wait and see whether this will be the case. Before these regulations, premiums were to rise to $51.50 per month by the year 2002. Under the new regulations, the increased benefits will increase these rates to $67 per month by the year 2002.

For the first time since Medicare was adopted, private insurers will be offering Medicare-type coverage with more generous pay schedules than Medicare offers. These policies came about because of complaints that the low payments under Medicare resulted in less attention being given to Medicare patients. Of course, this more generous schedule will result in higher copayments and greater premiums. Under the new law, if the Medicare patient pays the entire bill and the doctor agrees not to accept any Medicare reimbursements for at least two years, the doctor is allowed to accept these private payments. However, since almost all doctors who treat the elderly receive a substantial portion of their income from Medicare payments, it is unclear how many doctors will enter into this agreement.

Health insurance, along with the complex rules for Medicare and Medicaid, can be confusing. Some of these coverages overlap into the area of long-term care insurance. If you believe that you need more health insurance, review the following 11 tips carefully. Look to insurance counseling services (toll-free phone numbers are often available).

1. *Shop with care.* Don't pay for more coverage than you need. One broad policy is better than several policies that may duplicate coverage in one area and omit coverage in another area. It is unlawful for an insurance company to sell you a Medigap policy unless you sign a statement that you intend to cancel the prior policy when the new policy becomes effective. It is also unlawful to sell a policy that violates the antiduplication rules; the salesman, broker, or insurance company could be subject to criminal penalties, civil penalties, or both.

The federal toll-free telephone number to file complaints is 800-638-6833. Illegal market practices include high-pressure tactics to force or frighten a prospect into buying a Medigap policy or deceptive advertising such as mailings to those who may be particularly vulnerable to buying insurance. As with other expensive purchases, you should contact different companies and compare the costs and coverage. It is also helpful to ask friends, relatives, and acquaintances about particular companies to learn which ones are more cooperative.

2. *Evaluate your existing coverage.* You should not retain inadequate coverage simply because you've had it for a long time. Unlike most other coverages, when you replace a Medigap policy, you must be given credit for the period you held the old policy in determining whether any restrictions

for preexisting conditions apply under the new one. You have up to 30 days to decide whether to cancel the old policy and keep the new one or to return the new policy and retain the old policy. Delivery of the new policy or a refund if you decide not to purchase it should be within 30 days. Otherwise, contact the company and if there will be a further delay, ask for a written explanation. If there is no response from the company, contact your state insurance department. A list of the telephone numbers of the state insurance departments begins on page 177.

3. *Pay attention to maximum benefits.* A policy with lower premiums may offer reduced benefits. It may reduce the number of days of care or the dollar amount for the treatment of a particular condition. Some policies may eliminate certain coverages or provide less coverage.

4. *Remember, neither the United States nor your state are in the insurance business.* Do not be misled! The insurance companies that are selling the policies are privately owned. "State approval" means only that a company has met legal requirements. Insurance that supplements Medicare is not government-sponsored. If a salesperson tells you that the insurer is connected with the government in order to sell you an insurance policy, that insurer should be reported to federal authorities (800-638-6833) or to your state insurance department.

It is illegal to use names, symbols, and emblems of various government-supported programs including the Social Security Administration, the Health Care Financing Administration, and the U.S. Department of Health and Human Services. It is unlawful to mail solicitations that appear to be endorsed or in some way related to the U.S. government.

5. *Utilize your state insurance department. It should have a record of any company doing business in your state.* Call the department to confirm that an insurer is in fact licensed to do

business in your state. A salesperson contacting you should be able to give you confirmation of the name of the company that he or she represents and that that company is licensed. Be sure to get all salespersons' business cards and their addresses and telephone numbers and those of the insurance companies they represent.

If you do purchase a policy, make the check or money order payable to the insurance company, never the agent or anyone else. Get a receipt that acknowledges the insurance company, not the agent. Furthermore, it is a good idea to contact the insurance company to verify that the agent is affiliated with that company. Never pay cash.

Insurance policies are difficult to read. The salesperson is required to give you a summary that is easily understandable, and you should take the time to read and understand it.

6. *Check for exclusions for preexisting conditions.* You may have an existing health condition that the policy will not cover, while your existing policy *does* cover it. Generally, these are problems that you saw a doctor about within the six-month period preceding the effective date of the policy. Medigap policies must cover preexisting conditions after the policies have been in effect for six months. Some companies may offer a shorter exclusion period for a particular preexisting condition.

7. *Consider alternatives.* Rather than replacing a policy because it doesn't have long-term care with a new policy that does provide for long-term care, consider shopping for a long-term care policy that will *supplement* your coverage. Compute the cost and the coverage from this alternative with the cost of replacing your existing policy. Joining a managed care plan (HMO or PPO) may be preferable to a more costly alternative. Friends and relatives, particularly if they are health care professionals, may be very helpful.

8. *Be sure to compare rates among several insurance companies.*

9. *Get health insurance information from the Social Security Administration.* Call the SSA (800-772-1213) to order "The Guide to Health Insurance for People with Medicare."

10. *Don't be rushed into making a decision, but recognize there is a time limit.* If you are age 65 or older and qualify for Social Security benefits, you have a period of six months from the date when you meet both of these qualifications to buy a Medigap policy regardless of your health problems. If your birthday is on the first day of the month, your Part B coverage, if you buy it, starts on the first day of the previous month although you would still be 64 at that time, and your six-month Medigap open enrollment period also starts on that date. After that open enrollment periods ends, a person is limited as to the Medigap policy that is available, particularly if he or she has a preexisting health condition.

11. *Complete the application carefully.* Often an insurance salesperson is eager to complete the sale and may rush you to complete the application. Keep in mind that if you leave out any medical information, a later claim may be refused or delayed if you didn't specify a medical condition. The insurance company could also deny the claim completely or cancel the policy.

LONG-TERM CARE INSURANCE

Medicare and Medigap insurance may cover short-term periods in a nursing home when they are directly related to an illness or injury. Medicaid would pay additional amounts, but to qualify for Medicaid, personal assets must be substantially reduced. A long stay in a nursing home can be very costly. For those with more modest investment portfolios, long-term care insurance may be advisable. To determine whether you should insure against this type of risk, you or your advisor should do some projections. The potential annual expenses of $30,000 to $100,000 a year should be taken into account as well as the shorter life expectancy that may also be a consideration. The range of potential costs for extended long-term care varies greatly among the different sections of the country.

To purchase long-term care insurance you must be in reasonably good health. If you are not in good health but have life insurance coverage, review the discussion on life insurance later in this chapter. As you get older, the annual premium rate increases. Here are some of the factors to consider in evaluating an adequate long-term care insurance policy:

1. *"Qualified" or "nonqualified" policies.* The Health Insurance Portability and Accountability Act was passed in 1996. It created a category of policies with assured tax benefits ("qualified"), while leaving the other policies in a state of uncertainty relative to tax benefits ("nonqualified"). The qualified policies allow owners to exclude policy benefit payments from taxable income and to deduct part of the costs under certain circumstances.

In determining whether to purchase a qualified or nonqualified policy, an update on the tax status of the nonqualified policies should be obtained. Check with a knowledgeable source such as an attorney specializing in elder-care since the regulations are not always clear. Your tax advisor may also be able to help you.

At this time, qualified policies appear to be inferior to nonqualified policies. For example, under the qualified policy, a health care professional must certify that the insured will have the disabilities for at least 90 days to be eligible for coverage. Thus, if you are recovering from a fall and need care for five or six weeks, you would not be eligible.

To collect benefits, you must be unable to care for yourself in at least two out of six (or sometimes two out of five) of the following "activities of daily living": bathing, dressing, eating, toileting, continence, and transferring (e.g., moving from a chair into your bed). Nonqualified policies don't have the 90-day restriction. You may qualify for benefits under many of these policies if a doctor determines that it is a medical necessity for you to have help in taking care of yourself. One example is with very old and frail people who need help in taking medication or bathing, or who are so frail that the doctor determines that they can no longer live alone safely. It seems clear that there will be many fewer claims for both nursing home care and home care under qualified policies.

If you owned a long-term care policy before January 1, 1997, you have tax-favored status for your coverage; it is "qualified." You must be careful before replacing it or making any changes to the policy such as increasing the benefit level to avoid having it be considered the equivalent of a new policy. You should check on current tax status with both your tax advisor and the insurance company before making any replacements or revisions.

2. *The elimination period.* The choice of waiting periods is usually between 20 and 100 days. You have to decide whether the savings in premium costs justifies the need to self-insure for an additional period.

3. *The amount of "daily benefits."* Nursing home facilities vary in different parts of the country. Paying for daily benefits of $80 per day may not be adequate protection if expenses are incurred at the rate of $200 per day or more.

4. *"Inflation-adjusted" coverage.* If you are purchasing this policy at age 60 and you expect to need it at age 80 or 85, costs could be considerably higher. Some insurers give you the choice of providing for an inflation adjustment when

you initially buy the policy, while others periodically give you the opportunity to add inflation adjustment protection.

5. *Time period for benefits.* Should you receive benefits for a maximum of two to five years or for life? The longer the period, the greater the cost.

6. *Selection of the insurance company.* Select an insurer with care. Questions about the insurance company, the policies, and the agent should be directed to your state insurance department or insurance counseling program. (See Figure 9.1 beginning on page 177.) Certain companies may be easier to deal with when the time comes to put in your claim. Insurance agents with whom you have prior favorable experience or who are recommended by trusted advisors, as well as nursing home administrators, may be helpful. Contact several companies and compare coverages and costs. Generally, it's not advisable to buy multiple long-term care policies.

7. *Evaluate the financial strength of the insurance company.* Any policy purchased from an unsound company is a poor choice. The opinions of rating agencies cannot be guaranteed, but the opinion of two or more agencies should be very useful. Each rating agency has its own rating scale, so make sure you understand the rating system of each agency. Some of this information is available at public libraries, or you can call the following numbers. (Note that A. M. Best Company's 900 number is a long-distance call.) These rating agencies can also help you when you're considering life insurance policies.

NAMES OF AGENCIES AND TELEPHONE NUMBERS:

A. M. Best Co., Oldwick, NJ; 800-424-2378 or 900-555-2378

Duff & Phelps Credit Rating Co., Chicago, IL; 312-368-3198 (no charge)

Moody's Investors Service, New York, NY; 212-553-0377 (no charge)

Standard & Poor's Ratings Group, New York, NY; 212-208-1527 (no charge)

Weiss Ratings Inc., Palm Beach Gardens, FL; 800-289-9222

8. *Other considerations.* Nursing home benefits without prior hospitalization, home health benefits without prior hospitalization, restrictions on the number of days, coverage for Alzheimer's disease, some protection against rate increases, waiver of premium if you are in a nursing home, and restoration of benefits to the original maximum if after receiving benefits you go for a stated period without using further benefits. Both the insurance department of your state and the state insurance counseling program can provide you with information on long-term care coverage and other insurance (see Figure 9.1).

LIFE INSURANCE

Generally, if you have an adequate investment portfolio to fund retirement for yourself and your spouse, you do not need life insurance protection. The usual life insurance question is "who would suffer financially if I died?"

▆$▆ CASE STUDY 9.1—JACK AND JILL

Jack and his wife, Jill, believe that they have enough to retire on. However, they don't have long-term care insurance. Jack has had health problems and can't purchase long-term care insurance without paying excessive premiums. From time to time, they've considered cashing in a life insurance policy that they have.

In this case, it may make sense for them to review the policy provisions with their agent and determine whether that policy could serve as a surrogate for a long-term care policy for Jack. According to one 1993 study, the average cost of a year in a nursing home is about $38,000, and this cost varies widely in

FIGURE 9.1   STATE INSURANCE DEPARTMENTS, INSURANCE COUNSELING PROGRAMS, AND AGENCIES ON AGING

INSURANCE DEPARTMENTS	INSURANCE COUNSELING	AGENCIES ON AGING
Alabama		
Insurance Department Consumer Service 334-269-3550	800-243-5463	Commission on Aging 800-243-5463 334-242-5594
Alaska		
Division of Insurance 907-269-7900	907-562-7249	Division of Senior Services 907-563-5654
American Samoa		
Insurance Department Governor's Office 011-684-633-4116		Territorial Administration on Aging 011-684-633-1252
Arizona		
Insurance Department Consumer Affairs 602-912-8444	800-432-4040 501-371-2640	Department of Economic Security Aging and Adult Administration 602-542-4446
Arkansas		
Insurance Department Seniors Insurance Network 800-852-5494	800-852-5494 501-371-2640	Division of Aging and Adult Services 501-682-2441
California		
Insurance Department Consumer Services 916-445-5544	800-434-0222 916-323-7315	Department of Aging Health Insurance Counseling and Advocacy Branch 916-322-3887

Note: The 800 numbers shown can only be accessed by calls from within the respective state.

FIGURE 9.1 (CONTINUED)

INSURANCE DEPARTMENTS	INSURANCE COUNSELING	AGENCIES ON AGING
Colorado		
Insurance Division 303-894-7499, ext. 356	800-544-9181 303-894-7499, ext. 356	Aging and Adult Services Department of Social Services 303-620-4147
Commonwealth of the Northern Mariana Islands		
		Department of Community and Cultural Affairs 607-234-6011
Connecticut		
Insurance Department 203-297-3800	800-994-9422	Commission on Aging 806-424-5360
Delaware		
Insurance Department 800-282-8611 302-739-4251	800-336-9500	Services for Aging and Adults with Physical Disabilities Department of Health and Social Services 302-577-4791 800-223-9074
District of Columbia		
Insurance Department Consumer and Professional Services Bureau 202-727-8000	202-676-3900	Office on Aging 202-724-5626
Federated States of Micronesia		
		State Agency on Aging Office of Health Services Federated States of Micronesia Ponape, E.C.I. 96941
Florida		
Department of Insurance 904-922-3100	800-963-5337 904-414-2060	Department of Elder Affairs 904-414-2060

FIGURE 9.1   (CONTINUED)

INSURANCE DEPARTMENTS	INSURANCE COUNSELING	AGENCIES ON AGING
Georgia		
Insurance Department 404-656-2056	800-669-8387 404-657-5334	Division of Aging Services Department of Human Resources 404-657-5258
Guam		
Insurance Division Department of Revenue and Taxation 011-671-475-5000	671-475-0262/3	Department of Senior Citizens Department of Public Health and Social Services 011-671-475-0262/3
Hawaii		
Department of Commerce and Consumer Affairs Insurance Division 808-586-2790	808-586-0100	Executive Office on Aging 808-586-0100
Idaho		
Insurance Department SHIBA Program 208-334-4350	S.W.—800-247-4422 N.—800-488-5725 S.E.—800-488-5764 Central—800-488-5731	Office on Aging 208-334-3833
Illinois		
Insurance Department 217-782-4515	800-548-9034 217-785-9021	Department on Aging 800-252-8966
Indiana		
Insurance Department 800-622-4461 317-232-2395	800-452-4800 317-233-3475 317-232-5299	Division of Aging and Rehabilitative Services 800-545-7763 317-232-7020
Iowa		
Insurance Division 515-281-5705	800-351-4664	Department of Elder Affairs 515-281-5187

FIGURE 9.1 **(CONTINUED)**

INSURANCE DEPARTMENTS	INSURANCE COUNSELING	AGENCIES ON AGING
Kansas		
Insurance Department 800-432-2484 913-296-3071	800-860-5260	Department on Aging 913-296-4986
Kentucky		
Insurance Department 800-595-6053 502-564-3630	502-564-7372	Division of Aging Services Cabinet of Family and Children 502-564-7372
Louisiana		
Department of Insurance 800-259-5301 504-342-5301	800-259-5301 504-342-5301	Governor's Office of Elderly Affairs 504-925-1700
Maine		
Bureau of Insurance 207-624-8475	800-750-5353 207-623-1797	Bureau of Elder and Adult Services 207-624-5335
Maryland		
Insurance Administration Complaints and Investigation Unit— Life and Health 410-333-2793 410-333-2770	800-243-3425 410-767-1074	Office on Aging 410-767-1074
Massachusetts		
Insurance Division 617-521-7777	800-882-2003 617-727-7750	Executive Office of Elder Affairs 800-882-2003 617-727-7750
Michigan		
Insurance Bureau 517-373-0240 (General Assistance) 517-335-1702 (Senior Issues)	800-803-7174	Office of Services to the Aging 517-373-8230

FIGURE 9.1 (CONTINUED)

INSURANCE DEPARTMENTS	INSURANCE COUNSELING	AGENCIES ON AGING
Minnesota		
Insurance Department Department of Commerce 612-296-4026	800-882-6262 612-296-2770	Board on Aging 612-296-2770
Mississippi		
Insurance Department Consumer Assistance Division 601-359-3569	800-948-3090	Division of Aging and Adult Services 800-948-3090 601-359-4929
Missouri		
Department of Insurance Consumer Services Section 800-726-7390 314-751-2640	800-390-3330 573-893-7900	Division of Aging Department of Social Services 800-285-5503 573-751-3082
Montana		
Insurance Department 406-444-2040	800-332-2272	Division of Senior and Long-Term Care/DPHHS 800-332-2272 406-444-7781
Nebraska		
Insurance Department 402-471-2201	402-471-2201	Department on Aging 800-942-7830 402-471-2306
Nevada		
Department of Business and Industry Division of Insurance 800-992-0900 702-687-4270	800-307-4444 702-486-4602	Department of Human Resources Division for Aging Services 800-243-3638 702-486-3545
New Hampshire		
Insurance Department Life and Health Division 800-852-3416 603-271-2261	800-852-3388 603-225-9000	Department of Health and Human Services Division of Elderly and Adult Services 603-271-4680

FIGURE 9.1 (CONTINUED)

INSURANCE DEPARTMENTS	INSURANCE COUNSELING	AGENCIES ON AGING
New Jersey		
Insurance Department 609-292-5363	800-792-8820	Health and Human Services Division Department of Senior Affairs 800-792-8820 609-984-3951
New Mexico		
Insurance Department 507-827-4601	800-432-2080 505-827-7640	State Agency on Aging 800-432-2080 505-827-7640
New York		
Insurance Department 800-342-3736 (outside NYC) 212-602-0203 (NYC area)	800-333-4114 (outside NYC) 212-869-3850 (NYC area)	State Office for the Aging 800-342-9871 518-474-9871
North Carolina		
Insurance Department Seniors' Health Insurance Information Program (SHIIP) 800-662-7777 (consumer services) 919-733-0111 (SHIIP)	800-443-9354	Division of Aging 919-733-3983
North Dakota		
Insurance Department Senior Health Insurance Counseling 800-247-0560 701-328-2440	800-247-0560	Department of Human Services 800-755-8521 701-328-8910
Ohio		
Insurance Department Consumer Services Division 800-686-1526 614-644-2673	800-686-1578 614-644-3458	Department of Aging 800-282-1206 614-466-1221

FIGURE 9.1   (CONTINUED)

INSURANCE DEPARTMENTS	INSURANCE COUNSELING	AGENCIES ON AGING
Oklahoma		
Insurance Department 800-522-0071 405-521-2828	800-763-2828 405-521-6628	Department of Human Services Aging Services Division 405-521-2327
Oregon		
Department of Consumer and Business Services Senior Health Insurance Benefits Assistance 800-722-4134 503-378-4484	800-722-4134 503-378-4636 ext. 600	Department of Human Resources Senior and Disabled Services Division 800-232-3020 503-945-5811
Palau		
		State Agency on Aging Department of Social Services Republic of Palau Koror, Palau 96940
Pennsylvania		
Insurance Department Consumer Services Bureau 717-787-2317	800-783-7067	Department of Aging "Apprise" Health Insurance Counseling and Assistance 800-783-7067
Puerto Rico		
Office of the Commissioner of Insurance 809-722-8686	809-721-5710	Governor's Office of Elderly Affairs Gericulture Commission 809-722-2429
Republic of the Marshall Islands		
		State Agency on Aging Department of Social Services Republic of the Marshall Islands Marjuro, Marshall Islands 96960

FIGURE 9.1 (CONTINUED)

INSURANCE DEPARTMENTS	INSURANCE COUNSELING	AGENCIES ON AGING
Rhode Island		
Insurance Division 401-277-2223	800-322-2880	Department of Elderly Affairs 401-277-2880
South Carolina		
Department of Insurance Consumer Services Section 800-768-3467 803-737-6180	800-868-9095 803-737-7500	Division on Aging 803-737-7500
South Dakota		
Insurance Department 605-773-3563	800-822-8804 605-773-3656	Office of Adult Services and Aging 605-773-3656
Tennessee		
Department of Commerce and Insurance 800-525-2816 615-741-4955	800-525-2816	Commission on Aging 615-741-2056
Texas		
Department of Insurance Complaints Resolution (MC 111-1A) 800-252-3439 512-463-6515	800-252-3439	Department on Aging 800-252-9240 512-424-6840
Utah		
Insurance Department Consumer Services 800-439-3805 801-538-3805	800-439-3805 801-538-3910	Division of Aging and Adult Services 801-538-3910

FIGURE 9.1 (**CONTINUED**)

INSURANCE DEPARTMENTS	INSURANCE COUNSELING	AGENCIES ON AGING
Vermont		
Department of Banking and Insurance Consumer Complaint Division 802-828-3302	800-642-5119 802-861-1577	Department of Aging and Disabilities 802-241-2400
Virginia		
Bureau of Insurance 800-552-7945 804-371-9691	800-552-3402	Department for the Aging 800-552-3402 804-225-2271
Virgin Islands		
Insurance Department 809-773-6449, ext. 248	809-774-2991	Senior Citizen Affairs Division Department of Human Services 809-772-0930
Washington		
Insurance Department 800-397-422 360-407-0383	800-605-6299	Aging and Adult Services Administration Department of Social and Health Services 360-493-2500
West Virginia		
Insurance Department Consumer Service 800-642-9004 800-435-7381 (hearing-impaired) 304-558-3386	800-642-9004 304-558-3317	Commission on Aging 304-558-3317
Wisconsin		
Insurance Department Complaints Department 800-236-8517 608-266-0103	800-242-1060	Board on Aging and Long-Term Care 800-242-1060 608-266-8944
Wyoming		
Insurance Department 800-438-5768 307-777-7401	800-856-4398 307-856-6880	Division on Aging 800-442-2766 307-777-7986

different parts of the country. The life insurance policy could serve to replenish the portfolio for Jill's benefit if Jack should die after an extended period in a nursing home. An alternative, if there is substantial cash value, would be to cash in the policy to utilize its cash value to either help fund long-term care insurance costs or to increase the investment portfolio so that Jack and Jill can better cope with long-term care costs if they are incurred. If there is little cash value, maintaining the policy for its death benefit may make sense if the premiums are not too high.

$

TYPES OF LIFE INSURANCE POLICIES

What follows is a description of most, but not all, life insurance policies. (The summaries do not cover all policy features.)

TERM INSURANCE

These policies provide insurance protection only. If the insured dies, the beneficiary is paid. Generally there is no cash value to the policy and there is no borrowing against the policy.

LEVEL RENEWABLE TERM INSURANCE

The term, usually one year or five years, is covered by a fixed annual premium and a fixed face amount. Generally term policies are renewable; as long as you pay your premiums the insurance company will renew your coverage even if your health or occupational status has changed. Upon renewal, the annual premium is increased taking your age into account. Usually the insurance contract will allow you to reduce the amount of coverage, thereby reducing your premiums as well, but if you want to increase the coverage you will probably have to undergo a medical examination.

LEVEL NONRENEWABLE TERM INSURANCE

Usually this policy is not offered after you reach age 65 or age 70. You may have a limited time period when you can convert it to a cash value policy despite changes in health or occupation.

DECREASING TERM INSURANCE

The annual premiums remain fixed but the face amount gradually decreases. This type of policy is often used as *mortgage life insurance* so that the balance owed on your mortgage is paid upon death. Generally this type of insurance is not as good as a term policy that is large enough to cover your family's housing and other needs. Mortgage insurance must be used to pay off the mortgage, but if you have a favorable mortgage with low interest rates, your family may be better off not paying it off and utilizing insurance proceeds in another way. *Credit life insurance* is another kind of decreasing term insurance and is generally not advisable for the same reason.

CASH VALUE INSURANCE (WHOLE-LIFE)

This coverage is not limited to a certain term. Even if you don't die, it can build up cash value and act like a savings account. It is a form of forced savings. It costs more than term insurance in the early years of the policy so there will be a fund to help offset the cost in later years. As you and the policy get older, a more substantial portion of the death benefit consists of the cash value in the policy.

For example, if you take out a whole-life policy with a face amount of $100,000, the death benefit remains constant while the cash value of the policy gradually builds up. If the cash value or the policy has built up to a level of, say, $20,000, you can cash in that policy and take the money, but you no longer have life insurance coverage. If the cash value of the policy is $80,000 when you die, the insurance company only has to come up with an additional $20,000 to equal the $100,000 death benefit. The cash value of the policy is for the benefit of the insured, who can borrow on it or cash it in. Whole-life insurance is not a good buy if you plan to keep your policy for only a few years. Little if any cash value would be built up in that period. It usually takes about 10 years for cash value to build up substantially.

UNIVERSAL LIFE INSURANCE

This policy is also a cash value policy and is similar to whole-life in that it builds up cash value. While whole-life policies do not inform the holder about the effective rate of return being paid through accumulated cash value in the policy, universal life increases the rates of return on cash value accumulations. However, in recent years universal life policies have provided for a "surrender charge," and this reduces the cash value accumulations available if you drop the policy or borrow against it. Surrender charges usually gradually diminish and disappear sometime after the tenth year.

The policy may guarantee a certain minimum interest rate on your cash value, and in recent years the actual rate has been higher than the stated minimum. The interest rate fluctuates with prevailing interest rates.

VARIABLE LIFE INSURANCE

This is a wrinkle on the regular universal life policy. The insured chooses an investment or investments from stocks, bonds, money market funds, mutual funds, or a combination of these vehicles. The insurance company deducts the cost of insurance protection and expense fees from the cash value, usually monthly. However, if your cash value dips too low because you have not kept up premium payments, you may have to invest more money in order to keep your policy in effect.

"FINAL EXPENSE" POLICIES

These policies, aimed at senior citizens and sold through television advertising and by direct mail, have become popular in recent years. Although they seem attractive because they promise "guaranteed acceptance" regardless of the health of the insured, they're not good buys. Generally, the insurance does not provide full benefits if the insured dies from an illness within the first two years after purchase of the policy, and illness is the usual cause of death for the elderly.

"SECOND-TO-DIE" POLICIES

This type of policy is usually issued to a married couple. The face amount is paid when the surviving insured dies. Because the policy requires two people to die before payment, the annual premiums are less than if either spouse were the sole insured. Because the estate tax provides an unlimited marital deduction, most taxable estates are created at the

AN ALTERNATIVE TO LIFE INSURANCE?

There may be an alternative for those who rankle at the thought of buying life insurance. *Annual cash gifts to children or to an irrevocable trust for the benefit of the children with the gifts being invested to develop a diversified portfolio, may be preferable under certain circumstances.* For potential estates that would not be in difficulty by having to pay substantial estate taxes before the portfolio grew sufficiently, it may be a workable alternative. Perhaps a combination of both approaches could be used. The life insurance purchased by an irrevocable insurance trust could be converted to paid-up policies when the investment portfolio in the irrevocable investment trust grew sufficiently. A number of practical problems are involved, and your attorney can tell you whether a version of this alternative is workable for you.

time that the surviving spouse dies. Where insurance proceeds can pay all or a substantial part of estate taxes, the need to sell the family business and/or valuable property is avoided. When one spouse is otherwise uninsurable, this type of policy may still be available.

ESTATE TAX CONSIDERATIONS

Generally, life insurance is seen as providing protection for the spouse and children of the insured to meet the cost of living such as mortgage payments, college costs, medical expenses, and so on. If you're retired or nearing retirement, life insurance policy proceeds may be used to pay all or part of estate taxes, thereby avoiding selling a home or closely held business in order to pay taxes. How life insurance is purchased and held can make a substantial difference relative to estate taxes. See Chapter 10 for information on the formation and utilization of an irrevocable insurance trust.

Purchase of life insurance by children of the insured or through an irrevocable insurance trust can result in some interesting mathematics. For example, if Franklin has a $10 million estate and has his attorney prepare an irrevocable insurance trust that acquires a $2 million life insurance policy on Franklin's life, the proceeds of the $2 million policy will not be included in Franklin's taxable estate nor in his wife Elinor's taxable estate if the legal requirements for this treatment are met. Even if $1 million of premiums is paid over the years and this $1 million would have grown to $3 million if it had been invested, the adoption of this strategy could still prove very valuable to the trust's beneficiaries. The substitution of $2 million of insurance proceeds that is not subject to federal estate tax for $3 million that would have been included in the surviving spouse's estate is a good trade-off, because the $3 million would have been only $1.35 million after federal estate taxes applied at the

55% rate. $650,000 ($2 million – $1.35 million) would be gained.

Again, you must review the stability of the insurance company. Contact one or more of the five rating agencies (listed on pages 175 and 176) to get ratings on the prospective insurer or insurers. Where very substantial sums are involved, it may be wise to split the coverage over two or more insurance companies.

VIATICAL SETTLEMENTS OF LIFE INSURANCE POLICIES

Certain life insurance policyholders are able to receive accelerated death benefits on a tax-free basis. These proceeds would be received from a licensed settlement provider or individuals who meet insurance regulation requirements, and these proceeds would be tax-free. Policyholders who could qualify to sell or assign their life insurance for these benefits are terminally ill patients and chronically ill individuals. These provisions were enacted as part of the Insurance Portability and Accountability Act of 1996. "Terminally ill patients" are defined as physician-certified that their illness is reasonably expected to cause death within two years. "Chronically ill individuals" are generally individuals who cannot perform at least two activities of daily living—eating, toileting, transferring, bathing, dressing, and continence.

For the terminally ill or chronically ill, such an arrangement may provide funds when needed. Since payout rates vary greatly depending on the circumstances as well as who the provider may be, several proposals should be secured. The Viatical Association of America (800-842-9811), a nonprofit group, will provide a list of its members. Evaluate the proposal by asking whether the policy can be sold (the permission of the insurance company may be needed) and considering the life expectancy of the insured based on his or her medical records. The longer the life expectancy, the larger the discount on the face value of the policy. In other words, the longer the period that the provider will have to maintain the policy and wait for its money, the less it will be willing to advance.

Viatical settlements are fairly new and the opportunity for unscrupulous providers exists, in part because most states do not regulate settlement providers adequately. In 1994, CNA became the first large insurer to enter the viatical business. There are less than 100 firms providing viatical settlements. Fewer than 20 are firms with substantial funds for the purpose of funding benefits, while the others are brokers that charge a true provider a fee or commission, typically about 6% of the face value of the policy. Usually, there is no legal requirement that this fee be disclosed to the insured. Generally, the broker places the business where the broker will get the highest fee, rather than getting the best deal for the insured individual. *Even a hospital, clinic, or doctor may be an undisclosed broker.*

Make certain that the insured can receive the funds at the time that the policy is surrendered. After all, the point is to secure funds promptly from a nonliquid policy. Before entering into a viatical settlement, the insured should have a tax advisor establish whether the transaction will qualify for tax-free treatment under the Insurance Portability and Accountability Act of 1996.

PERSONAL UMBRELLA LIABILITY INSURANCE

Loss of a home could severely impact an investment portfolio by requiring substantial funds to be diverted to replace the home. Loss of an automobile would not be as major a financial setback as the loss of a home. However, both home-owners and automobile owners have even more substantial exposure.

For example, if a skilled surgeon slips on your icy porch and breaks a wrist so that his or her skills are substantially diminished, or if the seriously broken wrist results from an automobile accident where you were at fault, your home-owner's insurance or automobile insurance must provide critical protection for you.

Less well-known coverage is personal umbrella insurance. These policies raise the liability limits on certain underlying insurance if you are required to pay damages from a lawsuit or if you incur costs to defend against such a suit. President Clinton's umbrella policies have paid to defend him against a portion of the charges involved in Paula Jones's sexual ha-rassment suit. O. J. Simpson's umbrella insurer paid the legal bill to defend him in his civil trial.

In order to qualify for umbrella coverage, you must have basic auto and homeowner policy coverage, typically $100,000 per person and $300,000 per occurrence. Most claims are automobile-related. Some umbrella policies have an option you can add that pays for costs resulting from injuries resulting from the acts of an uninsured or under-insured driver. The premiums for umbrella cover-age are reasonable—reflecting the few claims against this coverage. Coverage for $1 million may be under $500 per year with $5 million of coverage being about $1,000 per year in most cases.

PROTECTION BEYOND INSURANCE

Those who have concerns relative to exposure that may not be adequately taken care of even by personal umbrella lia-bility insurance should discuss these concerns with their attorney. Professionals who may be subjected years later to substantial malpractice claims or others with substantial assets who could be subject to claims not covered by insurance or substantially exceeding insurance limits may consider certain sophisticated strategies. Only skilled, experienced attorneys with a thorough knowledge of creditors' rights should be relied on for advice. If an attorney does not have this expertise, he or she can refer his or her client to an attorney specializing in this area. Again, probabilities must be considered. Protection may be costly, incomplete, and extreme. Individual accounts in qualified employer retirement plans and to a lesser degree, IRAs and Keogh plans will often have a degree of protection from creditors that is based in part on the law of the state where the participant resides.

In Chapter 10, "Estate Planning," we cover certain trusts designed to accomplish estate planning objectives. Here we will also consider the protection that may be available by establishing an offshore trust.

The use of offshore trusts has grown tremendously recently. They are designed to protect substantial assets from legal claims arising from professional malpractice, divorce claims, and other lawsuits. To be legally effective, the transfer of assets to an offshore trust cannot be in fraud of creditors.

Both the doctor who amputates the wrong limb and the billionaire who is sued for divorce are subject to having any transfers that he or she makes without getting something of equal value in return set aside as being a fraudulent conveyance. However, if there are no claims in process or imminent, the transfer of assets to an offshore trust may successfully insulate the assets from activities that may arise sometime in the future.

Many people with concerns for the protection of their assets would not consider establishing an offshore trust because of the costs involved, which could be $15,000 or more, and having to rely on the laws of remote jurisdictions such as the Isle of Man or the Cayman Islands. Recently, Alaska and Delaware have passed laws that may afford the same kind of protection at a lower cost. Alaska and Delaware adopted their statutes in 1997, so the statutes haven't had much chance to be tested. There is some talk that the Delaware statute is deficient and is likely to be amended to resemble the Alaska law more closely.

The Alaska and Delaware trusts may not offer as much asset protection in some cases. However, there are estate planning advantages that may give the trusts more credibility as an asset protection device in other cases. The person establishing the trust may also be a "discretionary beneficiary" without having the trust assets included in the estate for federal estate tax purposes. However, the IRS has not yet ruled on these new trusts.

It may take years before the trusts' tax consequences are clarified, and even their usefulness as an asset protection device will probably not be tested for some time. At first, only the most adventurous and the most desperate are likely to utilize these devices. Just as offshore trusts often have been utilized together with such devices as family limited partnerships, it is likely that some of the earliest trusts established under these new state trust laws also will involve family limited partnerships. Please refer to Chapter 10 for more information relative to family limited partnerships. Again, you should seek the guidance of an experienced attorney who is knowledgeable in creditors' rights, if you are seeking to protect assets from substantial claims.

Part Four

PROTECTING YOUR FAMILY'S FINANCIAL WELL-BEING

Part IV deals with your financial well-being and also focuses on the well-being of your loved ones. Rather than examining your own finances, it addresses issues your heirs will face after your death.

With federal income tax, gift tax, estate tax, and generation-skipping tax, as well as additional state taxes, tax and estate planning oversights can be very costly. Conversely, intelligent strategies can result in spectacular tax savings.

Chapter 10 deals with estate planning strategies and the traps to avoid.

Chapter 11 deals not only with fraud and scams but also with how faulty logic and misinformation can lead you to make decisions that will hurt your portfolio. Included is an overview of the laws and legal principles that are designed to prevent scams and fraud.

Chapter 12 explains how to obtain effective professional advice. It details the different specialists including CPAs, CFPs, CFAs, and ChFCs.

CHAPTER TEN

Estate Planning

IN THIS CHAPTER

Here you will learn how to design a program that will satisfy your wishes for your beneficiaries following your death at the least tax cost. This chapter provides a brief overview of a subject that is inherently technical. It will focus on about 15 serious concerns most individuals face, including: how spouses should own their assets, what probate is and when is it required, how to avoid having your portfolio mismanaged after death, how to use estate planning tools, and when it pays not to give.

Generally, this book has concentrated on achieving and maintaining financial security for a couple's retirement years. We haven't addressed leaving an estate for loved ones; but, for many couples, that is an important issue. For some, it is a necessity. Some parents want to leave a family farm or business to succeeding generations of family members; some may want to leave a home or investments; and others will create or supplement an estate with life insurance for the needs and enjoyment of loved ones.

With estate tax rates reaching a current maximum of 55% and other federal and state taxes also being applicable at times, advanced estate planning can save hundreds of thousands of dollars, which can be the difference between success and failure.

Estate planning is the preparation of an individual's instructions about the disposition of assets upon death. If written instructions are not left in proper legal form, state law dictates disposition of the assets, probably not in a way you would choose. Furthermore, state laws would not have favorable tax consequences. A well thought-out estate plan can substantially reduce and, in some cases, eliminate estate taxes. The written instructions may be in the form of a combination of several of the following: will, trust agreement, durable power of attorney, death beneficiary designation of an IRA, life insurance benefits, medical instructions, and other documents.

Will estate planning cause marital disputes? It often does. To avoid this, many people simply do no estate planning, assuming they will "get around to it" or with a vague thought that "things will work out" after they die.

The first step in estate planning is for you and your spouse to discuss your respective concerns. Then, an inventory should be prepared. If, for example, your wife sees that she has fewer assets than you, your attorney will usually advise you to transfer ownership of sufficient assets to her in order to take as much advantage as possible of the Unified Credit of each spouse. Before 1998, the Unified Credit available to each spouse was $192,800. This meant that up to $192,800 of estate and gift taxes could be offset by applying this credit, equal to the estate (or gift) tax due on assets of $600,000. The Unified Credit provision has been revised to increase gradually from 1998 to 2006, when it will reach an equivalent of $1 million. (For more information on the Unified Credit, see Case Study 10.2 on page 211.)

Before consulting with an estate attorney, you should prepare a descriptive inventory of your assets and liabilities and details of the legal ownership of all assets. Both Case Studies 10.1 and 10.2 deal with the importance of precisely establishing ownership. Is the asset individually held or held jointly with one or more people? Also prepare a schedule of life insurance policies listing the owner of each policy, the beneficiary, and the face amount. Often overlooked is the face amount of life insurance policies. If the policy on you or your spouse is owned by the insured at the time of death, the face amount of the policy will be taxable for federal estate tax purposes.

Retirement plan accounts, Keogh plans, and IRAs should be listed. Copies of death beneficiary designations that are in effect for these plans should also be located. If you cannot find these beneficiary designations, ask your employer or plan sponsor (a broker, insurance company, or bank) for a copy. In addition, substantial expectancies should be considered. An expectancy is a property interest that you anticipate receiving as a gift or inheritance at some future date, usually from a parent or other close relative.

The mortgage balance on your home and any other debts that you may have should also be separately listed. (See Figure 10.1 on page 202). Separately note your concerns and desires as well as the ages of family members and other beneficiaries.

If you're worried that a spouse or child may be a spendthrift or have special care or financial needs, this should be noted. You and your spouse should give thought to what you consider to be appropriate provisions for these circumstances. Your attorney may also offer alternatives for you to consider.

Don't underestimate the importance of preparing this information before consulting an estate attorney. Not only will it help you clarify your wishes, but also the savings in

FIGURE 10.1   ESTATE INVENTORY

	CURRENT VALUE*		
	HUSBAND	WIFE	JOINT
Assets			
Bank accounts (checking and savings)	$	$	$
Other cash accounts (money market funds, cash accounts at brokers, etc.)			
Stocks, bonds, and mutual funds			
Retirement plan (profit sharing, pension) 401(k) Keogh SEP Other			
Annuities			
Business partnership interests			
Paintings, other art			
Other personal property (autos, furniture, and furnishings)			
Life insurance (face value)			
Home value			
Other real estate			
Total assets	$	$	$

*List amounts in the proper columns to show ownership.

FIGURE 10.1 (CONTINUED)

	CURRENT VALUE*		
	HUSBAND	WIFE	JOINT
Liabilities			
Mortgages and other debts	$	$	$
Loans on life insurance			
Other loans			
Total liabilities	$	$	$
Estimated taxable estate†	$	$	$
Federal estate tax (see Figure 10.2)	$	$	$
Amount available for your beneficiaries (net worth less federal estate tax)	$	$	$

*List amounts in the proper columns to show ownership.
†The exact value of the taxable estate will be reduced by funeral expenses and legal, probate, and other related expenses. Make copies of this blank form so that you and your spouse can make alternative calculations under different scenarios, varying the order of death and such factors as increases or decreases in values, the effect of an inheritance from a relative or friend, and so on.

time and cost for prior preparation and thought make the effort worthwhile.

You can refer to Figures 10.2 and 10.3 in estimating your federal estate tax.

SELECTING AN ATTORNEY

It is important to select a competent attorney who is experienced and trained in estate planning to advise you and prepare the appropriate documents. You can get referrals from a friend or an acquaintance who is an attorney or certified public accountant. CPAs and attorneys with a more general practice often have the opportunity to work with estate planning attorneys.

FIGURE 10.2   UNIFIED FEDERAL GIFT AND ESTATE TAX SCHEDULE

TAXABLE GIFT OR ESTATE		TENTATIVE TAX	
FROM	TO	TAX ON COL. 1	RATE ON EXCESS
$ 0	$ 10,000	$ 0	18%
10,000	20,000	1,800	20
20,000	40,000	3,800	22
40,000	60,000	8,200	24
60,000	80,000	13,000	26
80,000	100,000	18,200	28
100,000	150,000	23,800	30
150,000	250,000	38,800	32
250,000	500,000	70,800	34
500,000	750,000	155,800	37
750,000	1,000,000	248,300	39
1,000,000	1,250,000	345,800	41
1,250,000	1,500,000	448,300	43
1,500,000	2,000,000	555,800	45
2,000,000	2,500,000	780,000	49
2,500,000	3,000,000	1,025,000	53
3,000,000	—	1,290,800	55

Note: This schedule is for gifts made after 1983 and estates of persons dying after 1983.

At this point, it is important that you be candid about your own temperament. If you know that you are a procrastinator, it may be advisable for you to enlist someone to assist you or at least keep after you.

Now, do not get too smug if you are *not* a procrastinator.

FIGURE 10.3   ESTIMATING FEDERAL ESTATE TAX

1. Taxable estate*	$
2. Total of all post-1976 adjusted taxable gifts†	
3. Sum of #1 and #2	
4. Tentative estate tax on #3 (from Figure 10.2)	
5. Total of all gift taxes paid on post-1976 gifts	
6. Net tentative estate tax (#4 less #5)	
7. Estate tax credit‡	
8. Estimated estate tax	$

Note: This computation only provides an estimate. For example, the state death tax credit and other credits are not taken into consideration. We again give notice that we are not supplying legal advice. You must review your plans with a competent advisor before acting. Further detail is beyond the scope of this book.

*"Taxable estate" is the gross estate less all available deductions, including the estate tax marital deduction and charitable deduction subject to certain other qualifications.

†"Total of all post-1976 adjusted taxable gifts" means total amount of post-1976 taxable gifts [gross gifts less deductions including $10,000 annual exclusion per donee ($20,000 if spouse joins in gift), gift tax marital deduction, and charitable gifts] other than adjustments relating to certain gifts.

‡The maximum estate tax credit (the Unified Credit) is $202,050 for 1998; $211,300 for 1999; $220,550 for 2000 and 2001; $229,800 for 2002 and 2003; $287,300 for 2004; $326,300 for 2005; and $345,800 for 2006 and thereafter.

There is still room for you to make a critical mistake. Shopping for an estate planning attorney is similar to other types of shopping in many ways. If you are impatient, you are probably a poor shopper, and enlisting assistance would be a smart move.

It is strongly recommended that you enter into a written fee agreement with the attorney at the beginning. This is for both of your benefits. Also, detailed monthly statements are generally recommended. This will reduce the chance of costs getting out of hand. Depending on the degree of service involved, it is not unusual for an estate plan (including a revocable trust, pour-over will, durable powers of attorney, and transfers) to exceed $1,500. Where a married couple is involved, the cost for estate plans for both spouses is little more than for one spouse, since the provisions for the survivor of the two of them and for the children of their marriage usually will be identical. However, this is not the case where one or both spouses have children by a prior marriage.

Technically, there is a conflict of interest when both spouses have the same lawyer. This is clearly the case if either or both spouses have children from a prior marriage. On occasion, even with first marriages, there may be disputes where one spouse claims that the attorney favored the other spouse. If you feel that your spouse is being unduly restrictive, raise this issue and consider hiring independent counsel to review drafts of the proposed documents before they are signed. Obviously, this is a very difficult thing to do.

We can hear you saying that if there is anything worse than hiring one attorney, it would be hiring two attorneys. Very few couples feel the need for separate attorneys, but this possibility should be kept in mind.

NONCITIZEN ISSUES

If you or your spouse is not a U.S. citizen, the unlimited marital deduction is not available for property transferred to that individual. The unlimited marital deduction generally results in no estate tax being charged on the amount that is left to a spouse. The tax exposure can be huge. If a decedent has left his or her spouse a million dollars in excess of the credit exclusion amount, the estate tax on that million dollars could be as much as $550,000. (The theory behind the unlimited marital deduction is that federal estate tax will be collected when the surviving spouse dies.)

When the law was passed in 1988 to limit the use of the unlimited marital deduction to surviving spouses who are U.S. citizens, the objective was to give the IRS the same opportunity to tax the estate of a surviving spouse upon his or her death regardless of whether that spouse was a U.S. citizen. This opportunity could be lost if a noncitizen surviving spouse returned to his or her native land with the untaxed portion of the decedent's estate.

In the case of a noncitizen spouse, this problem can be solved through the use of a Qualified Domestic Trust (QDOT). At least one of the trustees of a QDOT must be a U.S. corporation or a U.S. citizen. The withdrawal of principal from the QDOT is taxed as if it had been part of the taxable estate of the deceased spouse. It is taxed on a cumulative basis so that successive distributions to the surviving spouse could be taxed at higher estate tax levels.

Again, the advice of an experienced attorney is necessary in this area. Transferring assets to the noncitizen spouse during his or her lifetime (a nontaxable event if both spouses are U.S. citizens) contains a limitation in that gifts above $100,000 per year to a noncitizen spouse trigger the gift tax. Still, much can be accomplished by giving less than $100,000 a year. Note that other gifts made to a spouse during the year are taken into account. A gift of $100,000 to the noncitizen spouse could be added to a birthday, anniversary, or other gift that will trigger the gift tax on the entire annual sum given. If the noncitizen spouse becomes a citizen prior to the spouse's death or within nine months of the spouse's death there is no need for a QDOT.

The noncitizen spouse may initiate proceedings within nine months of the death of his or her spouse by requesting permission to set up a QDOT. Then, the noncitizen spouse could begin proceedings to become a U.S. citizen and avoid the estate tax problem. IRAs, retirement plans, and life insurance owned by the decedent generally pass to the noncitizen surviving spouse apart from probate proceedings and may fall outside of QDOT protection unless specific action is taken to modify the beneficiary designation.

Also, jointly held property should not be overlooked. Although owned in both names, jointly held assets are treated as owned solely by the first spouse to die if the contribution of the surviving spouse is not proved.

THE DO-IT-YOURSELFER

And now for an observation and warning to the do-it-yourselfer. We suspect that many of you who are reading this book are do-it-yourself investors. The temptation to also be a do-it-yourself estate planner is great. An apparent savings of over $1,500 in legal fees is a strong incentive.

However, disastrous consequences may occur years later after the do-it-yourselfer dies. Serious errors by an attorney will usually result in his or her legal liability. Most attorneys carry professional liability insurance, but this relief is not available to the do-it-yourselfer.

Tax law related to estates can be convoluted. The potential do-it-yourselfer should be particularly aware of the need to regularly review case law and tax documents, since the law may have changed even if personal conditions have not.

Note: During the preparation of drafts of this chapter in 1997, the Tax Relief Act of 1997 was adopted, making material changes in the gift and estate tax laws. Both Case Study 10.1 and 10.2 had to be revised to take these changes into account. Both deal with unsatisfactory estate planning. The 1997 Act created potentially serious problems for many individuals with estate plans that were satisfactory immediately prior to its passage. For example, if Dagwood had a $2 million estate and his wife, Blondie, had a $600,000 estate, should he transfer up to $400,000 more in assets to Blondie because the exemption equivalent has been increased? If Dagwood's living trust provided that his Bypass or Credit Shelter Trust should be of a size to maximize the tax savings—a common provision—the change in law would seem to increase its potential size automatically by $400,000 by the year 2006 (from $600,000 to $1,000,000).

Would Blondie like the idea of Dagwood's potential Marital Trust for her benefit being reduced by $400,000 in order to shift this account to the Bypass Trust? If Dagwood should die without reviewing his estate plan with his attorney, could Blondie successfully challenge the shift of $400,000 from the Marital to the Bypass Trust as not being what Dagwood intended?

Charlton, Lana, Tyrone, and Hedy in Case Studies 10.1 and 10.2, as well as all of you, should be aware of the need to contact your attorney periodically to discuss the status of your estate plan.

▆$▆ CASE STUDY 10.1—CHARLTON AND LANA

Charlton and his wife Lana have combined assets exceeding $2 million in value. After being quoted a fee in excess of $1,700 to prepare an estate plan for himself and Lana, Charlton, a do-it-yourself investor, goes to his local bookstore and finds an estate planning book. He prepares documents for Lana and himself that paragraph-for-paragraph and page-for-page look every bit as impressive as the documents churned out by an estate lawyer's office. The documents are appropriately signed and witnessed, and the trust agreements are even notarized.

Upon Charlton's death after 2005, his loved ones discover that, although no federal estate tax is then owed since all of the assets were held jointly by Charlton and Lana, under state law the assets then become the sole property of Lana, and Charlton's trust is wholly ineffective. The eventual tax bill after Lana's death will probably be over $340,000 more than it would have been with correct planning. Attempts at corrective planning after Charlton's death are likely to be inadequate.

The trust agreement contained the appropriate language, but Charlton's failure to revise ownership properly before his death leaves a substantial problem. There are tax planning tools for corrective planning that may reduce or eliminate this additional tax exposure. However, it will involve transfers and expenditures by Lana that she may not feel comfortable doing, such as disclaimers of ownership, substantial gifts to the children during her lifetime, the purchase of life insurance policies, or a combination of all of these possibilities.

$

It is very important to promptly review the estate plan if you change legal residence to another state. In addition to changes in the law, changes in both personal and financial circumstances may make revisions necessary. Often, a call to your attorney and a brief telephone discussion will be all that is required. Do not count on your attorney to call you.

Because of the unlimited marital deduction, it is not unusual to have no federal estate tax owed upon death of the first spouse. Both Case Studies 10.1 and 10.2 deal with situations involving the death of the first spouse with no federal estate tax owed, but a difficult tax problem was created in both cases.

When initial estate planning has been inadequate, conservative planning devices may be available to at least partially undo the damage. Factors such as the life expectancy of a surviving spouse, the type or types of assets involved, and the financial needs of the surviving spouse and other beneficiaries have to be considered. Gifts of up to $10,000 per year (the annual exclusion amount) can be given to each donee by the surviving spouse without adverse tax consequences.

Perhaps the surviving spouse cannot afford to give substantial sums to the children and still meet possible emergencies and maintain the same standard of living. Prompt action is often necessary; a delay of several years in implementing a program can be costly. Proper planning could have avoided the tax problems being faced by the families in Case Studies 10.1 and 10.2.

▆$▆ CASE STUDY 10.2—TYRONE AND HEDY

Tyrone and his wife Hedy have over $2 million in assets. Tyrone is impressed when his friend Charlton tells him how he saved "thousands of dollars in legal fees" as a do-it-yourself estate planner. Tyrone buys the same estate planning book and prepares an impressive living trust agreement and will for himself and Hedy. Other than their home, nothing is held jointly, and almost all of the assets are in Tyrone's name. Upon Tyrone's death, everything would work out nicely. However, Hedy dies first—with only $5,000 in assets solely in her name. As a result, her Bypass (or Credit Shelter) Trust created under the living trust agreement that is equipped to initially shelter up to $1 million in assets from taxation will shelter no more then $5,000. This probably will cost Tyrone's estate over $340,000 in estate tax. This amount could have been saved if Tyrone had transferred assets to Hedy to bring her holdings up to at least $1 million at the time of her death. The added tax cost will occur upon Tyrone's subsequent death. (The Bypass or Credit Shelter Trust could generate a united credit of as much as $345,800 if Hedy had died after 2005. A gradual phasing in to reach this sum will occur during the 1998 to 2006 period.)

▆$▆

There are other ways to qualify for a maximum deduction than direct transfers to a spouse during life or upon death. These include: (1) adding your spouse as a joint tenant with right of survivorship or as a tenant by the entireties; (2) directly or indirectly designating the spouse as the beneficiary on a life insurance policy; (3) placing property in a Marital Trust for the sole benefit of the surviving spouse if certain requirements such as giving control over disposition of the remaining trust property after his or her death, are met;

and (4) placing property in a Qualified Terminable Interest Property (QTIP) Trust.

A QTIP Trust is unusual in that it enables an estate to obtain a marital deduction although it does not give the surviving spouse full control of the trust principal. The QTIP Trust is often utilized when someone has remarried and wants the second spouse to be provided for but that the principal of the QTIP Trust will be preserved for the children of the first marriage. When there is a second marriage under these circumstances, a written agreement describing this arrangement should be entered into by the couple prior to marriage. Otherwise, if the second wife survives her husband, she may have the right to claim a larger portion of his estate under state law. The premarital agreement is a technical document and before it is adopted, each party should obtain a lawyer's advice.

How property is held can be very important to estate planning. As Case Study 10.1 indicates, joint tenancy with right of survivorship can be disastrous. Yet, in other circumstances it may be helpful. Joint tenancy with right of survivorship between a husband and wife is referred to in most states as *tenancy by the entireties*. The survivor becomes the sole owner without any probate procedure. In very modest estates, it may serve as a substitute for more sophisticated estate planning. Even in large and complex estates, tenancy by the entireties or joint tenancy with right of survivorship can play an important part, particularly with regard to ownership of the personal residence.

Tenancy in common is another form of joint ownership. It does not involve the right of survivorship. When a tenant in common dies, the decedent's share of the ownership becomes part of the estate and subject to probate.

Community property law applies in Arizona, California, Idaho, Louisiana, Nevada, New Mexico, Texas, Washington, and Wisconsin. In these states, community property is property acquired during the marriage by either spouse. If a spouse dies during the marriage or the couple divorces, each spouse has a half interest in the property that is community property. There are variations in the law from state to state. Any person relocating to another state should have his or her estate plan documents carefully reviewed by a lawyer in the new home state. Moving to or from a community-property state, even to another community-property state, increases the likelihood that changes will have to be made to the estate plan documents. Changes often are advisable even where community-property law is not involved. A review of your documents should not be a costly process, but you should establish the fee beforehand in writing.

BEQUESTS

In almost all cases where there is a reasonable degree of family harmony, parents provide that upon the death of the surviving parent, the balance of the estate should be shared equally by their children. However, it may make more sense to spell out in the will or trust agreement that the children were loved equally but that their needs were unequal and that provisions were being made accordingly.

The documents should also provide that the surviving parent could make further adjustments to their children's shares if conditions warranted. One further point: If a surviving parent is considering remarriage, he or she may want to have a premarital agreement to deal fairly with all parties, including the children of the first marriage. The effectiveness of premarital agreements is controlled by state law, and its requirements may be technical. Last-minute arrangements or agreements entered into after remarriage may be ineffective in certain states.

Concerns may arise when some of the children are active in a family business or where all the children may be active in the business, but one or more of them show a much greater management ability than the others. What is fair treatment? These concerns should be discussed with your estate planning attorney and your CPA or other family advisor.

Maximum flexibility in dealing with alternatives must be preserved so revisions in your plans can be made later if expectations change. For example, the child or grandchild who decides to go into the family business after all instead of going to professional school, or the child or grandchild who, after being groomed to take over the family business, decides to do something else instead can raise problems. Usually it is best to get the opinions of several family members along with those of your advisors.

PROBATE

Probate is the legal procedure whereby the provisions of an estate plan are administered under a branch of the state court system. It covers the orderly valuation of a decedent's assets, the settlement of debts owed, and the payment of applicable taxes. The procedure is concluded by the distribution of the remaining assets. Completion of probate can take two years or more.

Depending substantially on the type of assets involved and the total value of your estate, certain delays may be unavoidable. If the probate procedure can be substantially reduced or eliminated, you will have substantial savings in time and money. If you have minor children at the time of your death and your spouse does not survive you, your will should designate your choice of a guardian. If your will does not provide for the naming of a suitable guardian, a judge will name the guardian, who may not be someone you would have chosen.

A will that is admitted to probate is part of the public record and is open to examination by anyone. A revocable trust, however, is not a public document. If there are matters that you want to keep private, such as provisions relative to the care of certain beneficiaries, these matters should be covered in a living trust agreement. By picking a competent trustee and successor trustee, administration of more detailed wishes over a period of time can be accomplished most efficiently by a trust. If you feel that there may be family disagreements, or that probate court supervision to protect the interests of certain loved ones is desirable, you should discuss these concerns with your attorney. Under these conditions it may be preferable to have all or part of the estate subject to probate procedures.

THE BYPASS (CREDIT SHELTER) TRUST

In most estates, the Bypass or Credit Shelter Trust is the planning tool that results in the greatest estate tax saving. Generally, the Marital Trust will postpone the estate tax until the surviving spouse dies. But the assets held in the Bypass or Credit Shelter Trust of the spouse who is the first to die will escape estate tax in both spouses' estates even though the surviving spouse can be protected as the primary beneficiary during his or her lifetime.

Here are a series of examples to illustrate how a Bypass (Credit Shelter) Trust reduces estate taxes.

ESTATE PLANNING: UTILIZING A BYPASS (CREDIT SHELTER) TRUST CAN REDUCE ESTATE TAXES

BACKGROUND

1. In example A, Paul leaves his entire $2,000,000 estate to his wife, Betty. Probate fees, legal fees, and other administrative expenses are not shown in any of these examples and vary substantially between states. They will generally run from less than 1% to as high as 5% of the assets in the probate estate. The expenses of administering a living trust are generally less but depend greatly on who the trustees are and the complexity of the trust.

2. Example B uses the same facts as Example A but assumes that Paul has a revocable trust agreement that establishes a Bypass or Credit Shelter Trust.

3. Probate fees are incurred under Example A and normally not under Example B. The combined costs incurred in Example B will usually be much less than the combined fees and costs under Example A.

4. Example C uses the same facts as Example B but assumes that during Betty's life, but after Paul's death, the assets in the Bypass Trust grow in value by $1,000,000. The point is that not only is $1,000,000 sheltered from taxation initially, the growth in value is also sheltered from federal estate tax in the surviving spouse's estate. (Annual income of the Bypass Trust is subject to federal income tax laws, however.)

5. If Example A, using the simple will, were changed to show growth in value from $2,000,000 to $3,000,000 in Betty's estate after Paul's death as in Example C, then

the federal estate tax that would have been charged to the estate of Betty as the surviving spouse would be $945,000 ($1,290,800 minus $345,800 Unified Credit). This would leave Betty's beneficiaries with $2,055,000 rather than $3,000,000 as shown in Example C.

EXAMPLE A

Paul has a will with bequest of all assets to Betty, his surviving spouse.

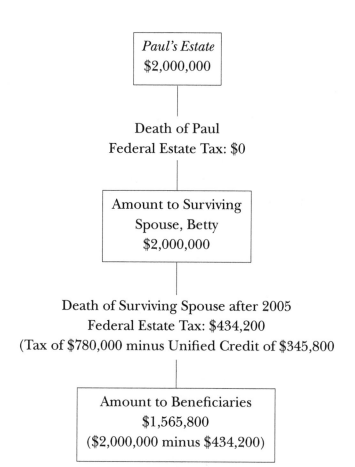

Paul's Estate
$2,000,000

Death of Paul
Federal Estate Tax: $0

Amount to Surviving
Spouse, Betty
$2,000,000

Death of Surviving Spouse after 2005
Federal Estate Tax: $434,200
(Tax of $780,000 minus Unified Credit of $345,800

Amount to Beneficiaries
$1,565,800
($2,000,000 minus $434,200)

EXAMPLE B

Paul has a revocable trust agreement with Bypass and Marital Trust provisions created in the trust agreement. Will "pours" all assets not already subject to terms of the trust agreement "over" to it.

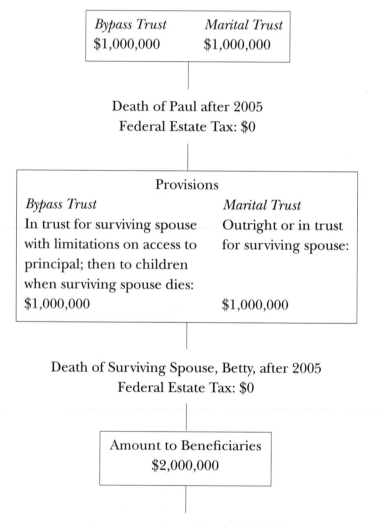

Bypass Trust
$1,000,000

Marital Trust
$1,000,000

Death of Paul after 2005
Federal Estate Tax: $0

Provisions

Bypass Trust
In trust for surviving spouse
with limitations on access to
principal; then to children
when surviving spouse dies:
$1,000,000

Marital Trust
Outright or in trust
for surviving spouse:

$1,000,000

Death of Surviving Spouse, Betty, after 2005
Federal Estate Tax: $0

Amount to Beneficiaries
$2,000,000

Savings over Example A: $434,200

EXAMPLE C

This example is the same as B, except assets in Bypass Trust increase in value during period beginning with Paul's death and ending with surviving spouse Betty's death.

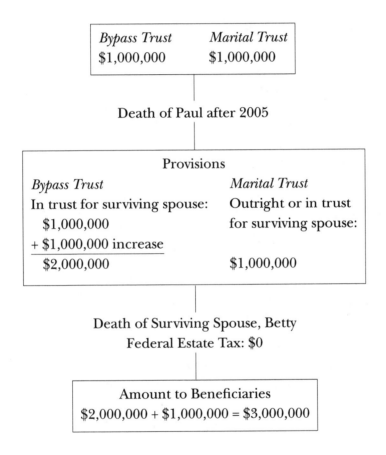

Bypass Trust	*Marital Trust*
$1,000,000	$1,000,000

Death of Paul after 2005

Provisions

Bypass Trust	*Marital Trust*
In trust for surviving spouse:	Outright or in trust
$1,000,000	for surviving spouse:
+ $1,000,000 increase	
$2,000,000	$1,000,000

Death of Surviving Spouse, Betty
Federal Estate Tax: $0

Amount to Beneficiaries
$2,000,000 + $1,000,000 = $3,000,000

THE TRUSTEE

In most instances, estate planning involving more than $1,000,000 in assets should involve the establishment of one or more trusts, whether subject to probate or not, that will be revocable during the lifetime of the creator of the trust (legally designated as the *grantor* or the *settlor*) and will become irrevocable upon the grantor's death or incompetency. A revocable trust is normally ignored for income tax purposes during the grantor's life. In many estates of less than $1,000,000, trusts can be beneficial for probate avoidance even if tax savings is not involved.

The trustee or trustees that the grantor appoints are required under state law to carry out the grantor's wishes as provided in the trust document. Confidence in the trustee's integrity and ability is a critical element in a solid estate plan. Generally, the grantor names himself or herself as the trustee during his or her lifetime, and upon his death or incompetency, an individual or a bank and trust company is named as the successor trustee or trustees. The advantage in using a corporate trustee such as a bank or trust company as your trustee or cotrustee is that there is continuity. That is, the bank will not become ill or die and it does not have any relationship with a beneficiary that could cause tax or other legal problems.

For example, the portion of your estate that will be held in a Bypass or Credit Shelter Trust so that it will be taxed in neither your estate nor your spouse's estate can be defeated if the IRS could show that your spouse had full control of that trust. With the phased-in increase in the Credit Shelter amount (based on the Unified Credit) that will reach $1,000,000 by the year 2006, an erroneous trustee provision or designation could be costly. Hundreds of thousands or even millions of dollars could be lost in additional estate taxes, since the surviving spouse may live many more years and the initial credit shelter amount may grow in value to many times its original size.

The major drawbacks in utilizing a corporate trustee or a corporate cotrustee can be both real and imagined. You may have a fine relationship with the people at the bank or trust company that you deal with, but in all likelihood these are not the people that your loved ones will work with after you die. Also, the costs that are charged by a corporate trustee are usually set by a schedule (subject to negotiation) and are often steep.

If the trust officers of the bank or trust company are competent and the fees are commensurate with the services and the responsibilities involved, the best interests of the trust beneficiaries may be served by the bank acting as the trustee or successor trustee. However, some banks and trust companies, because of the substantial turnover of personnel, lack experience as trustees.

In addition, the performance records of most banks and trust companies as asset managers and investment advisors are poor. Even when mutual funds are utilized as the primary or sole investment medium, banks sometimes rely heavily on their own mutual funds, which do not compare favorably with mutual funds that are managed by the most skilled advisors in the investment industry. Our experience is that a replacement of about 20% of the mutual funds during a 12-month period that is based on management performance is not unusual. You want to avoid being locked into a portfolio by a bank or other advisor.

In recent years, fewer prospective grantors have wanted to use a corporate trustee. Our experience is that in most cases where a bank or trust company was named in the original agreement as a trustee, periodic review of the trust agreement will result in the grantor naming an individual to be the trustee instead. However, even when an individual trustee or trustees are used, it is a good idea to have a mechanism for the use of a substitute corporate trustee if it is possible that all individual trustee candidates could die or be incapacitated before the trust would terminate. In almost all instances, trust agreements can be prepared to accommodate a grantor's first choice of a trustee. However, extreme care must be exercised when relatives are named as trustees or cotrustees.

For example, if your spouse is to be a trustee over that portion of your estate that is to be excluded from your taxable estate, your spouse should not exercise that degree of authority that will allow the IRS to successfully challenge the exclusion from his or her estate. It may be necessary to give the power of removal of a trustee to one person and the power of appointment of a successor trustee to another person. Otherwise the IRS may argue that having the power to both remove and replace a trustee should be considered the

UNINTENDED LOSS OF ACCESS TO YOUR INVESTMENT ADVISOR

An important point to discuss with your estate planning attorney is the management of your investments if you are either incapacitated during the term of the trust or die. Many people are unable to decide on a qualified individual whom they are comfortable to name as trustee. Still others are unable to choose a qualified individual as a successor trustee should the original trustee die or become incapacitated or resign. For this reason, a bank or trust company is often named as the trustee or the successor trustee.

In the absence of appropriate provisions, the bank or trust company will want to utilize its own investment department to manage the trust assets despite there being hundreds of better choices available. If you are satisfied with your current investment advisor, that advisor should be initially retained. To substitute unacceptable performance for acceptable performance, usually at a greater cost, does not make sense. On the other hand, if an investment advisor should underperform in the judgment of a majority of the adult beneficiaries, that advisor should be able to be replaced. These terms should be provided in your trust agreement, although most attorneys fail to include them unless requested by their client.

same as possessing sufficient powers that would make the assets includable in that person's estate, although the decided cases are favorable to the taxpayer.

THE IRREVOCABLE LIFE INSURANCE TRUST

The Irrevocable Life Insurance Trust (ILIT) is a separate type of trust that can result in substantial tax benefits. It is established to be both owner and beneficiary of one or more life insurance policies. Upon death, the proceeds are paid to the trustees of this trust. The trust agreement goes on to provide details for utilizing the policy proceeds for the benefit of loved ones. Existing life insurance policies can be transferred to the ILIT. Then, the policy proceeds will be removed from your potential taxable estate if you survive for at least three years (the three-year rule). The most immediate benefit can be secured when the ILIT is utilized to apply for and purchase a new life insurance policy. When properly accomplished under the careful supervision of an estate planning attorney, although you are the insured, you will never be the owner or beneficiary of the policy and the three-year rule would not apply.

Why would a person with assets purchase life insurance under these circumstances? If you own a business or undeveloped real estate, the purchase of life insurance may be a means to provide cash to pay all or a substantial part of the estate taxes and related expenses. Otherwise, your heirs and beneficiaries might be forced to sell valuable assets at distress prices. By utilizing an ILIT properly, the proceeds of the policies can be utilized for this purpose without being included in your estate for federal estate tax purposes.

The trust agreement will provide that funds can be loaned to your estate to pay taxes. In addition, it will provide that nonliquid assets may be purchased from your estate with these funds. In this way, cash can be used for tax payments and the family business or other nonliquid assets move your estate to the ILIT. The ILIT will then transfer the business or other assets to the beneficiaries tax-free. The agreement establishing this trust cannot be revoked or amended or it will lose its tax-preferred status.

The experienced estate planning attorney will include some escape hatches to cover certain situations. For example, if cash contributions to pay annual insurance premiums are discontinued, the insurance policies owned by the ILIT may be able to be converted to paid-up policies with reduced face amounts. If the grantor is still insurable, a new ILIT with newly purchased policies can then be established with terms that will take the prior ILIT's terms and insurance policies into account.

A second-to-die life insurance policy on the lives of you and your spouse is often utilized under these circumstances. The premium on this type of policy will be less than the premium on the life of either one of you. If one of you is uninsurable, this policy may provide the ideal solution. It should usually be purchased through an ILIT. Maximum utilization of the marital deduction will postpone taxes upon the death of the first spouse to die. The proceeds from this type of policy will be paid to the ILIT when the surviving spouse dies so that cash will be available for estate tax and other needs at that time.

PARTNERSHIPS AND BUSINESS INTERESTS

Putting business assets, investment assets, or both into a newly formed entity could enable you to retain control of assets while removing a substantial part of their value from your taxable estate. Limited liability companies (LLCs) and limited liability partnerships (LLPs) are recent additions to the laws of many states. They are hybrid entities that combine some of the characteristics of corporations with some of the characteristics of partnerships. Limited partnerships are not new. They also combine some of the characteristics of corporations with those of partnerships. We're discussing only those attributes that enable someone to retain control while establishing potential tax benefits by reducing the value of one's interest to a substantial degree.

Ignoring gift tax consequences for a moment, if you transferred your solely owned business to a partnership in which you retained a 52% interest, and your two sons each received a 24% interest, your interest in the business would be substantially reduced. If the business as a whole were worth $1 million, what would your 52% partnership interest be worth? $520,000 may not be the right answer. What would your sons' interests be worth? $240,000 each is probably not the right answer. What would an interested buyer of the business be willing to pay for your interest if your sons were not willing to sell—or pay them for their interests if you were not willing to sell? Lack of marketability of a business interest and minority interest ownership are both factors that reduce value.

Lack of marketability is not only looking for a buyer of a grocery store in a high crime area, but also seeking a buyer for a 52% interest in a business where the balance is owned by two brothers who seem difficult to deal with. Justification for a discount for a minority interest can be given to you by an interested potential buyer for a 24% interest in a business when the remaining interests are owned by strangers who would retain the power to control decisions. Lack of control could mean that: (1) one's share of the profits could be held back rather than distributed; (2) one would not be employed by the business; or (3) if employed, one would not determine anyone's salary. Discounts in value of 25% to 50% are often justified for the combination of a lack of marketability of an interest as well as it being a minority interest with little or no decision-making authority.

▆$▆ CASE STUDY 10.3—JERRY AND JERI

Substantial advantages can be obtained by utilizing valuation rules. Jerry and his wife, Jeri, have built a business with a value of over $3 million. Their adult children play important management roles in the business. Jerry and Jeri consulted with their tax advisors to establish a comprehensive program that will keep control of the business in their family after they die while substantially reducing potential estate and gift taxes.

The plan that was adopted will utilize the principles of creating minority interests with reduced market values so that these interests can be used to transfer ownership from Jerry and Jeri to their two adult children and their five grandchildren. Jerry and Jeri can each give a $10,000 per year gift, tax-free, to each child and grandchild. That would be $20,000 per year of interest in Jer-Jer, the new family limited partnership, to be given to each child and grandchild, or $140,000 per year given to the seven donees.

If valuation discounts for lack of marketability and for minority interests were supportable at a combined $33^{1}/_{3}\%$ rate, $210,000, not $140,000, would be removed from Jerry and Jeri's taxable estates each year. Over 10 years, $2,100,000 would be removed, saving more than $1 million in potential federal estate tax.

What if Jerry and Jeri are not in good health or their assets still have the potential of growing rapidly so that, in several years, their estates are still likely to increase greatly? Under these circumstances they don't have 10 years to achieve their goal of passing on their business to their loved ones instead of having it burdened with debt or sold in order to pay estate taxes. But Jerry and Jeri each has a Unified Credit that can shelter up to $1 million in gifts beginning in the year 2006.

Most estates have applied the Unified Credit in full when calculating federal estate tax liability after the death of the individual. However, in large estates it is more effective when it is utilized to shelter gifts during life. Jerry and Jeri also have $2 million in other assets. If they each give $1 million in partnership interests in 2006, the $2 million in gifts can remove $3 million from their potential estates because of the valuation discounts. If the $3 million in Jer-Jer doubled in value by the time that both Jerry and Jeri died, the use of their federal gift tax and estate tax credit (the Unified Credit), instead of being worth $1 million in exclusions to each of their estates, has become worth $3 million of exclusions to each of their estates.

Note: This case study does not cover all the technical problems that the competent attorney will have to deal with. For example, there is the generation-skipping tax (GST) to discourage gifts that skip a generation such as the gifts to Jerry and Jeri's grandchildren, but there are also cumulative $1 million GST exclusions for each of the grandparents.

$

If certain requirements are followed, everyone has the right to give up to $10,000 per year to anyone they wish to without incurring a gift tax or using up any portion of the Unified Credit. The primary requirement is that the gift is of a "present interest" rather than a "future interest." Generally, if there are restrictions on the donee's right to control the gift, it may be a gift of a future interest and the gift may not qualify for the $10,000 annual exclusion. How it can be used is shown in the tale of Jerry and Jeri above. After 1998, the annual exclusion will be indexed for inflation by a formula that will increase it in $1,000 intervals from time to time.

There may be additional estate tax relief under the Taxpayer Relief Act of 1997 where over 50% of a decedent's estate is the value of a qualified family-owned business. As the exemption equivalent of the Unified Credit increases from $625,000 in 1998 to $1 million in 2006, the combined Unified Credit and qualified business exclusion is capped at $1,300,000.

The rules under the 1997 Act are complicated and include provisions if one, two, or three families control the business. There may be situations where nonbusiness assets rather than business assets should be given during life in order for the estate to qualify for this limited relief. Failure to maintain family participation for at least 10 years after death can result in giving back the estate tax benefits. The complexity of this provision makes professional assistance necessary. Nontax problems such as the child who is not active in the business and the grandchild who should not be trusted with substantial assets are beyond the scope of this book. But, competent advisors can be helpful since they deal with these situations regularly.

ESTATE TAX BENEFITS FROM CHARITABLE GIFTS

There are a variety of charitable trust arrangements that can be established to benefit the qualified charity of your choice and result in significant tax benefits for you and your loved ones. There are different forms of charitable trusts, including a Charitable Lead Trust, which will pay income to a charity for a specific period and then distribute the trust principal to your beneficiaries.

Another variation is the Charitable Remainder Annuity or Unitrust, which pays a set dollar amount or a percentage of the trust assets to you or your beneficiaries and, after your death or after a specific period of time, the principal is donated to a charity. There are other variations, too. These are irrevocable arrangements that are generally utilized by the very wealthy who have a strong desire to assist a particular charity, coupled with a desire to obtain substantial tax benefits for their beneficiaries. Universities, religious institutions, and other charities maintain charitable giving departments that provide detailed information and assistance to potential donors.

DEATHBED PLANNING

Although it is a very difficult time, the terminally ill person should try some meaningful planning. Annual tax-free gifts of up to $10,000 per donee can be made without using any of the individual donor's Unified Credit. If it is late in the year, additional gifts of up to $10,000 per donee could be made for the new calendar year. Under these conditions, it usually does not make sense to make gifts of more than $10,000 to any donee since the gift tax paid within three years of death is added back into the estate and is also taxed.

Also, the annual exclusion amount will increase from time to time after 1998. Generally, cash or assets that have not appreciated substantially in value should be used for these gifts. Assets that have appreciated greatly achieve a stepped-up basis at death, which can save substantial income tax for the donor's loved ones. It is important to keep in mind that all gifts and other transfers by check are not complete unless the checks are deposited and cleared before the donor's death.

Also, if the terminally ill person is married, the potential Unified Credit should not be wasted as they were in Case Studies 10.1 and 10.2 earlier in this chapter. Figure 10.4 on page 230 sets out the amount that should be held by a terminally ill spouse at the time of death in order to maximize the tax benefits of the Bypass or Credit Shelter Trust.

A special alert should also be given to those terminally ill spouses who had Credit Shelter Trusts with up to $600,000 in their names pursuant to pre-1998 conditions. Their planning should be reexamined to take into consideration the phasing in of additional potential benefits for the 1998 to 2006 period. There is a requirement that the recipient of any transfers must live for at least a year and a day for the transfer to be effective. There is no penalty if the recipient

FIGURE 10.4   MAXIMUM ASSET
VALUE EXEMPTED FROM TAX USING
THE UNIFIED CREDIT

YEAR	AMOUNT EXCLUDED
1998	$ 625,000
1999	650,000
2000 and 2001	675,000
2002 and 2003	700,000
2004	850,000
2005	950,000
2006 or thereafter	1,000,000

Note: Prior to 1998, full use of the Unified Credit could exempt $600,000 in value from federal gift and estate taxes. From 1998 to 2006, a higher exempt amount is being phased in as shown above.

does not survive that long, so it should be tried if the tax saving is desired, whether it is additional funding for an existing Credit Shelter Trust or to establish a new Credit Shelter Trust.

Transfers of greatly appreciated assets to a terminally ill person may make sense even with the year and a day rule to cope with to achieve a step-up in basis of the assets that will reduce future taxes of surviving loved ones. In some cases, it is possible that the year and a day rule can be bypassed by utilizing certain trusts. This transfer planning makes sense if the potential savings in capital gains taxes of loved ones is substantial when compared to the potential increased estate tax of the terminally ill person.

Another area of deathbed planning to consider is IRAs and other retirement plans where the terminally ill person is a participant. The beneficiary designation and the distribution election should be reviewed for each account. Potential errors can be corrected. Also, it may be advisable to roll a retirement plan account into an IRA before death so that substantial income tax liabilities can be postponed for the benefit of the ill person's loved ones. Depending on who the beneficiary is and his or her age, income tax liability may be delayed for many years.

Tuition payments and medical care payments, even if they cause the annual per donee gift limit (currently $10,000) to be exceeded, are removed from the donor's estate if the checks are directly payable to a school, hospital, or physician.

If charitable gifts are contemplated, making the gifts before death will create an income tax deduction as well as remove the amount from the terminally ill person's estate.

Next, the disclaimer is an example of a postdeathbed device that a surviving spouse, heir, or beneficiary will sometimes find helpful.

Sol died leaving his wife, Sheba, with all $2 million of his assets. Sheba is a U.S. citizen, so there is an unlimited marital deduction, and no estate taxes are due. If Sheba should die with $2 million in her estate, only the Unified Credit amount (varying from $625,000 to $1 million depending on the year of her death) would be excluded from estate tax. But, if Sheba disclaimed a large sum from Sol's estate within nine months of his death, then that portion would go to Sol's next beneficiaries, who, under Sol's will, would be their children.

Sheba could even eliminate the entire estate tax that would be due on her death if she disclaimed $1 million and died after 2005. Sheba would be reluctant to disclaim an amount that she felt she might need to meet her financial needs, including potential emergencies. If Sol had had an estate plan with a properly prepared Credit Shelter Trust, Sheba still could have had the protection of the principal in that trust as well as the income. The children could have benefited by having the principal in that Credit Shelter Trust excluded from the taxable estates of both of their parents. By her disclaimer, Sheba is rescuing some of the tax benefits that would be lost by Sol having failed to include a Credit Shelter Trust in his estate plan. There are precise disclaimer rules that the knowledgeable tax advisor will utilize.

To illustrate how the step-up in basis rule works, let's take the case of Mr. Socrates on his deathbed on December 10. Mr. Socrates is a widower with a $5 million estate and 5 children and 10 grandchildren. Being able to give the annual exclusion amount (currently $10,000) to each of these potential beneficiaries would remove $150,000 from his taxable estate. If he survives to January 1, he can repeat the gifts for the new year, too. He is thinking of giving them either cash or common stock.

The stock is in Croesus, Inc. Bought for $1 per share many years ago, it is now worth $100 per share. If Mr. Socrates makes $150,000 in gifts of the stock (1,500 shares valued at $100 per share), when the children and grandchildren as donees sell the shares, they will have a taxable gain of $99 per share ($100 minus $1 cost). Using the capital gain rate of 20% for assets with a holding period of more than 18 months results in a capital gain tax of $29,700 when these donees sell the stock for $150,000. If Mr. Socrates gave $150,000 in cash instead, leaving the stock to be distributed after his death, this tax would be avoided entirely.

Upon receiving the stock, the children and grandchildren could sell the shares. If the shares were worth $100 each on the date of Socrates' death, the children and grandchildren as new owners could use $100 per share as their own cost basis—the step-up from $1 per share to $100 per share. Note that Mr. Socrates also owns securities that have dropped in value. They should be quickly sold so the losses can be claimed on his income tax return. The opportunity to claim these losses ends at death.

To this point, we have discussed federal estate taxes. Since 1976, the estate tax and gift tax has been integrated into a Unified Transfer Tax so that the IRS can have a measure of control relative to avoidance of taxes on transfers at death by those who make substantial transfers during life. Generally, the tax on gifts during life and transfers at death are taxed at similar rates. A principal difference is that a gift received during life is considered to have the same income tax basis as it had in the hands of the donor. As discussed, a transfer upon death receives a step-up in basis—that is, an income tax basis equal to the value of the property as of the date of death or as of an alternate valuation date thereafter.

The gift and estate tax rules are integrated to an extent to make them more effective, but there are still great potential advantages in gifts during life. As shown in the story of Jerry and Jeri (Case Study 10.3) and George and Martha (Case Study 10.4), if the gifts substantially increase in value, substantial tax savings can result. Assistance of a qualified attorney is advised when considering a program of gifts.

$ CASE STUDY 10.4—GEORGE AND MARTHA

George and Martha have three married children and five grandchildren. Annual qualifying tax-free gifts of up to $10,000 each to these donees by George would remove $80,000 per year (as well as the subsequent appreciation and income from these gifts) from George's estate. If George and Martha properly elect to treat the gifts as made equally by the two of them, the annual tax-free qualifying gifts can be increased to $20,000 per donee. If George and Martha want to add their children's spouses to the donee list, or anyone else, they can. Where the donee is a minor, the establishment of a Qualifying Trust should be considered.

Let's suppose George and Martha give $160,000 per year ($20,000 × 8 donees) for four years by using both of their annual exemptions. These gifts would remove $640,000 ($160,000 × 4 years) from their combined estates. If the date of death of the survivor of the two of them is 10 years hence, these gifts would have appreciated in value by $700,000. The result would be that $1,340,000 ($640,000 + $700,000) had been eliminated from the survivor's estate for a tax saving of $737,000 ($1,340,000 × 55%). Also note that, if desired, George and Martha could have used some or all of their Unified Credits for additional gifts.

$

$

CHAPTER ELEVEN

Foul-Ups and Fraud: The Laws That Protect the Public

IN THIS CHAPTER

Here we will examine some of the common money mistakes, frauds, scams, and rip-offs. We will also review the laws and legal principles that are designed to protect investors.

Most of us will admit to having made some monumental financial blunders, and those who won't make this admission are probably worse off than the rest of us. Fear and greed can be blamed for legions of investment mistakes. Thinking that you know more than you do is also a likely contributing factor. The worst foul-ups and mistakes are not necessarily the most obvious ones. Not acting on a favorable opportunity or acting on a poor one are common occurrences. Also, scams, rip-offs, and con jobs have cost investors billions of dollars.

FOUL-UPS

Probably more is lost through inertia than is lost through fraud. Young people make such mistakes as not taking advantage of their employer's retirement plan programs, incurring credit card debt, and purchasing whole-life insurance when term insurance would be better for their needs.

Although losing money through a scam or to high pressure will hurt more, putting all of your money or too much of your money in Treasury bills, certificates of deposit, and/or money market funds for a long period of time may be more damaging. You may want to be conservative and play it safe, but inflation might do more damage over several years than the one stock deal that goes sour. According to figures from Charles Schwab & Company, Inc., for the 70-year period ending in 1994, the *real* rate of return—that is, the annual average return rate in excess of the inflation rate—for U.S. Treasury bills was 0.6%, and for long-term U.S. bonds it was 1.7%. The average annual rate of return for common stock for the period was 7.1%.

In steering away from investing in equities, many retirees focus only on an investment yield or the dividend rate. You must also take into account potential price changes. Many investors have purchased long-term bonds without realizing that a substantial increase in interest rates will result in these bonds dropping in value.

A number of older people who grew up in the 1930s regard themselves as being very conservative when they limit their investments to money market funds, certificates of deposit, and fixed-income securities. Some of them may also add utility stocks. They believe that they are diversifying, because they do not have all of their holdings in one or two investments. But, they're not recognizing that all of their investments are interest-sensitive; when interest rates shoot up, the value of their stocks and fixed-income securities will quickly drop.

Another generation of people without investment experience may be participants in company retirement plans. Unfortunately, they translate their fears into selecting money market funds as the sole or principal investment vehicle for their retirement plan account. Following this strategy prevents them from benefiting from diversification, and furthermore these investors don't realize that inflation will usually do more damage than market fluctuations.

Another common investment mistake is overinvesting in the stock of an employer. Although loyalty is commendable—and we know there are many cases where employees did very well as their companies' fortunes surged during their employment careers—diversification will do much more for an investment portfolio than investing in any one company. With diversification, if one stock out of many fails, the performance of the other stocks can offset the loss. If you have little choice during your working years or feel that showing company loyalty is critical to your career, you should diversify your portfolio at the earliest opportunity once you stop working. With broad diversification, you will then have justification to sleep soundly at night.

Clinging to an unsatisfactory investment in the hope that you will eventually break even can be costly. Someone who waits for months or years for a stock to return to its purchase price is guilty of foggy thinking. If there is a better investment, switch. It may be a signal that you need help if you are not aware of investment basics. For many of you, selecting a professional advisor could be the most important step in your investment education. Most of you will be pleased with the results that a competent advisor can achieve for you. Some of you will learn not only from what the advisor is doing for you but will also start to study independently and become knowledgeable about investing. Age, health, and other interests will be factored into your decisions. You will learn that the knowledgeable investor takes advantage of opportunities such as those that present themselves when there is a market correction of 10% or more.

The strong skepticism that we encourage when you are tempted by business opportunities or get-rich-quick schemes should carry over if you attend financial seminars. Let's distinguish these seminars from educational meetings at the workplace relative to your retirement plan. But, you should still be vigilant even during an educational meeting about your retirement plan account. If you are approaching retirement, the investment advisor for the plan may also be soliciting your business outside of the plan, particularly if you're rolling over a substantial retirement plan account balance into an IRA. If you have been impressed with the advisor's abilities for a period of time and if other employees, particularly ex-employees who have utilized his or her services, are satisfied, he or she may be a better choice then someone whom you do not know. But again, don't be too lazy to investigate. If you can devote five hours in deciding which refrigerator to buy, how much time and effort should you devote when the equivalent of 300 to 1,000 refrigerators is at stake?

Often financial seminars will convey useful information, but remember that they have been arranged to serve the needs of the brokers or financial planners who are the sponsors. Your needs are only incidental to their needs.

Securities laws that have been designed to cope with fraud are reviewed later in this chapter. The establishment of the Securities and Exchange Commission (SEC) in 1934 created the federal agency charged with the duty of enforcing the securities laws and providing standards for disclosure of information about publicly traded stocks, bonds, mutual funds, and other securities. Not only investors but professional investment advisors, lawyers, and certified public accountants have depended on their intuition to sort out trustworthy individuals from con artists, although there are public records that may help investors avoid fraudulent operators. In recent years, computer programs have made searching public records easier.

FRAUD

If you are retired or about to retire, you are a particular target to many scam artists and high-pressure salesmen. Television ads and free seminars are used to peddle a variety of schemes including wireless cable licenses, rare coins, commodities, second mortgages, and the like. Remember the old bromide that "if it sounds too good to be true it probably *is* too good to be true." Don't give out your Social Security number, credit card information, or other personal information to people over the telephone unless you are convinced that the person has a legitimate need for the information.

Most of us assume that we are far too clever and wise in

THE FIRST CON JOB
ON MANHATTAN ISLAND

The story is told that the Dutch settlers bought Manhattan Island from the Manahata Indians for about $20 worth of trinkets in 1626. This has been regarded as one of history's great con jobs, and it was. Yet if the $20 or so in trinkets had been sold for their value and the proceeds invested by the seller for an average return of 7% per year for over 370 years, this investment would be worth over $1 trillion today. The Indians could now repurchase Manhattan Island with all of its improvements and have a huge sum left over to purchase several other cities as well.

the ways of the world to be swindled. Yet newspapers frequently carry stories about a "pigeon drop" or "bank examiner" fraud. These frauds are usually perpetrated on the naive and the elderly. In the "bank examiner" fraud, the victim gets a call from someone claiming to be a bank official who requests the victim's help in order to trap a crooked bank teller. The victim is requested to make a "test withdrawal" of several thousand dollars and to meet the "investigator" outside of the bank, being sure not to tell anyone. After the withdrawal, the victim meets the investigator and turns over the "evidence" that will be needed to expose the criminal. Of course that is the last that the victim sees of the investigator or the money. In the "pigeon drop," the victim comes upon someone apparently in the process of finding a great deal of cash. The "finder" offers to split the prize with the victim but requires the victim to make a "good-faith deposit," with predictable results. Authorities believe that these con games are often not reported to authorities by the victims because of the pain of embarrassment.

Sometimes, the criminal is a trusted advisor. To protect yourself, keep your investments in a custodial account with a bank or brokerage firm. Your account should not be accessible to the advisor or anyone else. Generally bank and broker custody accounts are insured against fraud for millions of dollars, but you must not let your guard down. Monthly statements from the bank or broker that are mailed directly to you will help you keep track of your holdings, but you should always be alert. Consider the tale of Terrence Hansen.

Terrence Hansen of Salt Lake City confessed to stealing over $400,000 from his clients. Mr. Hansen was a broker for eight years before he was caught in 1995. He used his computer to reproduce the logos of reputable brokerage firms and mutual funds. He had his clients make checks payable jointly to a legitimate firm and to "Income 36 Funds," which was the name on his private account at the bank. His bank accepted these checks after he had printed the name of the legitimate firm as well as "Income 36 Funds" and endorsed them. If a client requested a distribution from the client's brokerage account, Mr. Hansen sent out redemption checks from his private account, but these checks had the logos of the mutual fund company or securities firm instead. This is a version of what is known as a Ponzi scheme. When the scheme was uncovered, his bank paid out a total of more than $400,000 to several of Mr. Hansen's victims.

Mr. Hansen's con game lasted as long as it did because he was trusted; more funds came into the account than went out. The father of this type of swindle was Charles Ponzi, who after World War I set up shop in Boston. He promised investors a $2,000 return in 90 days for an investment of $1,250. When the 90-day period was about to expire, he encouraged investors to renew. Those who did not renew received their money. In all, Mr. Ponzi received $15 million but over $8 million of it was never accounted for. So great was the attraction and so skillful was Mr. Ponzi that when the con game was revealed and challenged, he had many supporters who refused to believe he was a crook. In fact, the publicity initially brought in huge amounts of additional cash to Mr. Ponzi.

What can we learn from Mr. Ponzi and Mr. Hansen? In Mr. Ponzi's case, a $750 return on $1,250 over a three-month period fails the smell test; it was just too good to be true. In Mr. Hansen's case, one of his clients happened to stop by the brokerage office where the client supposedly had an account. Of course, there was no record of the client's account, and that ended Mr. Hansen's Ponzi scheme. His clients learned that just relying on someone's good reputation was not enough to protect them.

Another common scam revolves around zero coupon municipal bonds. Bonds may sound safer than stock and zero coupon bonds sound very attractive because they sell at a huge discount from their face value. The reason for the discount is that with legitimate zero coupon bonds, the interest is paid in full on the date of maturity. Because the zero coupon bond does not pay any interest until maturity, it is an ideal setup for swindlers. Remember, buying securities without using a reputable broker or buying real estate without utilizing the services of a qualified lawyer are dangerous practices.

Another popular field for the con artist is business ventures. Among these so-called opportunities are placing and servicing display racks for candy, greeting cards, and other items, and servicing vending machines and pay telephones. These schemes are bait for the unemployed or people fearful that their retirement income may not be enough. Often the ads in the newspapers hold out the promise of making full-time income with little or no work. Once again, don't let your fears or greed cause you to fall for these cons.

You should not consider any of these opportunities without examining the proposal with your lawyer or CPA. You should also take the time to discuss the proposal with someone who has knowledge of the business. Check references carefully. Be alert to the possibility that the "reference" may be part of the scheme. Ask to see accounting records to support the claims and have your CPA carefully review these records. Be sure that all legal requirements have been met and ask for the opportunity to have your lawyer talk to the lawyer for the promoter. Keep in mind that even if everything checks out, there is no guarantee that you will make money. You should plan on giving at least as much time and attention to investigating a business venture as you would when you would buy a car.

GOVERNMENT REGULATION

Beginning in 1933, Congress passed a series of acts that created and empowered the Securities and Exchange Commission (SEC). The effect on investment in all securities has been substantial. The SEC has been active in the supervision and regulation of the issuance of new securities and trading both on the various exchanges and over the counter, accounting practices relative to the preparation of financial statements of corporations, corporate reorganizations excepting those of railroads, key financial matters involving public utility holding company systems, the activities of insiders, the conduct of investment companies, and the conduct of investment advisors. (This list is not all-inclusive.)

Among the statutes that the SEC is concerned with are:

1. The Securities Act of 1933, which deals with new issues of securities

2. The Securities Exchange Act of 1934, which covers trading on organized stock exchanges (expanded in 1938 to cover unlisted trading)

3. The Public Utility Holding Company Act of 1935, which allows and regulates public utilities

4. The Trust Indenture Act of 1939, which deals with the responsibilities of corporate bond trustees

5. The Investment Company Act of 1940, which regulates publicly held investment funds (including investment companies such as mutual funds)

6. The Investment Advisors Act of 1940, which requires registration of investment advisors and supervises their activities

These statutes are credited with revolutionizing and purifying investment activities. However, not only are there continuing activities of fraud and misrepresentation but some people design their activities to mislead and misrepresent by staying close enough to both sides of the boundaries of the law as to make them continuing problems for the uninformed and careless investor. Investors must keep in mind that the SEC's jurisdiction is limited. For example, relative to the regulation of new securities falling under its jurisdiction, it may refuse registration if there is not a "full and fair disclosure." If the offering is a bad investment because the underlying business activity is unprofitable or an unjustifiably high price is set, the SEC has no jurisdiction. Its activities are limited to the accuracy and adequacy of the disclosures, not the merits of the investment.

THE SECURITIES EXCHANGE ACT OF 1934

The 1934 Act substantially ended manipulation of stock prices on the stock market. There are occasional attempts at manipulation of stock prices and more frequent accusations, but the ability to clearly identify price manipulation in recent years makes it a rare occurrence. One result has been a tremendous increase in activity over the years as evidenced by huge increases in the number of stockholders, securities salespeople, and investment advisors.

Provisions of the 1934 Act, Section 16(a) require reports from insiders to be made to the SEC, detailing changes in their holdings of equity securities on a monthly basis. These activities are published in the financial press, which prevents unfair use of the information. A remedy is that profits realized by an insider from unfair use of information within a six-month period are forfeited to a corporation. Insiders are officers, directors, shareholders, and others who directly or indirectly own more than 10% of the voting securities of a company.

By making unfair profits of insiders forfeitable to a corporation, the 1934 Act generates the initiation of enforcement activity by the shareholders of the corporation and the corporation itself. The SEC does not have enforcement power relative to this provision. Section 16(b) has been criticized for not requiring proof of an abuse of trust. This can result in unfair litigation. For example, a director with other motives (such as to support the price of the shares for the benefit of the corporation and its shareholders) may be sued to return profits while not being able to present offsetting losses. Under current tax laws, wealthy directors would not be interested in taking short-term gains, so an improper motive is not likely.

The 1933 Act, the 1934 Act, the 1935 Act, and both 1940 Acts relate to providing requirements involving corporate statements and reports. Many of these requirements may be modified from time to time by the SEC. For example, registration statements for new securities must include financial information for the current year and the last three years. Form 10K requires figures for the registration of securities on a stock exchange.

THE PUBLIC UTILITY HOLDING COMPANY ACT OF 1935

The 1935 Act was enacted to give the SEC a great deal of authority with regard to public utility companies because of prior improprieties and the opportunity for abuse. The SEC broke up systems of holding companies that were deemed to be harmful and unnecessary. At one time, there were more than 2,000 companies involved, but by the end of 1960 there were fewer than 200.

THE INVESTMENT COMPANY ACT OF 1940

Back in 1940, the mutual fund industry, which was generally referred to at that time as the "investment fund industry," was a fraction of the size it is today. The Act of 1940 requires registration and regulates investment companies (mutual funds). The Act requires disclosure to afford investors full and complete information, prohibits the companies from changing the nature of their business or their investment policies without the approval of the stockholders, bars persons guilty of security frauds from serving as officers and directors, regulates the custody of assets, requires management contracts to initially be submitted to security holders for their approval, prohibits transactions between the companies and their officers and directors except on approval of the SEC, and prohibits pyramiding of such companies and cross-ownership of their securities.

THE INVESTMENT ADVISORS ACT OF 1940

This Act requires the registration of persons engaged for compensation in the business of advising others with respect to securities. Registration can be denied or revoked by the SEC if an advisor has been convicted or enjoined because of misconduct in connection with securities transactions or for making false statements in registration applications.

A person who has fewer than 15 clients and generally is not presented to the public as an investment advisor is not considered to be an advisor under this Act. Investment advisors may not engage in fraudulent or deceitful practices. They must disclose the nature of their interests in transactions that they execute for their clients. Profit-sharing arrangements are prohibited, and there are restrictions on the assignment of investment advisory contracts without the consent of the client. In 1960, the SEC's powers in the regulation of investment advisors were increased to include additional reasons for refusing, suspending, or canceling the registered status of an advisor.

THE TRUST INDENTURE ACT OF 1939

This Act was designed to protect the interests of bondholders, generally by strengthening the enforcement of obligations of corporate trustees (banks and trust companies) acting under indentures (agreements) relative to the issuance of the securities. It requires the corporate trustees to be free of conflict of interest and to make periodic reports to the bondholders, and gives them authority to file suits and proof of claims on behalf of the bondholders. It also prohibits provisions in the indenture that would reduce or eliminate the liability of the corporate trustee to the bondholders and "to use the same degree of care and skill in their exercise [of duties] as a *prudent man* would use in the conduct of his own affairs," according to a description by the SEC of the objectives of the Act (italics added).

The "Prudent Man Rule" was established as a legal principle in 1830 in the case of *Harvard College vs. Amory*. It has been described as requiring trustees to manage as "men of prudence, discretion and intelligence manage their own affairs, not in regard to speculation, but in regard to the permanent disposition of their funds, considering the probable income as well as the probable safety of the capital to be invested."

Different states have interpreted the Prudent Man Rule in different ways and adopted statutes describing in detail what that particular legislature considered to be permissible investments that could not be challenged as being improper. Over the years, most of the specific lists of permissible investments have disappeared, but there are a number of cases that have resulted in certain rules. Generally, speculation is not allowed. In addition, each investment must be judged separately as to whether it is appropriate for investment by the trust.

Concepts relative to safety through diversification are still in the process of being recognized. There are still places and situations where the trustee of a properly diversified portfolio may be successfully challenged because of the underperformance of an investment in a portfolio.

Fortunately, the law that governs qualified retirement plans—the Employee Retirement Income Security Act of 1974 (ERISA)—abandons the limitations of the more rigid versions of the Prudent Man Rule. This is doubly fortunate because ERISA, and not state law, is controlling in the area of qualified retirement plans. If qualified retirement plans were prevented from providing broad diversification because of the limitations of the Prudent Man Rule, millions of participants could be adversely affected. Which trustees would want to run the risk of having a particular mutual fund or a particular stock substantially underperform, although the overall performance could be substantially above average? The point of true diversification is that there will be underperformers at most, if not all, stages of the investment cycle. But the overall long-term performance will substantially benefit as a result of the diversification.

Before we summarize the Prudent Investor Rule, it should be pointed out that although forms of it have been passed in over half of the states in the past few years, the Prudent Man Rule is still a powerful influence. Just as the Prudent Man Rule took a number of years to develop, it may take a number of years before the Prudent Investor Rule substantially replaces the Prudent Man Rule. In the 150 years plus that the Prudent Man Rule was being developed and adopted, it was also being bent into different shapes for different areas.

For example, in many states where court-appointed guardians have been looking after the interests of minors and disabled persons, a separate list of permissible investments might govern that is more restrictive than even investments permitted in the same state under the Prudent Man Rule. Some courts may distinguish the applicable areas of new legislation and still apply a version of the Prudent Man Rule under certain circumstances.

In the past, some courts and state legislatures adopted different versions of the Prudent Man Rule for different circumstances. For example, they may have determined that a more restrictive list of permissible investments should be available for guardians appointed by the courts to look after the affairs of minors and legally disabled persons. If this rationale would continue, the benefits of more recent investment thinking may not be available in all cases where it should be and some fiduciaries may be penalized for following sound investment policies. Updating the investment knowledge of judges and state legislators is essential.

The Prudent Investor Rule was first set forth by the American Law Institute (ALI), which is a nonprofit group of legal scholars who are dedicated to developing statements of legal principles in an effort to improve the laws. Their proposals have been adopted by state legislatures and courts in a number of legal areas over the years. Their work in developing the Prudent Investor Rule filled almost 300 pages when it was published in 1992. The fact that the Prudent Investor Rule has been adopted in one form or another in over half of the states in less than 10 years as the Uniform Prudent Investor Act indicates the respect for the continuing work of the ALI.

The Prudent Investor Rule, as adopted in 1990 by the ALI, is lengthy. The heart of it is contained in Sections 227 and 228 of the ALI's restatement (3d) of trusts:

§227. **General Standard of Prudent Investment**

The trustee is under a duty to the beneficiaries to invest and manage the funds of the trust as a prudent investor would, in light of the purposes, terms, distribution requirements, and other circumstances of the trust.

(a) This standard requires the exercise of reasonable care, skill, and caution and is to be applied to investments not in isolation but in the context of the trust portfolio and as a part of an overall investment strategy, which should incorporate risk and return objectives reasonably suitable to the trust.

(b) In making and implementing investment decisions, the trustee has a duty to diversify the investments of the trust unless, under the circumstances, it is prudent not to do so.

(c) In addition, the trustee must:

(1) conform to fundamental fiduciary duties of loyalty (§170) and impartiality (§183);

(2) act with prudence in deciding whether and how to delegate authority and in the selection and supervision of agents (§171); and

(3) incur only costs that are reasonable in amount and appropriate to the investment responsibilities of the trusteeship (§188).

(d) The trustee's duties under this Section are subject to the rule of §228, dealing primarily with contrary investment provisions of a trust or statute.

§228. **Investment Provisions of Statute or Trust**

In investing the funds of the trust, the trustee has

(a) a duty to the beneficiaries to conform to any applicable statutory provisions governing investment by trustees; and

(b) has the powers expressly or impliedly granted by the terms of the trust and, except as provided in §§165 through

168, has a duty to the beneficiaries to conform to the terms of the trust directing or restricting investments by the trustee.

More detailed definitions of some of the terms contained in Sections 227 and 228 are contained in other sections of the proposed Act. Section 227(b) states that there can be an affirmative duty to diversify the investments of the trust while section 228(a) points out that the trustee has a duty to "conform to any applicable statutory provisions governing investment by trustees." Thus, the trustees should consult with their lawyer periodically since what has been true over most of the past 150 years is in the process of being changed. Incidentally, the reference in Section 227(b) to possible circumstances where it may not be prudent to diversify would cover such situations as tax planning by a terminally ill beneficiary or a beneficiary with controlling stock in a company where he or she has a high-paying position to defend.

It should be appreciated that the ALI, in its studies and preparation of the volume relating to the Prudent Investor Rule, did the intellectual work in understanding modern financial concepts. This is clear when the note and commentary in the volume are studied. Section 227(a) states that the evaluation of an investment is to be done on the basis of an overall investment plan that has risk and return objectives appropriate for the particular trusts. There is neither approval nor disapproval with regard to any single investment. The trustee must be able to justify the role if each investment plays in the overall investment program that is followed by the trust. Under these circumstances, it is necessary that a precise written investment strategy be adopted.

Unlike the Prudent Man Rule, the new standard does not prohibit speculation but recognizes that more speculative investments can play an important part in the overall investment strategy. The Prudent Investor Rule expressly negates a lack of care, indifference, or recklessness and requires a trustee of ordinary intelligence but, to the extent that greater skills are possessed, then the trustee must utilize these abilities.

The degree of care that is required is for the trustee to seek the twin goals of obtaining a reasonable return while protecting the capital. Generally, the trustees' reasonable efforts are what investors require of their investment managers. That is, after a risk level has been determined, it must be continually monitored. There is a duty to diversify under the Prudent Investor Rule. However, the trust agreement may provide certain standards that may limit or eliminate the rule to diversify. Retention of control of a family business is one example.

An important departure from the old Prudent Man Rule is that the Prudent Investor Rule requires the effects of inflation to be recognized. This was one of the great weaknesses under the old Prudent Man Rule which often led to an overemphasis on investments in certificates of deposit and fixed-income instruments in much larger proportions than were advisable. A continuing problem will be trust agreements that require the trustees to use fixed-income investments exclusively and the term of the trust may extend over many years in order to cover minor grandchildren or great-grandchildren. It will be helpful if lawyers preparing trust agreements for their clients will be able to advise them of the best provisions to protect the interests of the clients' loved ones.

Even clients who seek to have control of a family business retained may be making a big mistake. For every successful long-term business, such as the Ford Motor Company, there are hundreds of manufacturers of outdated products such as buggy whips and hula hoops that would have been better off sold than hung onto. Picking wise trustees and empowering them to be responsive to circumstances will usually be the best trust policy.

CHAPTER TWELVE

$

Investment Advisors

IN THIS CHAPTER

This chapter will help you select and work with professional advisors.

Your estate and tax planning will require the services of a qualified lawyer, and your tax reporting will probably require the services of a certified public accountant (CPA). Many of you will have a trusted insurance advisor and a number of you will be able to get sufficient objective insurance advice from one of your other advisors. Your attorney or CPA should be able to refer an honest, competent insurance advisor if necessary.

Most of you will also need an investment advisor because you probably do not have the expertise, temperament, or both to provide your own investment counsel. Probably less than 10% of you will have the knowledge and demeanor to manage your investments. Or, you don't have the time or want to devote the time necessary to manage an investment portfolio without assistance.

Those of you who have elected to oversee your investments must also take into consideration that your health and abilities will reach a point where a continuity mechanism should be in place and operating to protect you and those that rely on you *before* it becomes necessary. If you have an attorney, CPA, or both who have your complete confidence, you have strong allies in locating the other members of your team. It will be a balancing act: On the one hand you need advice so you don't take too much upon yourself, and on the other hand you are the leader of the advisory team; you are "watching the store." Whether looking for an attorney, CPA, financial professional, or other advisor, try to have several candidates to consider. Request a 30- to 45-minute meeting with the most impressive two or three candidates. In the interview look for a feeling of trust. Ask yourself, "Would I feel comfortable working with this person for the remainder of my lifetime?" Only as your final step, request references of clients who have similar financial circumstances to yours.

Generally you know what your attorney and CPA are doing for you, but what do CFPs, ChFCs, CLUs, and CFAs do? There are also PFAs, which may include one or more of the above. Who are these people, what do they do, and where can they be reached?

CFPs are Certified Financial Planners authorized by the CFP Board of Standards located in Denver, Colorado. Members of the Institute of Certified Financial Planners with the CFP designation who are practicing in your area can be located by calling the Institute of Certified Financial Planners (800-282-7526). Those who have a designation or an academic degree in planning and meet certain other qualifications can be located by calling the International Association for Certified Financial Planning (800-945-4237).

ChFCs are chartered financial consultants, a designation earned by life insurance agents who have already earned the chartered life underwriter (CLU) designation. They can be located by calling the American Society of CLU and ChFC (800-392-6900).

There are CPAs who provide planning services and have earned the Personal Financial Specialist (PFS) designation from the American Institute of Certified Public Accountants. They can be located by calling the Institute (800-862-4272) and requesting pamphlet G00616. In many states, there are attorneys who specialize in investment planning and advice and can be located by calling the local state bar office. Also, there are a number of attorneys and CPAs who provide considerable investment advice after years of experience although they do not have the official designation of their professional group. Many of these attorneys and CPAs are more qualified than those with the designation. Many are not. Your own experience and references from friends and relatives will be helpful in this situation.

Another designation is CFA, the Chartered Financial Analyst. Obtaining this designation is secured after completing a more rigorous program than the other financial planning or financial advisor designations. Generally, this is the preferred designation for those who hire security analysts, portfolio managers, and other investment professionals. The CFA candidates must pass three levels of examinations that are increasingly difficult, in addition to having at least three years of work experience in investment decision making. The CFA's focus is on the investment aspect, while the other designations are more directed to overall financial planning, and training in the investment advice area is not as intensive as it is with the CFAs. For reference, many of the top professionals in the investment world are CFAs, including: Abby Joseph Cohen, Mario Gabelli, John Neff, Gary Brinson, and Robert Sanborn. To locate a CFA in your area, call the Association for Investment Management and Research (800-247-8132).

Training and designations are important, but there is no question that the top performers with one designation will outdo mediocre performers with another designation. However, the combination of a designation that you are satisfied with, references (particularly from professionals whom you respect), and your own personal interviews should result in you meeting with candidates who are qualified and can interact effectively with you and your other advisors.

The fee arrangement should be discussed and given to you in writing before the planner or advisor is retained. Planners may have a conflict of interest if they offer their services on the basis of being informed and impartial but a substantial part of their income is in the form of commissions and fees for selling investments, insurance, or other financial products as licensed insurance agents, securities brokers, or both. Sometimes, apparently low advisory charges indicate that most of the advisor's compensation is earned from undisclosed sales commissions.

Generally, the fee-only planner is both more reasonable and less likely to be involved in a conflict of interest. It is best to have the entire fee arrangement in writing. Some fee-only planners are PFAs and belong to the National Association of Personal Financial Advisors (800-366-2732). To be a member you must have at least three years of comprehensive financial planning. This requirement may be met by CFAs, CPAs, ChFCs, and the other designations.

A HOBBY FOR THE INVESTOR WITH A NEW FINANCIAL ADVISOR— IT MAY BE BETTER THAN JOGGING

We believe that even an excellent do-it-yourself investor should rely on professionals at some stage—certainly before health and age interfere. But what should the individual do for a hobby if he or she loves investing? For the experienced do-it-yourselfers in their 60s, the investment career of Anne Scheiber should be considered. Ms. Scheiber averaged an annual return of 22.1%. Starting with $5,000, her portfolio exceeded $22 million when she died in 1995. Her strategy appeared to be investing in leading companies such as Coca-Cola and Exxon. She loved to go to the movies and invested successfully in movie studios. She kept informed, limited her investments, and did not invest in industries that she did not understand.

Her background was as an examiner for the Internal Revenue Service. If you could duplicate her performance, you would be doubling your portfolio every 39 months or so, and in $32\frac{1}{2}$ years (when you would be in your 90s), your portfolio would have doubled about 10 times. The initial $5,000 would then be over $5 million. Ms. Scheiber went on to live to 101. If you lived an additional $6\frac{1}{2}$ years or so, you could double your portfolio two more times to where it would be over $20 million. Considering cause and effect, perhaps having $5,000 grow to over $5 million in less than 33 years would be all the incentive that you would need to live to 101 as Ms. Scheiber did. Meanwhile, competent management of the balance of your portfolio would be protecting you and your loved ones while you enjoyed your hobby. You should also consider that Ms. Scheiber left almost all of her fortune to charities.

$

Conclusion

If you're a do-it-yourself investor, we hope that you'll read this last chapter, because eventually it will come in handy. Recall our table from Chapter 1, which showed that, although the S&P 500 Index gained 15.4% annually from 1984 to 1995, the average stock investor gained only 6.2% annually due to timing errors.

For those of you who want and need objective counsel now, read on.

There are three powerful reasons to obtain professional investment help:

1. *Procrastination.* Although you probably understand the theories of long-term investing and diversification and realize their importance, you may be a little lax at implementing a sound retirement plan—a delay that could cost you dearly in more ways than one (recall Chapters 5, 7, and 10). A true investment professional will objectively implement your retirement plan with neither hesitation nor emotion. Leave the deadlines to the professional and keep the peace of mind for yourself.

2. *Continuity*. At some point in your life, you may be neither willing nor able to diligently follow through with your financial issues. Your spouse may not have the inclination to take it on either. The continuity of professional management and oversight will allow you to sleep well at night and focus on other life issues. Most advisors will let you phase into a relationship over a period of time.

3. *Control*. After reading this book, you now have the tools, the background information, and a road map for finding a truly objective and seasoned professional. With this background knowledge, you can establish a true partnership with an investment manager and feel more in control of your finances than ever before. Think of this relationship this way: You are the owner of a corporation who's just entered retirement to spend more time with your family and enjoy what life has to offer. So you hire your investment manager to be the chief executive officer (CEO). The CEO provides you with detailed reports and updates that allow you to efficiently stay on top of your financial program while still having the time to maximize your retirement.

We conclude by extending our best wishes for a happy, healthy, and successful retirement. To avoid point 1, procrastination, we're giving you a gentle push to get you started on your retirement plan. We recall the insightful words of the Hebrew scholar Hillel who best summed it up: "If not now, *when?*"

INDEX

$